Research and Practice in Applied Lingu

General Editors: **Christopher N. Candli**
Macquarie University, Australia.

MW00723534

All books in this series are written by leading researchers and teachers in Applied Linguistics, with broad international experience. They are designed for the MA or PhD student in Applied Linguistics, TESOL or similar subject areas and for the language professional keen to extend their research experience.

Titles include:

Dick Allwright and Judith Hanks
THE DEVELOPING LANGUAGE LEARNER
An Introduction to Exploratory Practice

Francesca Bargiela-Chiappini, Catherine Nickerson and Brigitte Planken
BUSINESS DISCOURSE

Alison Ferguson and Elizabeth Armstrong
RESEARCHING COMMUNICATION DISORDERS

Sandra Beatriz Hale
COMMUNITY INTERPRETING

Geoff Hall
LITERATURE IN LANGUAGE EDUCATION

Richard Kiely and Pauline Rea-Dickins
PROGRAM EVALUATION IN LANGUAGE EDUCATION

Marie-Noëlle Lamy and Regine Hampel
ONLINE COMMUNICATION IN LANGUAGE LEARNING AND TEACHING

Annamaria Pinter
CHILDREN LEARNING SECOND LANGUAGES

Virginia Samuda and Martin Bygate
TASKS IN SECOND LANGUAGE LEARNING

Norbert Schmitt
RESEARCHING VOCABULARY
A Vocabulary Research Manual

Helen Spencer-Oatey and Peter Franklin
INTERCULTURAL INTERACTION
A Multidisciplinary Approach to Intercultural Communication

Cyril J. Weir
LANGUAGE TESTING AND VALIDATION

Tony Wright
CLASSROOM MANAGEMENT IN LANGUAGE EDUCATION

Forthcoming titles:

Anne Burns and Helen da Silva Joyce
LITERACY

Lynn Flowerdew
CORPORA AND LANGUAGE EDUCATION

Sandra Gollin and David R. Hall
LANGUAGE FOR SPECIFIC PURPOSES

Marilyn Martin-Jones
BILINGUALISM

Martha Pennington
PRONUNCIATION

Devon Woods and Emese Bukor
INSTRUCTIONAL STRATEGIES AND PROCESSES IN LANGUAGE EDUCATION

Research and Practice in Applied Linguistics
Series Standing Order ISBN 978–1–4039–1184–1 hardcover
978–1–4039–1185–8 paperback
(*outside North America only*)

You can receive future titles in this series as they are published by placing a standing order. Please contact your bookseller or, in case of difficulty, write to us at the address below with your name and address, the title of the series and the ISBN quoted above.

Customer Services Department, Macmillan Distribution Ltd, Houndmills, Basingstoke, Hampshire RG21 6XS, England

Children Learning Second Languages

Annamaria Pinter

Centre for Applied Linguistics, University of Warwick, UK

First published 2011 by
PALGRAVE MACMILLAN

Palgrave Macmillan in the UK is an imprint of Macmillan Publishers Limited,
registered in England, company number 785998, of Houndmills, Basingstoke,
Hampshire RG21 6XS.

Palgrave Macmillan in the US is a division of St Martin's Press LLC,
175 Fifth Avenue, New York, NY 10010.

Palgrave Macmillan is the global academic imprint of the above companies
and has companies and representatives throughout the world.

Palgrave® and Macmillan® are registered trademarks in the United States,
the United Kingdom, Europe and other countries.

ISBN 978–0–230–20341–9 hardback
ISBN 978–0–230–20342–6 paperback

This book is printed on paper suitable for recycling and made from fully
managed and sustained forest sources. Logging, pulping and manufacturing
processes are expected to conform to the environmental regulations of the
country of origin.

A catalogue record for this book is available from the British Library.

Library of Congress Cataloging-in-Publication Data
Pinter, Annamaria.
    Children learning second languages / Annamaria Pinter.
      p.   cm. — (Research and practice in applied linguistics)
    Summary: "ELT for children continues to be a big growth area worldwide.
    This is a comprehensive survey of key concepts specific to language
    teaching for children with up to date research findings, plus listings of
    resources for research and practice"—Provided by publisher.
    Includes bibliographical references and index.
    ISBN 978–0–230–20342–6 (pbk.)
    1. Language acquisition—Age factors.   2. Second language
    acquisition—Study and teaching.   3. Bilingualism in children.   I. Title.
    P118.2.P56 2010
    372.65—dc22   2010034190

Printed and bound in Great Britain by
CPI Antony Rowe, Chippenham and Eastbourne

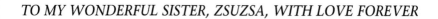

TO MY WONDERFUL SISTER, ZSUZSA, WITH LOVE FOREVER

Contents

List of Tables

General Editors' Preface

Research and Practice in Applied Linguistics is an international book series from Palgrave Macmillan which brings together leading researchers and teachers in Applied Linguistics to provide readers with the knowledge and tools they need to undertake their own practice-related research. Books in the series are designed for students and researchers in Applied Linguistics, TESOL, Language Education and related subject areas, and for language professionals keen to extend their research experience.

Every book in this innovative series is designed to be user-friendly, with clear illustrations and accessible style. The quotations and definitions of key concepts that punctuate the main text are intended to ensure that many, often competing, voices are heard. Each book presents a concise historical and conceptual overview of its chosen field, identifying many lines of enquiry and findings, but also gaps and disagreements. It provides readers with an overall framework for further examination of how research and practice inform each other, and how practitioners can develop their own problem-based research.

The focus throughout is on exploring the relationship between research and practice in Applied Linguistics. How far can research provide answers to the questions and issues that arise in practice? Can research questions that arise and are examined in very specific circumstances be informed by, and inform, the global body of research and practice? What different kinds of information can be obtained from different research methodologies? How should we make a selection between the options available, and how far are different methods compatible with each other? How can the results of research be turned into practical action?

The books in this series identify some of the key researchable areas in the field and provide workable examples of research projects, backed up by details of appropriate research tools and resources. Case studies and exemplars of research and practice are drawn on throughout the books. References to key institutions, individual research lists, journals and professional organizations provide starting points for gathering information and embarking on research. The books also include annotated lists of key works in the field for further study.

The overall objective of the series is to illustrate the message that in Applied Linguistics there can be no good professional practice that isn't based on good research, and there can be no good research that isn't informed by practice.

Christopher N. Candlin and David R. Hall
Macquarie University, Sydney

Acknowledgments

First of all, I would like to thank Chris Candlin and David Hall, for approaching me to write this book, and having the confidence in me that I would eventually complete this enormous task in addition to all my other commitments. They provided me with helpful suggestions and encouragement at every step of the way. Without their dedication and clear vision of the book, I could not have come this far.

I would also like to thank my colleagues, my students and my friends who have inspired me over the years and shaped my thinking about language learning, teaching and research. It is not possible to mention everyone but I would like to say a special thank you to Ema Ushioda for listening to me talk about this book over the months and years and for sharing ideas with me, especially about Chapter 4. Thank you also to Shelagh Rixon for providing me with additional sources and ideas and for being my mentor when I first took an interest in teaching English to young learners. My thanks also go to Helen Spencer-Oatey and Keith Richards for their support and understanding, and for sharing their valuable experience of writing for Palgrave. Finally, I would like to thank David Scott, who provided me with critical suggestions on previous drafts, and to Hugo Santiago Sanchez and Leo Vecchioli for their unfailing attention to detail.

Finally, and most of all, I would like to thank my family, my husband, Keith, and my son, Thomas, for supporting me and putting up with my absence at weekends and evenings when I was writing. Thomas has taught me many important lessons about children and childhood and continues to inspire and feed my interest in children. Without my family's support and love, I could not have written this book.

For permission to reproduce copyright material, I am very grateful to the following:

Oxford University Press, for an extract from Ana Llinares Garcia (2007) 'Young learners' functional use of the L2 in a low-immersion EFL context'. *ELT Journal*, 61 (1): 39–45.

John Wiley and Sons, for an extract from Christiane Bongartz and Melanie L. Schneider (2003) 'Linguistic development in social contexts: A study of two brothers learning German'. *The Modern Language Journal*, 87: 13–37.

Elsevier, for an extract from Merrill Swain and Sharon Lapkin (2002) 'Talking it through: Two French immersion learners' response to reformulation'. *International Journal of Educational Research*, 37: 285–304.

De Gruyter Mouton, for an extract from Rae Lan and Rebecca Oxford (2003) 'Language learning strategy profiles of elementary school students in Taiwan'. *International*

Review of Applied Linguistics in Language Teaching, 41 (4): 339–79, available for purchase in full via the publisher's website at www.reference-global.com.

Cambridge Scholars Publishing, for an extract from M. Devlieger and G. Goossens (2007) 'An assessment tool for the evaluation of teacher practice in powerful task-based language learning environments'. In K. Van den Branden, K. Van Gorp and M. Verhelst (eds.) *Tasks in Action: Task-based Language Education from a Classroom-based Perspective,* pp. 92–130.

British Association of Applied Linguistics, for an extract from the BAAL ethical guidelines.

Institute of Education, University of Warwick, for permission to reproduce their ethical clearance sheet.

Although every effort has been made to contact copyright holders, if any have been inadvertently overlooked, the author and publisher will make amends at the earliest opportunity.

Introduction

1 Why focus on children's second language learning?

Language learning in childhood is both similar and different from adult language learning. It is therefore important for language teachers who work with children to explore these similarities and differences so that they can make their work in the classroom as effective as possible.

The particular overview offered in this book is both timely and necessary, as the number of second and foreign language programmes (in particular English language programmes) for children is increasing at a very high rate globally. Governments all over the world are introducing English language programmes earlier in their education systems, typically during the primary school or preschool years. In addition to a general trend of introducing English, in many contexts of the world children already learn other second languages such as local official languages, majority second languages and/or heritage languages. The aim of this volume is to illustrate the variety of contexts where languages are learnt in childhood, to discuss links between existing research on child second language learning and classroom practice, and to enable practitioners to carry out their own locally based research.

Concept 1   Language acquisition and learning

..we *acquire* as we are exposed to samples of the second language which we understand. This happens in much the same way that children pick up their first language – with no conscious attention to language form. We *learn*, on the other hand, via a conscious process of study and attention to form and rule learning.

Lightbown and Spada (1999: 38)

While the two terms denote two clearly different processes, for individual language learners there is typically some overlap between natural acquisition

1

and instructed learning. In this book these two concepts will be used to denote these two tendencies where appropriate, but on the whole, where the distinction is not emphasised the terms will be used interchangeably.

2   What age range will be covered?

It is hard to fit 'childhood' into fixed age brackets. There are many different cultural interpretations of 'children' in different societies. Such cultural variation is further influenced by the type of definition we might be looking for. For example, legal and political definitions of a child refer to individuals who are not yet eligible to vote, drive, drink alcohol or get married. These are very different from biological definitions, or educational definitions. In this volume a broad educational definition will be used, focussing on children of preschool and primary or elementary school ages.

Even within this educational definition there is a tremendous variation from country to country, as will become evident in the studies in upcoming chapters. Typically, children start preschool at around the age of 3 and then they move to primary/elementary school at around the age of 5–7. Accordingly, some discussion will refer to the 'preschool years' and some to the so-called 'middle childhood' that covers the primary school years. Children may leave their primary school at around the age of 11 or 12, although in some countries this may happen later, at the age of 13–14. From age 13 years onwards children will be referred to as 'early adolescents'. Most of the discussion in this volume will be focussed on preschool and primary school years as well as on early adolescence, but occasionally, for example when comparisons of different age groups are discussed in particular studies (such as comparing 10-, 12- and 16-year-olds), it will be necessary and meaningful to report on learners who might be either younger than 3 years of age or older than 13 years of age. The three age groups are represented in table 1.

Table 1   Children: the three age groups

Education	Age	Capacities
Preschool	3–5	No formal learning experiences No literacy skills Large differences among children with regard to readiness for school
Primary school years	6–12	Primary/elementary schooling Often divided into lower primary and upper primary years
Early adolescence	13 onwards	Change of schooling to secondary or high school at around 11 or 12, but in some countries not until 14

The variation in school types and ages at which elementary education becomes compulsory shows a complex picture across different countries. This picture is further complicated by the fact that in research studies children are often described by referring to their grade level as opposed to their actual age. In the UK, for example, children start school at between 4 and 5 years of age, whereas in many other countries they start school much later, at 6–7 years of age. For the sake of consistency, wherever possible, children's chronological ages will be indicated in addition to their grade levels.

3   What is the scope of this book on child second/third language learning?

The general aims of the volume are:

- to offer a review of child development and language learning
- to tease out differences and similarities between adult and child language learning processes
- to illustrate what language learning entails for different children in different contexts around the world
- to relate the existing research in child second language learning (in different contexts and different areas of learning) to practice in classrooms and identify gaps and issues for future research
- to consider ethical and methodological challenges in research with children
- to offer a range of feasible topics for practitioners to research within child second language learning and teaching
- to offer a comprehensive list of resources.

To write a book on the topic of child second/third language learning, considering the range of different languages, age groups, learning contexts and research approaches that might be involved, is an impossible task. This is an enormously large and complex area and therefore it is not practical or feasible to cover all the research and practice in a comprehensive way. Instead, this volume gives a bird's eye view of some current research and debate. I hope that researchers, students and teachers, wherever they work and whatever their circumstances are, can find some useful ideas or inspiration to explore some topics further, while developing their own research interests.

Part I

Background to Child Second Language Acquisition and Pedagogy

1
Theories of Child Development

This chapter will

- consider three influential theories of cognitive development, i.e. those associated with Piaget, Vygotsky, and information processing, and some issues related to emotional development
- discuss the characteristics of different age groups
- consider links between cognitive development and second language learning/teaching

1.1 Introduction

This first background chapter is concerned with child development theories. As a language teacher working with children, you will find that basic understanding of the cognitive, social and emotional development of different age groups will be helpful in teaching, and in planning, implementing and interpreting research. Second language learning in schools or in less formal environments should not be seen as an isolated process but instead as closely intertwined with cognitive development, learning about the world and developing as a person.

Child development theories are interested in exploring the following questions. How do children mature as they get older? How do they think and learn differently from adults? To what extent is it nature that is responsible for these developments and what is the role of the nurturing environment?

Some theories are based on the premise that there are stages in development and that each stage is qualitatively different, while others maintain that development is more continuous. In terms of exploring the main forces behind development, some theories are more cognitive in orientation, while others are more social. The three main theories explored here are: (1) Piaget's stage-like theory of child development; (2) Vygotsky's socially mediated development; and (3) a more general approach, i.e. the information processing approach to child development. Some basic insights related to children's emotional development will also be reviewed.

1.2 Piaget's theory of child development

Jean Piaget (1896–1980) was a famous Swiss child psychologist who offered a systematic approach to the study of children's thinking and development from birth to adulthood. His name is associated with the 'stage theory' which has been extremely influential in educational circles throughout the twentieth century and remains relevant and popular today.

Piaget's theory grew out of careful observations of his own children and his interest in identifying aspects of child development that might be universal. This explains his interest in identifying stages in development. Piaget defined intelligence as a basic life function that helps organisms to adapt to their environment. During this process of gradual adaptation, children attempt to achieve a kind of balance or 'equilibrium' between themselves and their environment. Piaget observed that his own children were constantly exploring their environment and learning came naturally to them. They were curious explorers who were constructing knowledge through their own actions.

Concept 1.1   Piaget's organisation, adaptation, assimilation and accommodation

When interacting with the environment, children create mental structures or schemes (Piaget and Inhelder 1956). These schemes are being created all the time and they are also combined to make ever more complex schemes. This is the process of *organisation*. At the same time, children need to compare and adjust their developing schemes to match what they encounter in their environment. This process of adjusting is referred to as *adaptation*. Adaptation actually consists of two sub-processes: *assimilation* and *accommodation*. The first process refers to interpreting new knowledge in terms of old models/ schemes they already possess, and the second process refers to modifying these existing structures to fit the new knowledge. These processes work together to further cognitive growth.

How do these concepts actually translate into practice? Imagine a young child who already knows that creatures that live in water are fish, they have gills and their skin is covered by scales. This mental structure seems to fit well with what this child experiences in his environment (equilibrium) as he cares for his pet goldfish. One day however, the child will come across a book about whales, and realise that not all creatures that live in water are fish. Whales breathe air and they don't have gills or scales. At this point the child will have to reorganise the original mental structure for 'creatures that live in water' by adjusting it to accommodate the new information. With more and more experience of interacting with the environment over the years, the child can achieve more integrated and more differentiated levels of equilibrium. This will lead to a more and more sophisticated way of organising information.

1.2.1 Piaget's stages of development

Piaget argues that all children follow the same stages of development in the exact same order, hence he refers to these as 'invariant stages of development'. Within each stage the quality of thinking is relatively consistent across different tasks. A child's performance on one Piagetian task for a given stage will predict the performance on a range of other tasks for that same level. The stages of development are given in table 2.

Table 2　Piagetian stages of development

Stage 1　0–2 years: sensori-motor stage

Repetitive motor habits (e.g. kicking)

Goal-oriented behaviour (e.g. reaching out to grab)

Active curiosity (e.g. trying to put a block inside another one)

Imitation (e.g. actions of adult, accompanying a jointly recited nursery rhyme)

Object permanence (e.g. looking for an object where it was last seen)

Stage 2　2–7 years: pre-operational stage

Animism (attributing lifelike qualities to inanimate things, such as teddy bears)

Egocentrism (seeing the world from one's own point of view without appreciating others')

Centration (attending to one aspect of a task only)

At age 7: **intellectual revolution** (Wood 1998: 23)

Stage 3　7–11: concrete operational stage

Operational thought (ability to think in a logical fashion)

Using analogy competently (If A is smaller than B and C is smaller than B, then ...)

Full emergence of symbolic thought (e.g. an ability to make one thing stand for another, i.e. a map for a town)

Reversibility and conservation (e.g. mentally undo/change back an action)

Appreciating causality (reasoning from particular to particular)

Development of hierarchical classification (e.g. putting furniture and chair together rather than chair and breakfast)

Table 2   (Continued)

De-centration (ability to deal with more than one aspect of a task)

A gradual loss of/decline in egocenticity

Relational logic (mentally order a set of stimuli along a dimension)

Stage 4   11–12 and beyond: formal operational stage

Formal operational thought (ability to carry out mental actions on ideas and propositions without the need to rely on concrete objects)

Hypothetico-deductive reasoning (ability to reason by progressing from general ideas to specific ones by generating possibilities and hypotheses)

Thinking like a scientist (hypotheses are systematically tested in experiments, if-then statements)

Rational, systematic and abstract thinking

Our interest with preschool and primary school aged children leads us to focus first of all on the pre-operational stage. According to Piaget, the beginning of this stage is marked around the age of 2 and lasts until around the age of 7. During this stage children begin to use language and imagery as meaning-making systems and make huge progress in their intellectual development; but interestingly, Piaget describes this stage by largely focussing on deficiencies rather than achievements. When children in the pre-operational and operational stages were given the same tests and tasks, typically children under 7 were unable to do them, whereas those over 7 years of age were able to do them. In fact these two stages are best understood as divided by an 'intellectual revolution' (Wood 1998: 23) that, it is claimed, happens at around the age of 7.

Pre-operational children (2–7 years of age) do not yet follow the rules of 'formal logic'. Piaget characterised these children as 'ego-centric', i.e. unable to imagine any other perspectives but their own. One of the most well-known empirical studies conducted by Piaget and his associates to illustrate this point was the 'Three mountain experiment'. In this experiment a doll was placed facing a model of a mountain which had some snow on its top. The next mountain beyond the snowy one had a church on its top and beyond that the third mountain had a house. The children were asked to stand facing the third mountain, the one which had the house, i.e. directly opposite to where the doll was. Then they were asked what the *doll* could see. Children under the age of 7 tended to describe their own view rather than the doll's view, and they consistently responded that the doll could see the mountain with the house.

Another example to illustrate young children's failure to appreciate formal logic is their lack of ability to 'conserve', i.e. their inability to realise that the characteristics of an object will remain the same even if their outward appearance changes. For example, in experiments when water or sand is poured from a long narrow glass into a short wide glass, most pre-operational children say that the amount of the water or sand changed, as perceptually the level is higher in the first container, which is the taller and narrower one.

Similar findings were gathered in a range of different tasks (e.g. classification tasks, hierarchy tasks, see table 2) which all showed that young children can focus only on one aspect of the task at a time and they ignore all other aspects.

Quote 1.1   On pre-operational thought

Lacking operational thought means that...flexible, reversible reasoning which allows them to conserve, classify, seriate, coordinate perspectives and overcome misleading perceptual impressions' is not available yet.

(Meadows 1993: 24)

Overall, Piaget's assessment of young children under 7 is rather negative, as he describes them in terms of what they lack. The tasks that Piaget and his team used were all tasks that aimed to test formal logic. While it is true that young children are less able to do well on formal experimental tasks, children between the ages of 2 and 7 make important progress in their development. For example, they enjoy and participate effectively in repetitive games where the same scenario is acted out over and over again. 'Make believe' play, which over time becomes more complex, develops into socio-dramatic play (e.g. 'let's pretend we are mum and dad and we live with our 40 children in a double-decker bus'). Frequent engagement in different kinds of play situations contributes to cognitive, social and emotional development where children learn about feelings and points of view of others in meaningful and naturally occurring contexts. During play activities they participate in different culturally and contextually appropriate linguistic routines.

If you teach very young children, you may want to be reminded of their difficulties in coping with formal logic in de-contextualised situations. They cannot understand complicated instructions and they cannot work with tasks that require coordinating perspectives, evaluating options or reasoning in a formal manner. They enjoy spontaneous language play (Nicholas and Lightbown 2008) and simple, repetitive tasks, games and stories. Games and drama activities can stimulate these children's creative imagination and willingness to take on playful roles.

Following the so-called intellectual revolution at around the age of 7 (Wood 1998: 23), the beginning of the third stage marks the start of the most fundamental cognitive change, according to Piaget: the development of 'concrete operations'. While administering the experimental tasks to children, Piaget and his colleagues noticed that the majority of children who were older than 7 typically completed their tasks successfully. Children older than 7 years of age appreciate that pouring water from one container to another does not change the quantity of the water, because even though one glass is taller, the other is wider and these two characteristics compensate for each other. These children also appreciate that there may be more than one angle/perspective to a question or a task. They become competent at organising and sorting objects into hierarchical structures and they recognise that the same set of objects can be looked at and categorised in more than one way. Children's seriation also improves, which means that putting numbers of objects physically or mentally in a list according to their height or weight, progressing from smallest to biggest, is no longer a problem. They can work out puzzles of simple analogy such as 'if A is bigger than B and B is bigger than C, then A is also bigger than C (Chapman and Lindenberger 1988). Another area of development is spatial awareness. Understanding of distance, maps and directions improves. For example, at the age of 10 children can give clear, well-organised directions (Gauvain and Rogoff 1989).

A clear implication of these achievements in middle childhood for language teachers is that it becomes possible to use a greater variety of tasks and activities. For example, children can compare pictures and maps and sort different words into different categories. They can also use analogy to work out linguistic puzzles. A growing ability to appreciate other points of view allows teachers to include pair and group work, because children become more attentive while listening to one another and working collaboratively on tasks.

These are major strides in development but the concrete operational child still suffers from some limitations, according to Piaget. While children between the ages of 7 and 12 can use the rules of formal logic (as measured by the experimental tasks), they can only do so if the questions and problems are applied to concrete examples and objects in real life. Children overcome this limitation during the next stage of development, i.e. when they enter the formal operational stage. During this stage, children develop 'propositional thought' which enables them to become competent at discussing and evaluating problems without referring to the real world. Children at the formal operational development stage enjoy generating creative ideas and hypothetical propositions, i.e. they become interested in the 'what if' type of problems.

Example study 1.1   Shaffer (1973): Differences between concrete operational and formal operational thought

A study by Shaffer (1973) compared concrete operational and formal operational children's responses to the same task. The task invited the children to imagine how humans might benefit from a third eye and they were asked to draw some innovative solutions. Most younger children (9-year-olds in the concrete operational stage) drew a third eye in the middle of the forehead, between the two eyes and did not think of extra functions for it. Older children (13-year-olds, in the formal operational stage) were more creative, suggesting interesting new functions for the third eye, such as hiding it behind the hair at the back of your head, so that you can see things behind your back. Formal operational children were much more adept at generating more abstract and hypothetical solutions than were the younger children.

According to Piaget, the formal operational stage is the ultimate achievement of the human mind, which is characterised by hypothetico-deductive reasoning. Access to this type of reasoning enables adolescents to take an abstract/ hypothetical problem and carefully consider all possible factors that might affect the outcome. By considering all options in an orderly manner, the adolescent mind can propose hypotheses regarding what is most likely to happen, based on eliminating less likely scenarios one by one. One well-known experiment to illustrate formal operational thinking is the 'pendulum problem' (see Miller 1989). In this experiment the researchers asked children what factors they thought might affect the way the pendulum oscillated. By considering the strings of the pendulum of different lengths and the objects of different weights at the end of the strings, formal operators , i.e. children who had reached the formal operational development stage, discovered that it was only the length of the string that mattered. Younger children typically failed to test all options and came to a premature conclusion. Adolescents can take a systematic approach to this type of problem by holding all factors constant while testing just one factor at a time. Armed with an ability to think in abstract terms about hypothetical matters, adolescents are increasingly able to make decisions about complex problems by weighing up different alternatives. They also become adept at imagining creative alternative realities as opposed to what is given. This makes them question rules and procedures and ultimately adult authority.

If you are a teacher working with adolescents, the implications are that you can use more sophisticated tasks such as debates, role plays and various activities that involve evaluating different opinions. These learners can also appreciate linguistic challenges such as translation, or text analysis. Learners at this age are able to evaluate their own and their peers' progress in learning and they may be able to negotiate learning content with teachers.

1.2.2 Criticism of Piaget

Piaget's original stage theory has been scrutinised and criticised by many. In particular, two of his stages were criticised most: the pre-operational and the formal operational stages. It is widely accepted now that his claims about pre-operational children were too harsh and that he underestimated young children's mental capacities, whereas with regard to the formal operational stage, he somewhat overestimated young adolescents. (e.g. Donaldson 1978).

Since Piaget's original experiments, research on pre-operational thought has revealed that cultural practices influence the development of operational thinking significantly. Children from different cultures develop operational thought at different ages. In addition, in order to do well on the Piagetian tasks, children must take part in everyday activities which promote this kind of thinking and raise these kinds of problems of logic (e.g. Light and Perrett-Clermont 1989). Formal schooling itself facilitates the development of operational thought. Children's specific experiences and their unique motivations can also affect the emergence of operational thought (Ceci and Roazzi 1994).

So, what was so problematic with the Piagetian experiments for pre-operational children? Donaldson (1978) proposed that the language of the experiments was unnatural and difficult to understand. Some of the questions used in the experimental tasks were ambiguous and confusing. For example, in one of the task which tested children's ability to iden-tify categories of beads, the experimenter typically asked: 'Are there more brown beads or more wooden beads?' Donaldson argues that questions like this sound strange, unnatural and they are never heard in normal every-day conversations. Children, therefore, may have been confused about the interpretation of the questions rather than the task demand *per se*. When McGarrigle and Donaldson (1974) replicated one of the inclusion tasks with changes to the actual wording of the original questions, the results showed that the majority of the children were able to give the correct answer.

The context of the experiments was also problematic. For example, when the experimenter indicates the change by introducing a new container or rearranges the sticks in the conversion tasks, it is quite logical for the child to think that there is some link between the action (changing the display) and the experimenter's next question. A question asked without any change for a second time in everyday situations often carries the implication that the first answer was wrong or inadequate. It may have been this breakdown in mutual understanding between the experimenter adult and the child that contributed to these failures, rather than young children's complete lack of logic. This issue, namely, the potential lack of understanding between the child and an adult outsider/experimenter, can be problematic in all types of laboratory research contexts where the tasks are different from real-life experiences and events.

Overall, we can conclude that pre-operational children may be able to think in logical ways but only if the tasks are made meaningful and the instructions are clear and unambiguous. Donaldson also points out that 'ego-centrism' associated with the pre-operational stage is not just a young child-specific phenomenon. It is more a 'mode of thinking'. When we are familiar with the context, fully understand the task and have sufficient experience, we are more likely to demonstrate 'non-egocentric' ways of thinking, as opposed to situations where the task is not clear and the context is confusing.

Quote 1.2   On 'ego-centrism'

What is being claimed here is that we are all ego-centric through the whole of our lives in some situations and very well able to decentre in others. Piaget would not disagree with the claim that ego-centrism is never wholly overcome. The dispute with him is only about the extent – and the developmental significance – of ego-centrism in early childhood. I want to argue that the difference between child and adult in this respect is less than he supposes.

(Donaldson 1978: 25)

Differences between pre-operational and operational children are thus not quite as significant as was suggested by Piaget and his colleagues. The supposed abrupt change around the age of 7 seems more likely to be a gradual, continuous change, in that older children can achieve higher levels of within-stage consistency with fewer 'decalages' (slips, mistakes in the performance).

Quote 1.3   On the differences between pre-operational and operational children

It seems likely that, as far as the school years are concerned, the difference between younger and older children will turn out to be that the former can do what the latter can; but only sometimes, only under favourable conditions, only with help, only without distractions, only up to a point, without so much efficiency, without so much self-control, without so much awareness of the implications and without so much certainty.

(Meadows 1996: 29–30)

Piaget's assessment of the formal operational stage has also been criticised. It has been shown that even adults can be 'tricked into' giving the wrong answer in an operational problem-solving task, if the phrasing of the questions is misleading (e.g. Winer, Craig and Weinbaum 1992). In addition, as Wood (1998) and Donaldson (1978) both emphasise, adults do not always think according to the rules of formal logic. Indeed, this type of thinking is not generally necessary and practical in everyday life. Sometimes everyday rules may coincide with formal logic but other times they do not. Finally, one more point is significant. Piaget suggested that adolescents would reach the pinnacle of human development by about 12 years of age, yet there is plenty of evidence suggesting that development is nowhere near complete by this age. In fact Wood argues that many crucial improvements take place beyond 12 years of age.

Quote 1.4   On developments beyond the formal operational stage

Even though Piaget's claims, as they stand, seem overconfident regarding adolescent thought, there is plenty of evidence coming from other research to suggest that important developments take place around puberty (age 11–13). One line of evidence strongly suggests that literacy and especially the extended use of both reading and writing both trigger and facilitate important changes. Both reading and writing involve ways of communicating that transform the nature of children's knowledge of language and lead to more analytical ways of thinking.

(Wood 1998: 200)

Despite these criticisms, Piaget's legacy still lives on, albeit in significantly altered forms, i.e. with less rigidly described stages. Neo-Piagetian theorists (e.g. Karmiloff-Smith 1992; Halford 1992; Case 1991) still continue to argue that there are discrete stages of development in childhood.

1.3   Vygotsky's theory of development

Lev Vygotsky (1896–1934) was a Russian psychologist, a contemporary of Piaget. Just like Piaget, he has also been enormously influential in the field of education. As opposed to Piaget, his theory emphasises continuity in development rather than discontinuity or 'stages'. It focusses more broadly on the crucial role of social environment, and particularly on the role of expert helpers and the quality of their assistance to novice learners.

Quote 1.5   On the difference between Piaget's and Vygotsky's approaches to child development

Rather than being predominantly based on direct encounters with the physical world, for Vygotsky the construction of knowledge and understanding is an inherently social activity. Thus the child's interactions with other people, notably those who are more advanced and capable members of the society in which the child is growing up, mediate the child's encounters with the world-to-be-learned-about.

(Mercer and Littleton 2007: 13)

Vygotsky's interest is in the social processes of learning between people and how these processes contribute to and complement the individual's internal development. Any social encounter is situated in the local context but also in a particular historical and cultural setting. To describe how children learn from parents and teachers, Vygotsky proposed the 'law of cultural development' as an explanation. The adult and the child interact and together they construct new knowledge (*intermental* stage) and only following this stage is it possible for the child to internalise the new knowledge for individual reflection and understanding (*intramental* stage).

Quote 1.6   On Vygotsky's intermental and intramental processes

...processes of interaction between the child and others at the so-called intermental level, become the basis for processes that subsequently go on within the child – discussion, interaction and argument become internalised as the basis for intramental reflection and logical reasoning.

(Mercer and Littleton 2007: 14)

In order to clarify the relationship between intermental and intramental processes, Vygotsky proposed the concept of the *zone of proximal development* (ZPD). The ZPD is a metaphorical space between the child's level of current ability to solve a particular problem and the potential ability, which can be achieved with the careful assistance of someone else, usually a more knowledgeable expert, i.e. a parent or a teacher.

Concept 1.2   The zone of proximal development (ZPD)

[The ZPD] is the distance between the actual developmental level as determined by independent problem solving and the level of potential development as determined through problem solving under adult guidance or in collaboration with more capable peers. Intramental activity is accelerated by intermental (social) activity.

(definition in Vygotsky 1978: 86)

The ZPD captures Vygotsky's belief that learning and intellectual development are embedded in contextual factors and effective dialogue between the expert and the novice can accelerate individual learning processes. The ZPD also points to the fact that two learners who appear to be at the same level of development based on their individual achievements (e.g. as measured by test scores), can in fact be quite different in terms of how readily they may be able to respond to assistance within their ZPDs.

One implication of the Vygotskian approach for language teachers is that it is important to pay attention to individual differences and consider alternative ways and levels of assisting learners. It may be possible to start by offering only a small amount of assistance in case the learner is able to take some responsibility for solving the particular linguistic problem.

The concept of the ZPD has had immense influence on educational practices. It has also been the basis on which Wood, Bruner and Ross (1976) developed the concept of 'scaffolding'. Scaffolding is a special type of assistance that experts provide to novices while jointly engaged in a problem-solving task. The expert not only guides and supports the novice with information but may in fact intervene to simplify the task and to encourage the novice to persevere with the task. Effective interaction between expert and novice in the ZPD is crucial. Recognition of the importance of the quality of talk in classrooms has led to numerous approaches and techniques designed to enhance talk in interaction, such as 'guided participation' (Rogoff 1990) and 'teacher-led instructional conversation' (Tharp and Gallimore 1988). These techniques all imply that both the expert and the novice are active participants in the learning process:

- Learning is seen as a shared responsibility between tutor and student.
- Learners make unsolicited comments rather than just answer questions from tutors.
- Tutors provide a bridge between learners' existing knowledge and the new task.
- Tutors provide a focus and a structure to support the learners' problem solving (e.g. by offering reminders, simplifying the problem, removing distractions, highlighting crucial points and fading out when not needed any more).
- Tutors ensure that learners participate actively in the process of solving the task.
- Tutors build on learners' responses.
- Tutors encourage learners to use language effectively by paraphrasing learner utterances and introducing more formal phrases.

In order to highlight the importance of effective communication within the ZPD, Mercer (2000) introduced the concept of the *intermental development zone* (IDZ).

Concept 1.3   Intermental development zone (IDZ)

For a teacher to teach and a learner to learn, they must use talk and joint activity to create a shared communicative space, and intermental development zone (IDZ), on the contextual foundations of their common knowledge and aims. In this intermental zone, which is reconstituted constantly as the dialogue continues, the teacher and learner negotiate their way through the activity in which they are involved. If the quality of the zone is successfully maintained, the teacher can enable the learner to become able to operate just beyond their established capabilities and to consolidate this experience as new ability and understanding. If the dialogue fails to keep minds mutually attuned, the IDZ collapses and the scaffolded learning grinds to a halt.

(definition in Mercer 2000: 141)

From the language teachers' point of view important implications arise regarding effective teacher talk in children's second language classrooms. Teachers may want to explore their own target language use by recording their classes and examining features of effective communication – for example, how teacher talk may be adjusted to the needs of different learners, how paraphrasing or modifying instructions and explanations may help make input comprehensible to all learners in the class.

Vygotsky particularly highlighted the central role of 'language' and identified two main functions for language use. On the one hand, we use language as a communicative tool. In this way, we can jointly share and develop knowledge. On the other hand, language is also a psychological tool which helps us organise, plan and review thoughts and actions. In second language classrooms both these functions are relevant. In addition to using language to communicate with one another, learners can also use language to reflect on their learning. For example, when learners are given tasks and they collaboratively negotiate linguistic structures and forms, e.g. correct use of tenses, or phrases, or in the process of debating, negotiating and trying out different linguistic alternatives, they use language to reflect on their own knowledge and on others' contributions.

Swain's study (2000) illustrates how two students can benefit from the process of jointly negotiating a task in their L2. The learners in this study were recreating a piece of text after listening to it together. In order to recreate it to be as close to the original as possible, the learners have to work together and negotiate linguistic solutions together, focussing on those in particular that they are not sure about.

Quote 1.7   On why joint problem solving generates new linguistic knowledge

Our data showed that these actions generated linguistic knowledge that was new for the learner, or consolidated their existing knowledge. In line with van Lier, one might hypothesise that learners seek solutions to their linguistic difficulties when the social activity they are engaged in offers them an incentive to do so, and the means to do so. The important point however in this context is that it was the act of attempting to produce language which focussed the learner's attention on what he or she did not know, or knew imperfectly.

(Swain 2000: 100)

In the process of working together learners are using language (L1 or L2) as a psychological tool and they offer assistance to one another within their respective ZPD. Ohta (2001) argues that even learners who are at the same level of L2 development are able to assist one another in helpful ways.

Quote 1.8   On peer assistance

By working together learners collaboratively build utterances that are a bit beyond their reach and that of the interlocutor. Assistance is responsive to the partner's need for support. Learners wait patiently for the interlocutors to finish their utterances and step in to help at an appropriate time rather than interrupting. The assistance provided is overwhelmingly helpful.

(Ohta 2001: 125)

It is important to note that not all talk between learners during task-based interactions is necessarily helpful or leads to learning. Sometimes learners may mislead one another or come to solutions that are incorrect linguistically. Moreover, not all learners can communicate in pairs or groups effectively and it may be important for teachers to prepare their learners by providing explicit training in how to use effective strategies for talking and working together.

The following study is an example where 9–10-year-old children were exposed to a set of training materials that helped them become better communicators, and this in turn led to further individual benefits.

Example study 1.2   Mercer, Wegerif and Dawes (1999): 'Thinking Together' materials

'Thinking Together' is a set of materials that the researchers specially designed to enhance children's abilities to talk together effectively in groups. The research project was carried out in year 5 classrooms with 9–10-year-old children in primary schools in Milton Keynes, UK. Altogether 124 children participated. 'Thinking together' was aimed at training children how to use exploratory talk effectively, i.e. exploring each other's ideas, challenging assumptions, and debating solutions while working towards solving puzzles collaboratively. The researchers compared two sets of children: those who were in target classes where 'Thinking Together' was taught and those children who were of the same age but did not use the materials. Before and after the intervention, The 'Raven Progressive Matrices' (Raven *et al.* 1995) were used to measure children's general non-verbal reasoning. Non-verbal reasoning tasks are visual puzzles with geometrical shapes where children need to be able to notice patterns and complete missing items. During the intervention the children worked with these puzzles and received training in effective ways of working with them in groups. After the intervention, the researchers compared the quality of the children's talk, using video-recordings of groups where children participated in group tasks. The study showed that the 'Thinking Together' materials were changing the way children were using language in groups. Those in the target groups discussed issues for longer and in greater depth and they provided reasons and justifications more frequently than children who were following the ordinary syllabus. The researchers also noticed that children who increased their exploratory talk improved their

---

joint problem solving. Finally, as a result of the treatment, the target children became significantly better at solving these problems individually, which suggests that the collaborative activity accelerated their individual learning.

This project report underlines the importance of fostering effective group and pair talk in L2 classrooms and the importance of helping children to develop ground-rules and useful strategies. One of the most important implications from the Vygotskian approach to learning is that classroom talk involving both teachers and learners deserves a great deal of attention. In fact, classroom talk is where learning happens.

Quote 1.9   On the centrality of talk in learning

...it is in the talk through which tasks are defined, negotiated, and evaluated, and by means of which the students' participation is monitored, and assisted, and students and teachers engage in the dialogic co-construction of meaning, which is the essence of education.

(Wells and Chang-Wells 1992: 33)

1.4   The information processing (IP) approach

The 'information processing approach' is a more recent development in the study of cognition and, unlike the theories of Piaget and Vygotsky, it is not associated with a single name or a researcher. The IP approach to researching cognition is associated with the computer as an analogy to illustrate how the human mind works. Here we are interested in the mind in its development. Following the computer analogy, the human mind is studied both in terms of its hardware, consisting of the nervous system and the brain, sensory receptors and neural connections, and its software, comprising various mental programmes such as rules and strategies for remembering, organising and evaluating incoming information.

Quote 1.10   On the development of hardware and software systems in childhood

As children's brains and nervous systems mature (hardware improvements) and as they adopt new strategies for attending to information, interpreting it, remembering what they have experienced, and monitoring their mental activities (software improvements), they are able to perform increasingly complex cognitive feats with greater speed and accuracy.

(Shaffer and Kipp 2010: 299)

One of the most important aspects of hardware development is brain growth. At birth, the brain weighs only about 30 per cent of its adult weight. By the age of 2 the weight of the brain is about 70 per cent and by year 6 it is 90 per cent of its adult weight (Thatcher *et al.* 1996). While brain development is continuous and extends beyond childhood, researchers have identified spurts of brain growth based on brain weight and skull size and in electrical activity of the cortex (Epstein 1980; Thatcher 1994). Specific growth spurts seem to occur at the age of 1.5–2 years, 7.5–9 years, then between the ages of 12 and 15, and finally another spurt around 18–20. The first spurt coincides with major increases in L1 development and the second spurt happens around Piaget's pre-operational/operation shift. The next growth spurt may signal significant developments in abstract thinking and literacy development, while the last one can be associated with the development of the mature adult capacity for reflective thought (Fischer and Rose 1995; Kitchener *et al.* 1993).

In order to appreciate the different components and processes of the computer-mind, it is a good starting point to consider the mind as a multi-store model (Atkinson and Shiffrin 1968). According to this model, when input reaches the mind and the individual chooses to attend to it, it gets stored and processed, first of all, in the short-term memory store. This memory store is of limited capacity. Originally it was thought that the human working memory was capable of storing only seven pieces of unrelated information, such as seven random numbers (Miller 1956). This, of course, is not quite true, as the basic capacity can be increased dramatically according to what strategies the individual applies, such as categorising the seemingly random numbers in a meaningful way. According to Baddeley (1994), the capacity of the short-term memory store can be stretched to as many as 20 items in this way.

If the incoming new information is important, the individual needs to transfer it from the short-term memory store into the long-term store, which has infinite capacity. According to the 'levels of processing model' (Baddeley 1992), when information enters the mind, it can be stored in different ways. Information interpreted meaningfully or deeply will be linked to other information and will be retained more permanently in the long-term memory store. When a particular link is strengthened, it becomes automatised. Automatic processes demand little or no attentional resources and they can free up spare capacity for new tasks. Automatisation in language learning helps speakers retrieve huge chunks of language from their long-term memory store without having to consciously think about the separate constituent parts. This allows speakers to develop fluency in a second language.

1.4.1   Attention

Before any information can be stored or processed, individuals must notice it and attend to it. Children's attention improves over time. Sustained attention improves with age, which means that children get better at keeping their attention on the core features of the task. Cognitive inhibition, i.e. cutting out distractions while working at a particular task, also improves with age. Gains in cognitive inhibition are particularly marked from early to middle childhood but further improvements occur in adolescence (e.g. Riderinkhof and van der Molen 1997). Planning makes attention more effective and goal-directed.

Example study 1.3   Vurpillot (1968): Children's attentional strategies

In this study the researcher explored the attentional strategies of children between the ages of 3 and 9 years. The children were invited to look at two drawings of houses. Each house had six windows but there were some small differences between the two houses. Some windows were drawn with curtains, some without, some were open and some were closed. The children were invited to look at the two drawings to decide whether the houses were the same or not. Considering the task, the most appropriate strategy is to look at each window one by one in the first house and compare all windows to their corresponding pair in the second house. The researchers recorded the children's eye movements to gain insights into the ways which they directed their attention. The findings showed that all children aged 5 or younger only examined a few windows and quickly concluded that there were no differences, that the houses were exactly the same. Children from age 6 onwards were more likely to examine pairs of windows and those children older than 6 started to use the systematic strategy of comparing windows one by one, i.e. effectively and exhaustively.

Attentional strategies improve particularly sharply in middle childhood (Strutt, Anderson and Well 1975). Older children are more adaptive, adjusting their attention to the changing requirements of the situation. The ability to focus attention on the basis of previous experience of similar tasks continues to improve into adulthood as studying at tertiary level puts new challenges on attention allocation (Brown, Smiley and Lawton 1978).

From the language teacher's point of view, it is important to remember that young children under 5 or 6 years of age may not enjoy tasks such as 'Spot the differences' or other types of problem-solving puzzles, because they are not able to direct their attention in ways that may be required by such tasks. It is better to plan activities that involve routine patterns of active participation.

1.4.2   Processing capacity and memory store

The total processing capacity of the hardware system increases with age, according to Kail's studies (1993, 1997). He gave individuals between the ages of 7 and 22 a variety of cognitive tasks and found that the average processing time decreased with age for all tasks. A steady decline across the ages eventually trailed off at 12 years of age. This pattern was repeated for motor tasks such as tapping, clapping, and many other tasks. The patterns were very similar. These findings are particularly robust because the same patterns of declining processing speed can also be found among different nationalities and cultures.

Research into measuring memory stores shows that age differences are highly reliable, as children can store more information as they get older. Among the forerunners of modern memory research were Brunswick, Goldscheider and Pilek (1932), who found that a linear and steep rise in memory store development occurred between the ages of 6 and 11 years of age. This was followed by a plateau in performance during pre- and early adolescence. The basic memory span of a 2-year-old is just two items, the span of a 5-year-old is four items, the span of a 7-year-old is five items and the span of a 9-year-old is six items, as compared to the adult's span which is seven items.

Case (1985) found that as cognitive processes (e.g. multiplying 12 by 8) are executed more efficiently with age, they require less operating space. In turn, this means that there is more resource available in short-term memory to manipulate information. In children (between the ages of 3 and 16) the amount of resource available to store information about how to perform a task (storage space) is a function of their chronological age. (Case 1972; Scardamalia 1977). However, the resource necessary to process instructions and store task information (operating space) develops very slowly in younger children (aged 3–8) and more rapidly from 8 onwards.

1.4.3   Expertise

In addition to a gradual increase in capacity with age, domain-specific knowledge, i.e. expertise in a particular area, can enhance our ability to store, remember and retrieve information. A widely cited study by Chi (1978) compared recall results of chess positions of adult novices and expert children. Both adults and children were asked to remember a range of chess positions for recall. The experiment demonstrated that the chess-expert children had significantly better memory spans for chess positions than did chess-novice adults, despite the fact that adults showed larger memory spans for digits in an earlier task. This finding supports the argument that domain-specific expertise is an essential element of recall success. Experts have a more organised memory. Wood (1998: 35) argues that both experts and novices share the same channel capacity, but an expert manages to encode the six to seven items as a meaningful configuration rather than as seven isolated pieces. Another study by Schneider and Bjorklund (1992) confirmed the importance of domain-specific expertise. They investigated novice and expert soccer specialists' ability to recall lists and found that experts remembered far more items on the soccer list than did non-experts. Having large amounts of knowledge and experience in a particular area can aid memory functions although domain knowledge might not be the only factor, because these children are often highly motivated too.

Quote 1.11   On the importance of expertise

Several studies demonstrated that rich domain-knowledge enabled a child expert to perform much like an adult expert and better than an adult novice – thus showing a disappearance and sometimes reversal of usual developmental trends. Experts and novices not only differed with regard to quantity of knowledge but also regarding the quality of knowledge, that is, the way their knowledge was represented in the mind.

(Schneider 2006: 247)

Increasing levels of processing and growing expertise both have implications for language teachers. Children's gradual ability to cope with increasingly complex tasks which require storing and retrieving larger amounts of information (e.g. memory games and reading tasks) allows teachers to select more and more challenging tasks with older learners. Teachers can explore their learners' interests and expertise so that L2 learning may focus on these areas.

1.4.4   Mental representations

How does incoming information get represented in children's minds? In terms of the representations in the mind for concepts, facts and ideas, the number of representations and the strength of associations are increasing throughout the developmental process. Simon (1974) pointed out that older children seem to include more information per chunk than younger children. In terms of the nature of links among items, children progress from a more *perceptually* organised representation base to a more *conceptually* organised representation base. Young children form groups of similar objects on the basis of perceptual similarity. Older children however are most likely to invoke super-ordinate relations to explain similarity, moving to a more advanced, abstract, conceptually based approach. For example, in a word sorting exercise, younger children would put together *banana* and *monkey*, whereas older children would put *banana* with *apples* in the super-ordinate category of *fruit*. These developmental trends have implications for teaching L2 vocabulary.

Quote 1.12   On the development of hierarchical word relationships

The words for basic level concepts are the most commonly used words, they are learnt by children before words higher or lower in the hierarchy, they are the shortest words, and they are the words used in neutral contexts e.g. *We have always kept dogs* is more likely to be used than *We have always kept spaniels.* Conceptually, the basic level is the highest level at which objects have similar shapes, are used in similar ways and at which a single mental image can be used for the whole category (Lakoff 1987). So we can create a single image of a chair but not of furniture, and we interact physically with all chairs in the same way (by sitting on them), but interact differently with different examples of furniture. At a basic level, a child's experience with the physical world links directly into the development of concepts and vocabulary, serving as an 'entry point' for learning.

(Cameron 2001: 79–80)

Younger children's knowledge is not represented in the same way as older children's and adults' knowledge. They have fewer features or dimensions with which to represent concepts. Older children tend to have more numerous, more varied and more abstract dimensions. Category boundaries of young children's concepts are restricted and less well-defined. Children do not lack hierarchical structures entirely, but rather, their hierarchy is perhaps less reliable and contains incomplete information. Even preschool children's categorical representations are hierarchical (Keil 1981) but less complete and systematic. Overall, the development is the constant reorganisation of existing knowledge so that the more salient and more abstract attributes are stored at higher levels of hierarchy.

The following study illustrates the importance of the development of hierarchical relationships between concepts.

Example study 1.4   Verhallen and Schoonen (1993): Lexical knowledge of bilingual children

This study explored Dutch-speaking (monolingual) and Turkish-speaking (bilingual) children's lexical knowledge in the Netherlands. The participants were 80 children between the ages of 9 and 11. The researchers used a definition task where children had to express all the meanings of words that they knew. This allowed the researchers to analyse more in-depth how meaning structures were represented in children's minds. In definitions it is possible to refer to vertical relations between concepts which are hierarchical (such as the relationships between *dogs, animals* and *mammals*), or horizontal relations (such as the relationships between *dogs, they sniff, they are used for protection,* or *they have four legs*). The results showed the older children used more hierarchical categories whereas younger children used more horizontal categories and subjective descriptions. The study also showed that bilingual (Turkish-Dutch) children lagged behind monolingual children in their ability to produce effective definitions.

1.4.5   Memory strategies

Memory strategies can be divided into two categories: those related to short-term, and those related to long-term memory.

Concept 1.4   Short-term memory strategies: rehearsal, organisation and elaboration

These strategies are used to store information effectively so as to help recall. *Rehearsal* means repeating the information in some way orally or in writing. *Organisation* means to manipulate the information so that it is more meaning-ful, for example, by putting similar words together. *Elaboration* means extending the meaning of the items in some way, such as by using metaphors or analogies, to impose personal meaning on random information.

(adapted from Berk 2000)

Concept 1.5   Long-term memory strategies: recognition, recall and reconstruction

Once the information has been stored effectively, it will be available for retrieval. *Recognition* is noticing whether an image or concept is the same as or different from a given stimulus. Recognition is a fairly automatic process by the preschool years and it does not require a deliberate search of the long term memory store. *Recall* stands for generating a mental image of something that is no longer present. The better an item was stored, the easier it is to search for it. *Reconstruction* is a complex process of recalling information but it also requires interpretation.

(adapted from Berk 2000)

Children's memory strategies become more effective with age, helping them to remember/store information as well as retrieve information from storage when necessary. Strategies are acquired as a result of deliberate learning and training efforts but children need a significant amount of time and practice to perfect them.

The first memory strategy to develop is rehearsal or repetition for memori-sation, followed by organisation and elaboration. It appears that younger children, between 3 and 4 years of age do not rehearse at all. Children aged 7–10 can rehearse but only with help, while 12-year-olds can rehearse without help. According to Flavell (1992), rehearsal and organisation strategies develop quickly between 5 and 10 years of age.

Even when young children are encouraged to rehearse, their rehearsal efforts have little effect on their memory performance until about the age of 6 (Baker-Ward, Ornstein and Holden 1984). Some young children can be trained to rehearse, but when given the opportunity to do so without prompting, most children abandon the strategy (Bjorklund *et al.* 1997). Schneider and Bjorklund (2003) argue that young children may be taught to rehearse and this improves their performance, but this is a short-lived advantage and even with sustained training they cannot do as well as older children who rehearse spontaneously.

Quote 1.13   On rehearsal strategies

Even after being taught how to rehearse and having experienced evidence of its success, children will not usually rehearse spontaneously when they are asked to memorise other material. The use of rehearsal as an aid to memorisation might appear to be a simple, self-evident and obvious way to aid learning. But children learn how to do it gradually, throughout the early years of school.

(Wood 1998: 76)

The way children rehearse makes a difference, too. Simply repeating words is less effective than trying to organise them in some way: 8-year-olds repeat single words to try and remember them, whereas older children connect words within a list and repeat the list instead of individual items. This approach improves recall (Kunzinger 1985; Orstein, Naus and Liberty 1975).

Quote 1.14   On organisational strategies

Children younger than 10 years do show evidence of organising material which has to be remembered but often they do so in only a partially effective way – for example, organising a list of items is achieved best if all the items can be grouped into a small number of categories, but young children may use a large number of categories, and have several 'categories' which only include a single item.

(Smith, Cowie and Blades 1998: 377)

By the time children are 9–10 years of age, they can often consider the nature of the list before deciding on how to memorise it (McGilly and Siegler 1990). Unless items are highly familiar and strongly associated, children under the age of 8 do not group them at all (Best and Ornstein 1986; Bjorklund and Jacobs 1985). Until they are 9–10 years of age, children are no better at recalling items that can be semantically organised than those that are difficult to organise because they are unrelated (Hasselhorn 1992).

Quote 1.15   On emerging organisational strategies

It has been suggested that whereas older children and adults enter a memory task with a deliberate strategy to organize material for recall, the organization seen in the protocols of younger children may not represent an intentional strategy per se. Rather, the categorical relations in a list may be discovered only at output, while a child is in the process of retrieving individual items (Bjorklund 1980, Bjorklund & Hock, in press)[=1981: AP]

(Bjorklund and Zeman 1982: 800)

Ornstein *et al.* (1985) propose that children gradually transfer a strategic approach to settings in which the interim connections may be less salient.

Long after learning rehearsal and organisational strategies, elaboration is developed. Elaboration rarely appears before the age of 11. Children's working memories must expand before they are able to use this strategy (Schneider and Pressley 1997). With age, they are able to create more and more meaningful and memorable relationships between items that need to be remembered.

Children's ability to remember and retrieve experiences also develops steadily in childhood. General representations of events, called 'scripts', help children interpret familiar experiences (Berk 2000: 295). Young children develop 'scripted memory' of events by gradually absorbing what happens at significant events such as birthday parties, in the playground or at restaurants. Then they organise and interpret these experiences so as to make predictions about similar events in the future. Novel experiences are embedded into familiar ones slowly and gradually. Autobiographical memory is built up gradually, too. Parents play an important role as they help children construct increasingly complex personal narratives by frequently talking through important events in the child's life.

Older children and adults represent a large volume of information relying on their 'fuzzy trace memory' (Brainerd and Reyna 1990). This means creating a vague *gist* that concentrates essential content without the non-essential details rather than trying to remember everything word by word.

Concept 1.6   Fuzzy trace theory and gist

A theory that proposes two types of encoding, one that automatically reconstructs information into a fuzzy version called *gist*, which is especially useful for

Concept 1.6   (Continued)

reasoning and a second, verbatim version that is adapted for answering questions about specifics.

Gist is a fuzzy representation of information that preserves essential content without details, is less likely to be forgotten than a verbatim version, and requires less mental effort to use.

(Berk 2000: 293)

Young children are biased towards storing and retrieving verbatim traces. For example, 4-year-olds are better at answering verbatim whereas children at the age of 7 are better at gist (Brainerd and Gordon 1994). Fuzzy traces help retention a great deal and in most everyday life contexts fuzzy gist is sufficient. Fuzzy traces are also less likely to be forgotten than verbatim memories.

By the age of 6–7 children can recall the important features of a story, and they can combine information into a coherent story and reorder the sequence of events to make it more logical (Mandler 1984). Over time, school-aged children become more adept at drawing inferences about actors and actions, adding information to the story to help the listener to make sense of it, increasing the coherence of the story and its memorableness (Thompson and Myers 1985). Identifying and summarising main ideas is not produced spontaneously until high school years (Bjorklund and Douglas 1997).

How do strategies develop? Strategy development is a gradual process and at the initial stages children exhibit some deficiencies. There are some stages in development that seem to occur in many areas of development with many different tasks (e.g. attention, memory).

Concept 1.7   Strategy deficiencies

Production deficiency: at this first stage a child cannot use a strategy even though it would be helpful, e.g. not using rehearsal strategies when asked to remember some words.

Control deficiency: at this stage the child can sometimes use the relevant strategy but not always; usage is not yet consistent.

Utilisation deficiency: at this stage the child applies the rehearsal strategy consistently, but despite this his or her performance on the task does not seem improve.

Siegler's model of strategy choice (1995, 1996) maintains that children generate a variety of different strategies while they are working on any one task. Siegler presented children with different problems over an extended period of time and recorded their strategy use. Large numbers of different problems (i.e. reading, spelling, time-telling, word decoding, memory for word lists and basic maths) were used and children's strategy choices were recorded in different circumstances. Siegler concluded that children's strategy development follows an 'overlapping waves pattern', which means that multiple strategies are present at any one time, with some becoming less frequent, others more frequent, and still others rising and falling over time.

Quote 1.16   On overlapping waves of strategy use

Within this overlapping wave conception, some ways of thinking are prevalent early on and then decrease in frequency, others rise from infrequent to frequent use, and then fall to infrequent use again, others grow from infrequent to frequent use and remain frequent, still others are only used occasionally even at their peak. The advantage of this conception is that it allows depiction of the diversity of children's thinking over time and the introduction of new ways of thinking into children's cognitive repertoires.

(Siegler 1995: 267)

There are many implications that arise here for teachers. For example, fuzzy trace theory suggests that young children cannot cope with traditional listening exercises such as comprehension questions and it is best to develop tasks that allow them to listen and join in with a story, a rhyme or song as they feel ready to do so. The cyclical development of strategy use implies that teachers should consider helping children discover new strategies and encourage the use of different strategies related to the same task.

1.4.6   Knowledge about thinking and the mind

Concept 1.8   Metamemory and metacognition

These terms describe what children understand about their own memory and mind. *Metamemory* refers to our knowledge and understanding about memory functions while *metacognition* refers to our knowledge and understanding about thinking, how the mind functions. *Metacognitive strategies* are those that allow us to plan, monitor and evaluate our learning and thinking.

Preschoolers often confuse remembering, knowing and guessing, and their understanding of their own mind is incomplete and limited. Very young children believe that the mind is static and passive. So 5-year-olds still think it is possible to think of nothing, whereas 8-year-olds understand that it is not, because the mind is always active (Flavell 2000). Children younger than 6 have problems recalling what they were thinking just a minute before, whereas school-aged children make big gains in their understanding of their own memory functions and capacities. They begin to view the mind as an active constructor capable of selecting and transforming information. They are also more conscious of strategies for processing information and understand more about task variables that influence performance.

Knowledge about memory increases between the ages of 4 and 12. Children younger than 8 do not have a well-developed sense of self and an ability to self-evaluate (Harter 1998). The ability to evaluate one's performance particularly increases after the age of 11 or 12 but self-esteem generally decreases until mid-teens and this may have an effect on self-reporting (Muñoz 2007). There is a strong relationship between children's growing memory capacities, i.e. how much they can remember, and their metamemory capacities, i.e. how much they know about their own memory functions. This relationship appears especially strong in children 10 years of age or older. For example, Schneider (2004) reported that there are important correlations between metamemory, memory behaviour and memory performance. Children who can reflect on and explain why a memory strategy works show better recall (Justice *et al.* 1997).

It is clear from a teacher's point of view that these learners are ready to be engaged in self- and peer-evaluation and may be able to take some responsibility for their learning through planning, monitoring and evaluating learning processes.

1.5   Emotional development

Language learning is not just a cognitive activity concerned with remembering words and using effective strategies to recall, retain or reconstruct information. It is also important to acknowledge that children's language learning is embedded in their emotional development. Learning a new language may involve negotiating new identities and it is bound up with who we are, who we would like to become, how we feel about ourselves and how we form social relationships.

Quote 1.17   On the importance of identity in child L2 learning

Language is the most salient way we have of establishing and advertising our social identities (Lippi-Green, 1997). Young language learners, particularly second language learners, are developing new identities in the community and at school… Looking at children's progress in language learning through the window of identity has provided powerful messages that language learning is more than the development of language knowledge (see e.g. Toohey 2000; Miller 2003).

(McKay 2006: 30–1)

1.5.1 Emotions and sense of self

In the preschool years, young children are not yet able to control their emotions and their self-concepts are very basic. When asked to say who they are, they describe their physical appearance, their possessions and perhaps their everyday behaviours (Harter 1996; Watson 1990). Their self-esteem is very high and they are described as 'learning optimists', as they rate their own abilities high. They typically underestimate task difficulty and have clear expectations of success. They cannot yet differentiate between causes of success and failure. In the primary years children rapidly gain control of their emotions. Their self-concept becomes more complex and sophisticated. When they describe themselves, they will mention both positive and negative personality traits. They become competent at comparisons and frequently compare themselves to their peers. Through these comparisons they create a more realistic picture of the self and thus their self-esteem adjusts to more realistic levels. In adolescence, the control of emotions develops further but older children have much lower self-esteem and lower levels of motivation (e.g. Victori and Tragant 2003). Self-concepts become more sophisticated. In addition to physical characteristics and personal traits, older children emphasise interpersonal relationships when they are asked to describe themselves.

1.5.2 Friendships

Preschoolers consider everybody who is available to play as a friend. Children who play together at this age often play parallel games without much mutual engagement. Yet, friendship is very important to young children even at this early age and some research (e.g. Field 1984) indicates that even kindergarten children as young as 3–4 years of age go through a period of grief response when their friends leave.

In the primary school years children begin to develop more complex friendships. Friends like each other and respond to each others' needs. Trust becomes an important aspect of friendships. Children become more selective about friends and typically end up with just a few good friends. Sex segregation in friendship groups becomes very common and typically boys' friendship groups are different from girls' groups. Berndt (1982) suggests that boys' groups are competitive and grow out of team games that are increasingly more complex in their rule structure. Boys practise leadership and other social roles through participating in these games, whereas girls emphasise intimacy and exclusivity in friendship.

Bigelow and La Gaipa (1980) asked children to write essays about their idea and understanding of 'friendships'. The researchers noted that three different stages of development emerged with regard to the changing nature of friendships during the primary school years. When talking about friendships, children between the ages of 7 and 8 tended to focus on common activities or emphasised living nearby, whereas children between the ages of 9 and 10 began to mention shared values. Finally, by 11–12 years of age children mentioned the importance of understanding, self-disclosure and shared interests among friends. A similar study (Selman and Jaquette 1977) that used interviews to gain insights into children's conceptions of friendship, found that mutuality and reciprocity as important features of friendships emerged during the primary school years gradually. Children between the ages of 4 and 9 often said that a friend is someone who helps you but they did not talk about reciprocating. Between the ages of 9 and 15 an awareness of mutuality develops slowly and from 12 onwards children become more aware that relationships change and they accept that their friends need other relationships.

Quote 1.18   On features of children's friendships

A considerable body of research over the last 20 years has been summarised by Newcomb and Bagwell (1995) and Hartup (1996). Newcomb and Bagwell conclude that relations between friends, compared with non-friends, exhibit four particular features: reciprocity and intimacy; more intense social activity; more frequent conflict resolution; and more effective task performance.

(Smith, Cowie and Blades 1998: 121)

The following study illustrates how important friendship groups may be in terms of children's success and wellbeing at school.

Example study 1.5   Azmitia and Montgomery (1993): Benefits of working with friends

This study was carried out with 11-year-old children in California, USA. The researchers compared 18 pairs of close friends (who had each nominated each other as friends) and 18 pairs of acquaintances (who had not nominated each other as friends but who did not dislike each other either). All children had same-sex partners. The researchers gave all the children some scientific reasoning tasks to work on and video-recorded their performances. Interestingly, the results showed that friends did much better than non-friends. In particular, the problem-solving accuracy of friends was better than that of non-friends. The researchers noted that friends appeared more able and willing to evaluate and critique each other's reasoning and whenever they disagreed they managed to resolve the conflict successfully.

By adolescence, friendship represents greater depths of intimacy, loyalty and mutual understanding. Friends may help to relieve loneliness, sadness and fear. Forgiveness is part of friendship and only major upsets will lead to ending friendships. Adolescent friends tend to be very similar to one another, with the same educational aspirations, same family background and similar taste in music, clothes and hobbies (Berndt and Keefe 1995).

Overall the implications for language teachers are clear. It is important to consider friendship groups for group and pair work as well as classroom research, as children tend to respond better to tasks in a secure, friendly environment.

1.6 Conclusion

What can children's language teachers' learn from these theories? Combined with teachers' own experiences, these ideas, propositions, research findings and debates can spark new interests, encourage investigations and help explain successes and failures in everyday teaching. The best way to view these three approaches is to focus on how they complement our understanding about children. Table 3 attempts to summarise some implications that language teachers may consider, but it is important that we all draw our own conclusions and insights.

Table 3 Implications for language teachers

	Some implications for teachers
Piaget	Taking developmental stages into account when planning tasks, and teaching materials for different age groups
	Anchoring young children's tasks in the here-and-now and planning simple, one-dimensional tasks
	Encouraging hands-on tasks for young children
	Taking care with planning the language of task instructions and explanations
	Creating opportunities for creative explorations
Vygotsky	Importance of the tutor/teacher in guiding children's thinking
	Encouraging collaborative learning to create opportunities for peer scaffolding

Table 3   (Continued)

	Some implications for teachers
	Expecting wide variations across cultures but also across individuals as they interpret the same task
	Taking into account where the current level of the learners is so that they can learn effectively within their ZPD
	Paying attention to the process of learning rather than just the product/ outcomes
	Thinking about effective language use, both the teacher's and learners' in classrooms
Information processing	Teaching and practising strategies, not just one but different ones
	Encouraging different approaches and offering alternatives
	Encouraging students to monitor their behaviour and learning processes
	Building on an increasingly more powerful memory store capacity between the ages of 6 and 12
	Taking into account what children are knowledgeable about when planning teaching content
	Encouraging self-assessment, especially with children of 10 or over
Emotional development	Building positive self-esteem and a positive L2 self-image
	Encouraging pair and group work among friends

2
Language Learning Processes in Childhood: First and Second Languages

This chapter will

- outline some important aspects of L1 development in childhood
- consider the 'age factor' in L1 and L2 acquisition
- review the debate around the Critical Period Hypothesis (CP)
- discuss evidence from both naturalistic second language and formal foreign language contexts

2.1 Introduction

How are first and second languages learnt? Some theories stress universal/biological foundations and processes, others focus on cognitive aspects, such as memory functions and strategies, and yet others focus on social and cultural influences. Table 4 summarises some popular approaches.

Language acquisition research is a heavily contested area and no one theory is universally accepted. Each approach offers a different point of view and a different emphasis to explain language acquisition phenomena. Together they contribute to our ever-increasing understanding of language learning.

2.2 First language acquisition in childhood

Exploring L1 development is crucial to second language teachers. In order to make your teaching effective, you will need to familiarise yourself with the linguistic background of your pupils. How far have the children progressed in the acquisition of their L1? How much do they already know about the formal properties of their L1? What grammatical terminology are they familiar with? What vocabulary might still be unfamiliar in L1? Can they read fluently in their L1? How much writing do they do in L1? Questions like these will influence second language teachers' day-to-day decisions about how to

Table 4 Some language learning theories/approaches

Behaviourism (e.g. Skinner 1957)	Stimulus and response connections build habits
	Complex behaviour is shaped by breaking it into parts and drilling each element, adding new elements gradually
	Children are born as 'clean slates' and the role of the environment is significant in shaping them
Universal Grammar/ nativist approach (e.g. Chomsky 1987)	Humans are biologically pre-programmed to learn
	Language has an innate blueprint
	Universal Grammar contains a set of specifications for permissible structures in any language
	Children do not violate UG rules
Cognitive approaches (Anderson 1985)	The human mind is a computer
	Learning is information processing
	Learning involves storing and retrieving information
	Learning leads to automatisation and developing declarative and procedural knowledge
Input and interactions (e.g. Larsen- Freeman and Long 1991)	Both comprehensible input and interaction are necessary for language learning
	Meaning negotiation drives language learning forward
	Focus on form and feedback are also essential
	Learners need opportunities for input, interaction and output
Socio-cultural perspectives (e.g. Lantolf 2006)	Language learning is socially mediated
	Dynamic relationship between individuals and environment
	Interactional routines are culturally determined
	Linguistic and cultural knowledge are inseparable

approach aspects of L2 teaching. Children's L1 knowledge and competence also has consequences for researchers (see Chapter 6).

2.2.1 Preschool years

Babies begin their journey of becoming communicators (Berk 2000: 368) as they learn to use eye-contact, smile and begin to gaze in different directions. At around 3 months vocalisation and turn-taking begins and by the end of the first year most children realise that they can communicate effectively by using two basic forms of preverbal gestures: 'protodeclaratives' (i.e. making declarative utterances such as 'there' meaning 'My car is there') and 'pro-toimperatives' (i.e. asking for things such as 'koko' by stretching out to reach toward some chocolate, meaning 'Give me that chocolate').

The last quarter of the first year is an important turning point in development.

Quote 2.1   On the development of joint attentional behaviours

At nine months of age human infants begin engaging in a number of so-called joint attentional behaviours that seem to indicate an emerging understanding of other persons as intentional agents like the self, whose relations to outside entities may be followed, directed or shared.

(Tomasello 1999: 61)

The second year is characterised by more and more turn-taking and ges-tures. Typically 2-year-olds recognise about 200 words but would actively use fewer. Initially, they can produce only a small number of sounds: words with repeated syllables such as 'mama, dada, bye-bye'. Simplified language input from parents with words such as 'tummy, choo-choo' reinforces this phenomenon. Around the middle of their second year, toddlers begin to use sound patterns and rhythm in creative ways. This is linked to early encoun-ters with nursery rhymes and songs in the company of their parents, siblings or even the media. Many toddlers with busy parents spend a great deal of time watching TV or educational DVDs and learn new language in this way.

With regard to vocabulary acquisition, children first learn so-called mini-mal words (two sounds) then add an end consonant, change the length of the vowel and finally produce the word. Word learning is fast during the pre-school years and children's pronunciation improves steadily. Phonological development is largely complete by the time children go to school but aspects of intonation and stress patterns will be acquired much later. Babies say their first words at around the age of 12 months, although there is a large variation across individuals. By the time children go to school they know many thousands of words. It has been assessed that children pick up an average of 5–8 new words a day (Berk 2000). The earliest words they learn refer to important people, objects, familiar actions and their outcomes (e.g. 'mummy gone'). Between the ages of 18 and 24 months a spurt of vocabulary learning takes place. Nelson (1996) points to the centrality of naming and referring that is first achieved in non-linguistic ways (pointing and gesturing). Parents keep naming things and much of this early language learning is related to common vocabulary that will serve as a basis for further communication.

Quote 2.2   On the importance of naming things

Events are non-linear and dynamic – action, actor and object are only three aspects of the complex situation in which many objects are visible at once and many actions take place at the same time. The practice of drawing attention to a specific object and naming it places it in a privileged class of named things that can be talked about in any situation.

(Nelson 1996: 338)

Nelson suggests that this kind of naming and referring is later extended to abstract categories such as places, events and time. These abstract concepts are embedded in local cultures and they are learnt gradually over the years.

One strategy for word learning is 'fast mapping' which means acquiring words after hearing them used in familiar contexts. Both under-extension and over-extension are common strategies in early word acquisition. For example, 'bear' may be used to refer only to a teddy (under-extension) or 'chicken' might be used to refer to a duck (over-extension). Around the age of 2 coining words is common. Children use novel ways of expressing themselves by building on analogies, such as a child aged 3–4 years calling a Dalmatian 'a dog with chicken pox'. Another strategy for word learning described by Clark (1990) is the 'lexical contrast' strategy. When learning a new word, children contrast it with other words they already know. This works well for early vocabulary because many basic words refer to separate entities that are non-overlapping (such and 'big' and 'small'). A further strategy is 'syntactic bootstrapping' (Gleitman 1990) which implies deducing word meanings from how the words are used in syntax. For example, in the sentence 'the cat caught the mouse' and the 'the cat and the mouse are singing' the child can work out that the first verb requires an object whereas the second one does not. The first sentence implies that the cat is doing something to the mouse whereas in the second sentence they are doing something together. Learning new vocabulary is a cyclical process. Children hear a word in a relevant context but they may not immediately understand it. It may take encountering the word many times before they begin to use it themselves.

A variety of different factors influence word learning, such as children's cognitive foundations (their memory capacity, their ability to recall), the rate of their neurological maturation, personal styles, the quantity and quality of adult–child communication, individual differences and even cultural differences are important. Interestingly, birth order makes quite a big difference. First-born children are used to a more referential style of labelling objects while later-born children learn a more expressive style of language as they listen to their parents and older siblings regulating others' behaviour (Oshima-Takane, Goodz and Derevensky 1996). Overheard conversations between adults and older siblings may be a useful source for development. For example, it would not be unusual for a 3-year-old to say to an older sibling 'Stop making a fuss about everything', as he would copy what parents often say to older children. The younger sibling can pick up phrases like that, whereas a first-born would not have had this opportunity. On the other hand, other research cited by Foster-Cohen (1999) suggests that second-born children may be slower at language development in general because their older siblings can work out what they mean and take care of their needs without the younger ones needing to communicate their needs clearly and explicitly.

There are also interesting cultural differences in the way parents talk to their children and thus in the way children learn new words.

Quote 2.3   On cross-cultural differences

English-speaking mothers tend to use more nouns than verbs and this is reflected in the infant's tendency to learn nouns before verbs. By contrast, Korean- and Mandarin-speaking mothers tend to use more verbs, and their infants' early words are as likely to be verbs as nouns (Gopnik and Choi 1995, Tardiff 1996). English-speaking mothers tend to focus on objects and activities, giving their babies directions and asking them questions, whereas Japanese mothers focus on the child's feelings and emotions (Fernald and Morikawa 1993, Toda, Fogel and Kawai 1990), differences that are reflected in their infants' early word learning.

(Thornton 2008: 192)

In terms of grammar, the first sentences tend to appear at around 1.5 years of age. Initially toddler talk is described as telegraphic speech (no articles, prepositions or auxiliary verbs are used). Telegraphic speech is remarkably similar across many languages, although, for example, in highly inflected languages such as Turkish or Russian, important grammatical markers are acquired early. Telegraphic speech is often ambiguous because of its fragmented nature and this is why children need to use gestures and intonation to make their early utterances clearer and more effective.

At first, two-word utterances are used and then a third word is added. UG researchers believe that an elaborate grammar is already present in the background and this is why children do not violate certain rules of grammar. Others, such as, for example, Tomasello (1995) argue that two-word utterances are copies of adult language. By the age of 2–3 children begin to add grammatical markers such as plurals. Acquisition of less complex morphemes is followed by more complex ones (e.g. Johnston and Slobin 1979). The acquisition of grammatical morphemes is vital as these will help to give more precise meaning to utterances. In English, grammatical morphemes seem to be acquired in more or less a consistent order. Brown (1973) reported that the three children in a study learnt 14 grammatical morphemes in English in exactly the same order. Children over-extend grammatical rules as well: for example, the irregular past tense in English is often produced by using the regular marker (e.g. *go* **goed*). [The asterisk as usual indicates an incorrect form.] Initially children might use *went*, the correct form, because this is what they hear others use, but at a later stage when they learn to apply the '*-ed*' marker for regular past tense, they over-extend this rule to irregular verbs: '*go-goed*'. This is a very good example of a developmental error which shows active analysis and an attempt to apply rules. Negatives and questions also take a cyclical developmental path. Toddlers' first questions are declaratives with rising intonation such as 'where mummy go?' At the next stage they learn to use the copula 'where mummy is going?' and finally they correct the word order to 'where is mummy going?' The negative construction is similar. Development occurs in a step-like fashion. Three steps are common, such as 'No I go', 'I no go','I don't go'. By the age of 3 more negatives and questions are used. Sentences get longer as children learn to use coordination ('and'). Later, subordinate connectives are added such as 'if' and 'when'.

Research shows (e.g. Snow 1986) that speech addressed to young children (18–36 months) is both simpler and more grammatical than ordinary adult speech that is characterised by ill-formedness, hesitation and ungrammaticalities. As parents talk to their children, they constantly try to teach them about language. Children have a salient acoustic basis for separating out declaratives, imperatives and questions early on and because parents' utterances are restricted to the 'here and now' contexts, it is easy to follow the gist of the intended meaning. Parents are experts at fine-tuning their utterances to the needs of their children. Conversations are generally unequal, i.e. dominated by the adult interlocutor, although effective interlocutors follow the child's lead and let them guide the line of conversation. Parents expand on the child's utterances by reformulating telegraphic utterances, turning them into correct utterances. This may also be a source of syntactic development for children. Parent talk is an important source of continuous language development and the quality of the talk is particularly important in preparing children to become effective communicators.

Quote 2.4   On the importance of parent talk

Children whose parents were more prone to instruct made less than average progress whereas those whose parents were more concerned to ensure mutual understanding and, above all, to extend the children's topics through related questions, comments and explanations, were likely to make faster than average progress. These parents, it is suggested, as well as providing clear evidence from which the child can construct his control of the language, also increase his motivation to communicate and to acquire the means to do so more effectively.

(Wells 1986: 137)

Engaging children in dialogue, such as joint picture-book reading, enhances their language skills, but in addition to the linguistic benefits it also helps children learn about people's mental states, motives, emotions and different cause and effect relationships.

Young children's communication in the preschool years is very much related to their everyday experiences and they are not yet able to communicate in a de-contextualised manner. De-contextualised communication requires an acute awareness of the listener's needs. When a young child is talking on the phone and expects the listener to see his new pyjamas, it is clear that this child cannot appreciate yet that the person on the other end of the line cannot see the pyjamas and will need a description. According to Lloyd, Baker and Dunn (1984), younger children show inadequacies both as speakers and as listeners. As speakers they have difficulty in constructing unambiguous messages and as listeners they can't judge the adequacy of simple messages. Robinson and Robinson (1983) demonstrated that young children automatically blamed the listener for unsuccessful communication, regardless of the message quality. The authors showed that the shift from listener-blaming to speaker-blaming was a phenomenon which was related to coming to understand the importance of the message in referential communication. Most 3-year-olds give ambiguous descriptions of objects and places, and the ability to send a clear message (describe objects unambiguously) develops with age (Deutsch and Pechmann 1982). As they get older, children become better at communicating with unfamiliar people and people who are out of sight. They give fuller explanations to people they are not familiar with than to people who they know (Sonnenschein 1986).

The development of metalinguistic awareness is slow in young children. The ability to think about language as a system is emerging gradually. For example, most 4-year-olds are aware that word labels are arbitrary but some may confuse a long word with a long object: for example, they might say a long word is 'snake' because of the shape and length of the actual animal. Metalingustic awareness, just like metacognitive awareness (see Chapter 1), develops fast during the years of primary school as a combined result of factors such as physical maturation and school-induced strategies and thinking skills.

2.2.2   Primary school years

According to Berk (2000), between the start of the elementary school and adolescence, vocabulary increases four-fold, to about 40,000 words. Children's ability to understand and give definitions improves with age and synonyms appear, and 10–11 year olds can add new words to their vocabulary by simply being given a definition. Individual variation is still important and children who read regularly will accelerate their learning of words. School-aged children begin to appreciate multiple meanings of words, subtle mental metaphors, humour and puns, and they begin to develop a capacity for abstract reasoning. Understanding non-literal meaning and irony is a fairly late development, emerging after the age of 10.

Until the late 1960s it was assumed that a 5-year-old had already completed his acquisition of the syntactic features of the L1 and any further development was devoted to the expansion of the lexicon. However, given Piaget's findings about fundamental cognitive changes after the age of 5, it seemed reasonable to hypothesise that the child's linguistic competence must also reflect these changes. Equally, Carol Chomsky's (1969) work made it clear that there were very important developments taking place between the ages of 5 and 10. She drew a distinction between 'basic tools of language' (e.g pronominalisation) which she maintained were acquired by age 5, and 'specialised syntactic tools' for complex constructions gradually mastered between 5 and 10 years of age. Children during the middle school years acquire a range of complex structures, for example the full passive construction in English, by gradually extending the passive forms to different nouns, first animate, then inanimate. They also begin to form understanding of the pronoun reference systems and the conditional structures. Syntactic development is slow and continues into young adulthood.

One aspect of grammatical development is related to understanding that two or more functions can be represented by the same linguistic form. One study that showed this is focussed on the use of determiners in French-speaking children. Karmiloff-Smith (1986) proposed that children acquire just one function at a time and the development is stage-like. In French *le* and *les* have several related but different meanings: 4-year-old children can understand that 'le chien' makes reference to a single dog, and 'les chiens' to more than one dog. However, 'les' can also mean all the dogs, referring not just to 'plurality' but also to 'totality' (to all the dogs in a picture, for example). The ability to use 'les' to refer to 'plurality' and 'totality' simultaneously only emerges in French children at around the age of 8. It is not that children do not understand the concept of totality because they can express this meaning in a different way, but it is simply that they do not yet appreciate the multiple, simultaneous functions of the same linguistic form.

In addition to lexical and grammatical development, children during the school years become more explicit, more precise and more listener-friendly when constructing messages. At home, children are typically supported by sympathetic listeners who are familiar with their lives. Most of the early talk is about the immediate environment, about directly perceivable and observable aspects of everyday life. In fact, children often do not need to understand the precise meaning of a word because they can work it out from the context. It is this primary reliance on context and contextual cues which makes communication in a familiar setting a stress-free enterprise for the young child. School represents the first unfamiliar context for many children, where a totally different type of communication is required. At school, in conversations with teachers and peers over tasks, at least some of the time, the precise meaning of words can matter a great deal.

Quote 2.5   On switching to using talk in an intellectual way

When we as adult questioners, use language in ordinary conversational ways, we expect that children will do likewise. We would be quite annoyed if they did not. But when we set someone an intellectual problem (and even a very simple construct-mode problem may be genuinely 'intellectual') we switch, often without noticing it, into using language in an intellectual way – that is, with the expectation that the precise wording is to be definitive. We intend that language shall be given primacy over other clues as to the nature of the task. However, the trouble is that young children do not necessarily know this.

(Donaldson 1992: 119)

During the primary school years children experience and practise language in different contexts. They listen to the teacher talking at school, they talk together with their peers during groupwork and they chat in the corridor and in the playground. Those children who have siblings spend a considerable time talking and playing together. Some children will be learning and using two languages simultaneously during these years. For example, at home they may be using their L1 while at school they may be learning some or all subjects in another language (L2). Chapter 3 reviews many similar examples.

It is important to have a great deal of practice in participating in different types of school talk. Mercer (1995) distinguishes three types of peer talk in school activities. The first type is *disputational* talk which is characterised by disagreements, short turns offering suggestions, assertions and counter-assertions. The participants are in competition with each other and each seems to have a strong desire to win the point. The second type of talk is *cumulative* talk, where the speakers build positively on what the previous speaker says. This sort of talk is characterised by repetition, agreements, confirmations, elaborations. The third type of talk is *exploratory* talk, where the partners are engaged in critically constructing the discourse. This is a very important type of talk to experience. In this talk, children offer suggestions to each other for joint consideration and the suggestions are carefully examined, challenged and justified. In the process, alternatives are offered and reasons are requested. Talking with a partner is an opportunity to put half-formed ideas into words. Having to say what you mean, thinking aloud, is a way of making your thoughts clear to yourself and having to say things to a partner is a way of developing a shared understanding of ideas. Learning to analyse and clarify one's own thoughts and learning to express oneself clearly and explicitly are very important for different school tasks, and children make great progress in this respect during middle childhood.

According to Rodino and Snow (1997), this explicit way of talking is similar to the reflective and distanced stance that is required when working on writing tasks.

Successful participation in referential communication requires the development of an ability to appreciate different points of view. As children mature in their roles as communicators they begin to act more deliberately rather than spontaneously. They learn that message quality affects the success of communication, that as a listener you have to respond to both adequate and inadequate messages to help the speaker. The tendency to give more information after listener feedback also increases with age (Patterson and Kister 1981). Just as in other areas of strategy development (Siegler 1981), children go through certain stages to achieve ever-more effective strategies in handling referential tasks. Whitehurst and Sonnenschein (1981) explain that in a typical referential communication task a speaker can give three types of description. The first one is a 'contrastive description' when the speaker provides the minimum necessary information, not more and not less. This is the most effective strategy in describing. The second type is 'redundant description', when the speaker says more than necessary. Finally, the third type is 'incomplete description' when the speaker provides less than necessary information for the listener to act upon. Preschoolers are uninformative: they frequently give incomplete information in description tasks. Then, as they mature they become redundant, and finally contrastive speakers. Lloyd's study (1991) showed that 10-year-olds and adults behaved very similarly on a task that required communicating route directions to each other. However, 7-year-olds produced fewer adequate messages than the older children and adults.

De-contextualised communication and exploratory talk both place demands on children that are similar to the demands of literacy. The introduction to, and an increasing reliance on, literacy in primary school helps children make further developments in their L1. In the earlier years of primary school, children's writing does not much differ from their speaking. However, by the time they are 9–10 years old (Perera 1986) their writing differs from their speech in that it is largely free of mazes, i.e. circular arguments and repetitive descriptions, and colloquial constructions such as tag statements or vague clause completers. There is, however, great variation among children. Writing helps to develop many aspects of children's language such as relative clauses, parenthetical constructions, clause length, and subject and noun phrase complexity. All of these continue to improve into adulthood. The middle childhood is also the period of rapidly developing metalinguistic thought. Children are able to reflect on their thoughts and language use, bringing implicit knowledge to consciousness and examining it by using language. This leads to understanding new relationships and new theoretical propositions. They are also able to analyse unknown words and make inferences.

2.2.3   Post-primary school years

L1 development continues after the primary school years into adolescence and adulthood.

Quote 2.6   On developing one's L1 across the lifespan

... in terms of Piagetian cognitive maturation, adolescents have attained abstract thinking and have well-established metacognitive skills, developments that both enable and are fostered by advances in linguistic knowledge. This does not mean that later language development culminates in a clear end state. Rather, the process continues across the lifespan ...

(Berman 2007: 348)

During the post-primary years, many further, subtle structural refinements take place in addition to the massive acquisition of more marked lexis. The most important changes that occur in this period are strongly related to the acquiring of new, more sophisticated forms of literacy.

Vocabulary increases by thousands of words each year (Anglin 1993). Late elementary/early high school students will learn 3,000 to 5,400 words per year. This advanced vocabulary store contains more marked forms which are greater in length, less frequent and semantically more specialised or more formal. Adolescents are able to use more affixing, compounding, synonymy and polysemy. They also develop an increasing sensitivity to different registers. They are able to alternate between colloquial, everyday expressions and words which are more formal, more distanced and academic in style. These words in English tend to be of Latin origin, e.g. *alternate* instead of *switch*. In writing, their lexical diversity and the mean length of sentences will increase. Adolescents appreciate jokes, riddles, similes, idioms, metaphors, proverbs, and they understand figurative language and irony. Different types of linguistic humour ranging from obvious to subtle become available.

Complex grammatical structures are used more often, such as, in English, the past perfect tense. The use of infinitives, gerunds and participles will also increase together with non-finite subordination, as in 'Being close friends, they decided to attend the event together'. Tighter connectivity appears in discourse. Passives and modals are used a great deal. Complex noun phrases and sophisticated sentence connectors appear.

According to Berman (2007), multifunctional structures take on ever more sophisticated forms, such as those demonstrated in the following example. One of the earliest inflections acquired in English is the *-ing* ending that is initially used in young children's speech to describe present and past progressive events, such as the 'the children are swimming/were swimming'. Then, at the next stage, the non-finite form appears, such as 'watch someone swimming'. Much later again, the nominalised form is acquired, such as 'swimming is healthy'. Next, non-finite subordination appears, such as 'swimming fast to save his life, he swallowed a lot of water'. Finally, a relative construction with the *-ing* form appears: 'an issue requiring attention'. This illustrates well the route of development of a single structure from preschool to mature, proficient speakers/writers.

Quote 2.7   On the route of development

Clearly no single factor can explain the complex and protracted route from preschool interactive language use to command of formal book language. Growth in command of linguistic forms and structures is an obvious prerequisite but its pattern is not simply cumulative. Rather, forms previously used in restricted contexts and for limited functions are extended to new metaphorical and communicative contexts, while initially restricted discursive functions are expressed by means of an expanding repertoire of linguistic forms.

(Berman 2007: 359)

Wood reminds us that spoken fluency, for example in telling effective narratives, is not an automatic skill but something that adolescents acquire parallel to learning sophisticated literacy skills. To tell a story coherently requires orchestrating a range of different skills:

Quote 2.8   On adolescent spoken fluency

The child that is fortunate enough to achieve fluent levels of literacy has at her disposal a whole new range of words, linguistic structures and skills in planning which enable her to create interesting, informative, dramatic and *coherent* narrative. Such a child may draw upon and exploit two powerful bodies of expertise. On the one hand, she has her voice, perhaps the most versatile of musical instruments, rich in prosodic melody and embedded in bodily movements that help to orchestrate her interactions with her listeners. On the other hand, she has command over a range of literacy devices and structures that can be exploited in speech to make what she says dramatic, flexible, variable, versatile, and should she so wish, fast and efficient.

(Wood 1998: 211)

Adolescents are continuously exposed to new social experiences. Their extensive participation in peer culture and their more independent lifestyle will offer new opportunities to develop their L1, combined with the effects of promoting more formal styles of language in classrooms. Those preparing to apply for places at college or university will experience yet new, more academic ways of using their L1 in interviews, tests, essays and reports.

2.3   Second language acquisition in childhood

Children are believed to be more successful second language learners than adults. Parents all over the world put their children in language schools at an early age, convinced that the earlier they start learning, the better. But what is the actual research evidence behind this widespread belief about young children? Are young children superior language learners as compared to older learners? What are children's advantages over adults, if any?

When it comes to pinpointing the exact effects of age on the processes of second language acquisition, research to date has produced rather complex results. Although age is inevitably important, it is clear now that other factors may also play equally important parts in the process of learning a new language. For example, factors such as supportive contexts, opportunities to practise, motivation and the quality of formal instruction all make a difference, and age simply cannot be separated and examined in isolation.

Quote 2.9   On the age factor

...while everybody agrees that the learner's age does influence the SLA process, scholars have not been able to establish the exact pattern or nature of age-related change, let alone identify the specific causes and mediators of the process.

(Dörnyei 2009: 233)

2.3.1   Critical Period Hypothesis

The Critical Period Hypothesis (CPH) is a term taken from biology and it refers to restrictions on the development of some skill or behaviour. When timing is critical, a particular development can only take place within defined periods of time. For example, new-born ducklings will bond with the mother duck only if they have a chance to see her and follow her within a few critical hours after their birth. The question is whether acquiring languages to native-like levels can happen within a similarly defined critical period.

Concept 2.1   The Critical Period Hypothesis (CPH)

In its most succinct and theory-neutral formulation, the CPH states that there is a limited developmental period during which it is possible to acquire a language, be it L1 or L2, to normal, native-like levels.

(Birdsong 1999: 1)

CPH in L1

There is more or less unequivocal agreement about the existence of a weak form of a CPH for first language acquisition. If a child is deprived of their first language from birth, they will certainly suffer serious negative consequences. Studies of children who were for some reason abandoned or grew up in isolation (e.g. Curtiss 1977) and deaf children who did not learn sign language early in life, show that trying to learn L1 after puberty is a difficult achievement which leads to rather poor outcomes that cannot be described as comparable to 'native-like' competence. Mayberry, Lock and Kazmi's (2002) work with deaf children also illustrates that there definitely is a critical period for L1 acquisition.

Quote 2.10   On CPH in L1

Our results show that the ability to learn languages arises from a synergy between early brain development and language experience and this is seriously compromised when language is not experienced during early life...

(Mayberry, Lock and Kazmi 2002: 38)

These authors conclude that missing out on the opportunity of learning one's first language in early life has irreversible consequences. Others argue that depriving a child of language in the early stages of life also affects their cognitive development and it may be the case that the combined psychological and cognitive effects cause these problems rather than a critical period for language *per se*. (Peterson and Siegal 1995; Lundy 1999).

CPH in L2

Is there a similar critical period for second language learning? This question is much harder to answer. A great deal of research has been completed both to support and to refute the CPH. Birdsong states that the CPH occupies an 'unmistakeable centrality' in SLA research (Birdsong 1999: 1) and it continues to engage researchers today. Originally, the Critical Period Hypothesis in L2 was based on neurological arguments based on Penfield and Roberts (1959). They proposed that L2 acquisition was most efficient before the age of 9, at which point the brain becomes stiff and rigid and loses its capacity for natural acquisition. Progressive lateralisation of cerebral functions and ongoing myelination in the Broca area will eventually cause such stiffness. (Penfield and Roberts 1959; Lenneberg 1967). Lenneberg (1967) proposed that the critical period is associated with a 'heightened plasticity' in the brain which is lost, at least partially, once the brain becomes lateralised and stiff.

Age ranges for child/adult SLA

If there is a critical period for SLA, how can it be tested? At what ages should children be tested? At what age can we separate child SLA from balanced bilingual acquisition that starts at birth? Not unexpectedly, different age ranges have been proposed by different researchers. According to Schwartz (2003), in early bilingual acquisition the two systems of grammar develop at the same time whereas in early L2 acquisition one system of grammar is already formed at the time the child encounters another language. Dimroth (2008a) proposes that most important aspects of morphosyntax and phonology are not yet all in place before the age of 4, and therefore child L2 acquisition starts at 4 years of age. Other researchers, such as Nicholas and Lightbown (2008) claim that early child SLA starts earlier, at about 2 years of age, arguing that L1 grammar is already well established by then, and children who begin an L2 at age 2 already rely on their L1 as a resource, as evidenced by code-switching. Another relevant question is about how long the critical period might last. Some argue it is complete by the age of 7, while others think it lasts until the age of 15, with each period being critical for the acquisition of different aspects of the second language; 7 years of age is also often referred to, following Piaget's famous cut-off point.

According to Singleton (2003), the CPH in L2 acquisition has been interpreted in different ways and there seem to be three commonly held views. First, after a certain maturational point learners are not able to attain native-like levels of proficiency; second, after a certain maturational point successful learning requires more effort than before; and finally, after a certain maturational point the processes of L2 acquisition are qualitatively different from before.

These suggestions imply that comparisons between the L2 acquisition processes of adults and children of different ages are important. First of all, some evidence points to the finding that at least in some respects, grammatical development is very similar across children of different backgrounds. Dulay and Burt (1974) claim that children pass through some 'universal' develop mental stages at least with regard to the development of morphology. They compared the developmental paths of children learning English from two different L1 backgrounds, Spanish and Chinese. They used a 'bilingual syntax measure' instrument (BSM) which consisted of picture stimuli to elicit responses from the children. There were no correct answers but the questions were constructed in such a way that it was almost unavoidable to use certain structures. They administered the BSM to 55 Chinese- and 60 Spanish-speaking children, all aged 6–8 years. The speech samples elicited in this way were then analysed to investigate 11 morphemes (such as pronoun case, articles, the copula, *-ing* for progressive tenses, plural forms, past regular and irregular and possessive and 3rd person singular forms). The results showed that the acquisition of these for Spanish and Chinese children were virtually the same. The authors acknowledge that their claims cannot be extended to other areas of English grammar; however, they also suggest that the grammars of Spanish and Chinese are so widely different that these children must have universal mechanisms to guide them to be able to perform in such an uniform manner. What about adults? Or is this only specific to children? In fact, the area of morphosyntax is so robust that even adults show a similar path of acquisition. Bailey, Madden and Krashen (1978) replicated the procedures used by Dulay and Burt (1974), with 73 adult subjects who were between the ages of 17 and 55. The results showed that despite the differences among adult learners in the amount of instruction, exposure to English and use of mother tongue, there is a high degree of agreement with regard to the difficulty of grammatical morphemes. Adults also use common, universal strategies for language learning. In addition, the relative accuracy of the different forms in adults is similar to the relative accuracy observed in children. Many other studies also attest to the fact that the developmental order is very similar in all learners (Cancino, Rosansky and Schumann 1978; Clahsen 1984).

Some universal processes are shared across L1 and L2 acquisition for young children (especially in the area of morphosyntax), although more recent research that compared L1 and L2 development found that even at a very young age, children's first and second language acquisition processes are not actually identical. There is plenty of evidence for L1 transfer into L2, just as in the case of adult learners. For example, Haznedar (1997) studied the L2 acquisition of English by a Turkish boy (Erdem) who was just 4 years old when he started at a nursery in an English-speaking context. Data collection began after a month in the new environment and it showed that Erdem's utterances were influenced by transferring Turkish structures into English. Similarly, Whong-Barr and Schwartz (2002), who studied Korean- and Japanese-speaking children (between the ages of 4 and 10) learning English as an L2, showed that L1 transfer was an important feature of their L2 interlanguage, not just at the beginning of the acquisition process but throughout the period of study, which lasted several years.

Some recent longitudinal research with untutored children (Dimroth 2008b) also shows differences in the way children of different ages process a second language: in particular, important differences were discovered with regard to the order of acquisition of different aspects of grammar. In Dimroth's study, two Russian beginners of L2 German (aged 8 and 14) were compared with one another but also with adults with regard to the acquisition of negation and finiteness in German sentence grammar. The study showed that the adolescent learner was more similar to the adults than the younger learner. The child learner was faster and she acquired the grammatical features in a different order. Dimroth (2008b) suggests that younger children assimilate input patterns in a different way, i.e. without analysis, whereas older learners analyse the input more carefully.

Current neurological experiments point to important differences in the way older and younger learners process second languages. For example, Weber-Fox and Neville (1996, 1999) explored the different brain patterns of younger and older second language learners. They found that older learners processed L2 in different ways from younger learners, although it may be that the different proficiency levels of the groups influenced the results. Similarly, a study by Kim *et al.* (1997) looked at the differences in the location of two languages in the brain in bilingual learners, using functional magnetic resonance imaging (MRI). Both very young beginners and older beginners were given a sentence generation task and their brain activity was monitored while they were engaged in the task. The results indicated that the older beginners had two distinct areas of activity in the Broca area whereas in the case of the early bilinguals there was no separation between languages. This seems to point to the fact that there is neurological difference between how younger and older children process language.

2.3.2   Rate of development: older learners' advantage?

Krashen, Long and Scarcella (1979) suggested that in order to tease out young learners' advantages over adults' in second language learning we should explore both the rate of language learning and the ultimate attainment that learners achieve. With regard to the rate of language development in an L2, research evidence seems to be clear, and clearly in favour of older learners. Studies that focus on measuring learners' rates of development typically compare learners of different ages.

One of the most famous and most often cited examples in a naturalistic setting that compared the rate of development across different age groups was a series of studies in the Netherlands. It was conducted by Snow and Hofnagel Höhle (1978a, 1978b/1982).

The first study (1978a) was conducted with 69 English-speaking subjects of all ages (from very young children to adults) who were all classified as new arrivals to the target country (The Netherlands). At the time of testing, some subjects had been in the country for one year, while others only for three months. The first group of subjects who had been there for a whole year were tested only once, at the end of their first year while the second group was tested three times within the year, at four-month intervals. This grouping allowed the researchers to compare subjects with different lengths of residence (albeit all quite short). A variety of different tests were used which tapped into subjects' pronunciation, auditory discrimination ability, morphology, vocabulary, sentence repetition and translation. The findings were clear-cut in that adults and adolescent beginners showed a clear advantage over the younger beginners in all areas of competence, although this advantage began to disappear by the end of the year. The instruments overall favoured the older learners because they tapped into more abstract and explicit knowledge. There was only one test related to phonological and phonetic skills that did not show significant differences between younger and older learners.

In the follow-up study (Snow and Hofnagel-Höhle 1978b/1982), exactly the same way as in the first study, 51 beginners (within six months of arrival) were tested three times and 30 'advanced' speakers with at least 18 months in Holland were tested only once. This time the researchers included a greater variety of tests such as pronunciation, auditory discrimination, morphology, sentence repetition, translation, sentence judgment, vocabulary, story comprehension and storytelling. On the first testing occasion significant age differences were noticed among the beginners, and in all cases the adolescent and adult subjects outperformed the younger ones, except for the imitation condition of the pronunciation test. The advantage of the older learner over the younger seems to be especially high for aspects of the second language that are dependent on rule acquisition, i.e. in syntax, morphology and metalinguistic ability. Differences in pronunciation, auditory discrimination, story comprehension, and spontaneous fluency tests diminished earlier than in morphology and sentence translation tests.

In another study, Snow and Höfnagel-Höhle (1977) combined a laboratory test with a more naturalistic component. In the laboratory test, the participants were asked to imitate Dutch words which were judged by native speakers for accent. In the naturalistic study participants in their first year in the Netherlands were tested every four to five months using both an imitation task and a spontaneous production task. These were again recorded and evaluated by native-speaker judges. The researchers found an initial advantage for older subjects but younger learners were catching up and became better at pronouncing some words than the older learners after 10 to 11 months of residence. After 18 months of residence, some adults showed lower scores than the children.

Many other studies indicate that, overall, older learners progress faster and do better on measurement tests. In The French immersion programmes older learners have a clear advantage over younger ones except for pronunciation and oral fluency (Cummins 1983; Harley 1986; Swain 1981). Turnbull *et al.* (1998) clearly show that those who started earlier (i.e. at a younger age) outperformed those who started at a later age on a range of spoken tests.

Pronunciation and oral performance, especially face-to-face communication and listening, seem to be the areas in which young learners do relatively better, but even here their advantage is not completely undisputed. Olson and Samuels (1973) investigated the German pronunciation of three different age groups of English speakers: 20 elementary school pupils (aged 9.5–10.5), 20 junior high students (14–15 years of age) and 20 college students (18–26 years of age). The participants' pronunciation was tested using a German phoneme pronunciation drill task, which took about 15–25 minutes to complete. All subjects' performances were recorded and the results clearly showed that the two older groups, i.e. the junior high school students and the college students, performed significantly better than the younger ones.

In an attempt to confirm adults' initial advantages, Aoyama *et al.* (2008) compared phonetic measures in Japanese adults and children learning English in Canada during the first two years of immersion in an L2-speaking environment. The point of this study was to tease out whether adults did have any advantage over children and if yes, was this short-lived or sustained. The children's mean ages were around 10 years while the adults' mean age was 40. Altogether, 16 adults and 16 children were included. All adults learnt English in Japan starting between 11 and 13 years of age but none of the children knew English when they arrived in Canada. In the study, 26 English words (frequently occurring familiar words) were elicited three times. The tests were administered three times over a 1.6-year period. The results showed that adults' intelligibility scores were higher but children improved between time 1 and time 2, and thus in the end no significant differences were shown. All scores, however, remained significantly lower than the native English speakers' scores. While the children's production improved more rapidly than the adults', it is still the case that after 1.6 years of exposure, all children still had a noticeable foreign accent.

In sum, it seems to be the case that in natural contexts older learners have an initial advantage over younger learners but younger learners tend to catch up in the long run. What happens in formal contexts where children are learning second languages as school subjects? Will older learners progress faster? If yes, how can we protect and justify early foreign language learning?

In the 1960s when French was introduced in primary schools in England and Wales, the Burstall report (Burstall *et al.* 1974) which evaluated the project found some interesting benefits gained by younger learners. They compared children who started French early at the age of 8 (experimental group) and those who started later at 11 years of age (control group). Comparisons between the two groups were made twice, once at the age of 13 and a second time at 16. The first time around the findings showed that the experimental pupils outperformed the control pupils on speaking and listening but the scores on reading and writing in the control group were just as high, or higher, than the experimental group. Three years later, when the same children were tested again, the only test the experimental group scored higher on was the listening test. The rest of the tests did not show a difference. This was taken as evidence for the overall superiority of the older learner and the funding for the programme to start a foreign language early was cut. The conclusion of the report was that early foreign language learning in formal contexts was not a worthwhile activity because initial advantages would disappear by the time the children study the language more seriously in secondary school.

A much larger study, The Barcelona Age Factor project (BAF 1995–2002), compared different age groups of English language learners in Spain. Data were collected from over 2,000 participants after approximately 200, 400 and 700 hours of instruction in English. To compare the results of those who began learning English at the age of 8 and those at the age of 11, a large range of different measures were used including measures of speaking, listening, writing, reading and comprehension tests in L1 (which was Spanish for some and Catalan for others). Several measures were meaning-focussed, such as an oral interview and a role play. The results showed that late starters, i.e. those who started English at 11 rather than 8, always obtained higher scores than the early starters. After 200 hours (time 1 testing) the difference between the two groups was marginally significant on many tests. This initially small difference reaches significance after 400 hours (time 2 testing) in favour of the older learners. After 700 hours (time 3 test) significant results on all tests in favour of the older learners were obtained. Muñoz (2006) concludes that there exists an age-related difference in the rate of foreign language learning in a school setting in that older learners indeed showed the most rapid initial progression. A distinction emerges between two types of tests used: more cognitively demanding tasks, with tapping into the morphosyntactic component, and the less cognitively demanding task, tapping into speech perception and production and fluency tasks. A strong increase in the development of morphosyntactic ability can be detected at around the age of 12. The progression seems much faster between ages 11 and 13 than between ages 14 and 16.

Quote 2.11   On the advantage of older learners in foreign language settings

In sum, differences in cognitive development play an important role in explaining why older learners in a formal foreign language situation are faster and more efficient than younger learners, especially in tests in which the morpho-syntactic component is important. The older learners' superior cognitive development also allows them to take greater advantage of explicit teaching processes in the classroom. In contrast, young learners seem to favour and to be favoured by implicit learning. Implicit learning improves with practice but occurs slowly and requires massive amounts of exposure.

(Muñoz 2006: 32)

Muñoz's findings fit well with the 'older the better' conclusion. Older learners and adults are indeed very different from younger children. What is the underlying reason? Felix (1985) proposes that the co-existence of a UG (Universal Grammar) and a domain-specific cognitive function becomes untenable in adults and the competition between these two systems results in the dominance of the cognitive function, leaving no room for the innate acquisition system. This is known as the 'Competition Hypothesis'. Bley-Vroman

(1989) proposed the 'Fundamental Difference Hypothesis' which also denies adults' access to UG. In agreement with Bley-Vroman, DeKeyser (2000) comments that between the ages of 6/7 and 16/17, we all lose the tool for implicit induction to human language.

Although there are indications in the BAP data that by time 3 testing the youngest learners seem to be catching up on some measures, in foreign language contexts children simply do not receive enough contact hours for this catching up to be completed. Interestingly, Singleton and Ryan (2004) calculate that comparing the amount of exposure in naturalistic and formal language learning contexts, it would take approximately 18 years for foreign language learners to catch up with older beginners, if at all. This is well beyond the length of time we can follow participants in a research project. In fact this would stretch well beyond the period of schooling in most people's lifetime.

While the Barcelona study offers convincing results because of the size and the length of the project, it is important to add that the actual quality of materials and teaching were not really evaluated. What if good quality teaching can make all the difference? A small project in Croatia (Mihaljević Djigunović and Vilke 2000), which ran for eight years, reported important benefits for younger children. In this project 1,000 first graders (age 6–7) learning one foreign language (English or French or German or Italian) were investigated and compared to a group that started later, at the age of 10. The experimental language programmes were focussed on the intensity of exposure and offered natural content-based conditions. The tests that were used included oral interviews, classroom observations, storytelling and proficiency tests. Young learners were developing fast at the phonological level (Kovačević 1993), mastered prototypical language elements faster than other parts of the language, and interestingly, a number of learning and communication strategies also emerged. In the final evaluation the researchers found that the experimental project students were significantly better at pronunciation, orthography and vocabulary than the older beginners. The researchers concluded that the project learners outperformed the other groups on tests of implicit knowledge. The most important variable to explain the younger learners' success was the quality of input/teaching, but also the tests themselves were more naturalistic.

2.3.3 Ultimate attainment: younger learners' advantage?

Older learners progress faster initially, due to their superior strategies, cognitive capacities and strong motivation – but younger learners often overtake them in the long run. This implies that younger learners are likely to have an advantage when it comes to ultimate attainment.

Studies that explore ultimate attainment of learners who started an L2 at different ages often use native speakers both as control subjects and as judges of non-native performance. If those learners who started younger compare more favourably with native speakers, then it could be argued that an early start contributes to higher, native-like levels of ultimate attainment. Ultimate attainment research to date has produced very complex results. Most of these studies have been conducted with immigrants and a large proportion of them have focussed on pronunciation and on grammar. This is partly because these are aspects of language competence that can be tested easily and quickly in experimental circumstances. Pronunciation and accent have also been particularly popular because a native-like accent is believed to be more difficult to attain than other aspects of competence for older learners.

Pronunciation/accent

The superior ultimate attainment of younger children was confirmed in a study conducted by Oyama (1976, 1978). In the first study (1976), 60 male immigrants participated whose age on entering the USA ranged between 6 and 20. The first variable in this study was the age of onset (AO) of second language acquisition of these subjects. The subjects' length of residence ranged from 5 to 18 years and this was the second variable under investigation. The participants' pronunciation was tested using two 45-second extracts from a reading task and a free speaking task. A group of native speakers (NS) also performed the same tasks. All performances were recorded and the NS' and non-native speakers' (NNS) recordings were randomly mixed up on a tape. Then NS judges were asked to rate the 'nativeness' of the extracts. The judges rated the performances on a five-point scale from 'heavy accent' to 'no accent at all'. An extremely strong effect for age of arrival was found but almost no effect for the number of years spent in the USA. The youngest arrivals within the NNS group performed within the range of the NS controls whereas those above the age of 12 did not. In a second study (1978), listening comprehension scores were compared, based on the performances of the same subjects. Twelve short English sentences were recorded by native speakers and the participants had to repeat these. Subjects of 11 years and under were native-like whereas older subjects were not. Those arriving after age 16 performed markedly worse than natives, suggesting that there may be a second cut-off point. These results suggest that pronunciation in the long term is probably affected by age of arrival but not by length of residence. The cut-off point for pronunciation seems to be around the age of 12.

In their studies, Flege, Monroe and McKay (1995) and Flege, Yeni-Komshian and Liu (1999) also showed that the degree of authentic accent and age of arrival correlated. The authors studied Italian immigrants in Canada who had lived there for at least 15 years at the time of testing. In 1995, 240 Italian immigrants were tested. They were asked to read out five short English sentences and their performances were mixed up randomly with the performances of 24 native speakers. These tapes were presented to native speaker judges. The ratings increased systematically with the decline in age of arrival, indicating a clear effect of age of onset in ultimate pronunciation attainment. The 1999 study used the same design but with Korean speakers: 240 immigrants and 24 native speakers were asked to participate. Once again, ratings for authentic accents tended to decline with increasing age of arrival. The authors claim that once learners firmly established the categories of their L1 sounds, L2 sounds can only be perceived according to these original categories and this leads to a foreign accent. L2 speakers will have particular difficulty with those sounds that are similar to their L1 sounds but not quite the same.

While young children's native-like accent and authentic pronunciation cannot be denied, there is at the same time a great deal of evidence in the literature that older learners, even adults, can master accent and pronunciation to native-like or near-native levels with dedication, motivation and formal training.

An interesting series of studies was conducted in the Netherlands by Bongaerts and his colleagues (Bongaerts 1999). These studies focussed on successful adult learners who started English at high school at 12 years of age, typically studying it for just two hours a week, taught by non-native speaker (NNS) teachers. After high school they continued specialising in English at university, which meant a large amount of input from about 18 years of age. This included formal training in pronunciation and phonology. When they graduated, they typically spent a year abroad in Britain in a fully English-speaking environment. In the first study the participants were asked to read aloud a text, ten sentences and 25 words, alongside some native speakers. The unexpected results showed that many advanced NNS were rated higher than the native speakers (NS) themselves, some of whom had heavy regional accents. In the second study the same groups of subjects participated but the judges and the NS were better matched in terms of regional accents. The advanced NNS received very high scores from the judges, (means ranged between 4.18 and 4.93 as opposed to NS scores which ranged between 4.67 and 4.94.) and five out of 11 individuals from the advanced group were judged to have native speaker-level pronunciation. These NNS participants reported in a questionnaire that they were highly motivated: it was important for them to have good pronunciation in English and they consciously worked on improving it. Following criticisms that the participants' L1 (Dutch) is very close to English, in the third study a new second language was investigated. The same research procedures were repeated but this time French learners rather than English learners were asked to participate. Similar results were obtained in that three out of the nine participants were judged to be at NS level. Bongaerts claims that the cause of these learners' success is threefold, following Klein (1995). Firstly, it is of vital importance to them that they should sound native; secondly, they have continued access to massive amounts of authentic input; and thirdly, they had focussed training in phonetics, targeting the differences between their L1 and L2 systems. Similar studies where advanced level adult L2 learners were mistaken by NS judges for native speakers continue to be reported in more recent research, such as Urpunen (2004) with Finnish women in Canada and Nikolov (2000) with learners of Hungarian.

Some researchers (e.g. Bley-Vroman 1989 or Selinker 1972) maintain that successful adult L2 learners are rare, exceptional, and even peripheral among the total adult L2 population. The perceived low levels of success in adulthood could be explained by the fact that many L2 learners abandon their L2 learning well before they come anywhere near their ultimate attainment. This often happens for practical reasons, i.e. they simply do not need very high levels of L2 in their jobs, for example. These learners are not motivated to achieve their full potential. So, in terms of ultimate attainment it does make sense to focus on those language-learning individuals who make every effort and whose target language context affords favourable circumstances, as they are the only ones who exemplify 'true' ultimate attainment levels.

Grammar

In addition to pronunciation, the grammatical competence of second language subjects has also been investigated. Patkowski (1980–90) conducted a study using quantitative analysis of English grammatical competence. He studied 67 highly educated immigrants from various L1 backgrounds who had lived in the USA for at least five years. Fifteen native-born Americans (with similar backgrounds) were used as controls for the comparisons. A multiple choice test of syntactic competence revealed age effects, but not quite as sharp as expected: those entering before the age of 15 did better. They were showing evidence of being more systematically proficient. With regard to the effect on their performance, the amount of informal exposure was significant but the amount of formal instruction was not.

Perhaps the most well-known study in this area pointing to the ultimate advantage of young learners is the one conducted by Johnson and Newport (1989). These authors were also looking for a correlation between age and test results in different areas of English grammatical competence. They tested 46 native Chinese and Korean speakers. All subjects had resided in the USA for at least five years but they all arrived at different ages. The researchers used grammaticality judgment tests. These tests require subjects to make judgments about the grammatical correctness of English sentences. The participants were given 276 taped English sentences and they had to decide whether they were grammatically correct or not. About half of the sentences functioned as 'distractors' (which means they were incorrect). The sentences exemplified basic surface contrasts in English such as regular verb morphology and particle placement. Younger learners achieved better scores. Those who arrived before the age of 7 performed within the range set by native speaker controls. Performance levels declined between 8 and 15 years at age of arrival, and among those who arrived at around age 17 performance was claimed to be random. This accordingly suggests that in addition to the first sensitive period between 0–7 years of age (particularly ripe for acquisition) there is a second maturational sensitivity between the ages of 7 and 17, during which time the ability to acquire L2 is gradually diminishing. After age 17, age of arrival ceases to have any effect at all. In contrast, however, when Birdsong and Molis (1998) replicated this study they found a strong age effect but with no cut-off point at all. Rather, the 'earlier the better across the lifespan' seemed to be the pattern emerging for the whole group. This means that performance of those arriving after the age of 17 was not random but continued to decline steadily.

More recent studies that employ longitudinal designs do not seem to confirm young learners' advantages when it comes to acquiring grammar. Jia and Fuse (2007) report that none of the ten Mandarin-speaking immigrant children that they followed mastered past tense *-ed* at an 80 per cent accuracy level after being immersed in the English environment for five years. In addition to the regular past tense, other morphemes were measured, such as the irregular past tense, 3rd person singular, progressive aspect *-ing*, the copula *be*, and the auxiliary *do*. All these were measured in both obligatory and spontaneous contexts. Overall, the researchers found that the children's language environment was a stronger predictor of individual differences than their age of arrival. Younger learners were not better at acquiring grammar simply because of their age.

Quote 2.12   On failure to master past tense *-ed*

By the end of the 5th year of immersion, only one structure (progressive aspect -ing) was mastered by all participants and one structure (regular past tense -ed) was mastered by none of the participants. Performance on other structures fell in between. In other words, all participants still spoke English with various degrees of morphological errors, after having lived in an English-speaking country for 5 years.

(Jia and Fuse 2007: 1293–4)

While previous studies only measured attainment at one point of time, this study was longitudinal and it measured grammar performance over time using 13 testing times altogether.

In contrast, adult learners have been shown to acquire grammar successfully. For example, White and Genesee (1996) investigated the acquisition of English by French native speakers in Montreal, Canada. These participants started English after the age of 12. They were asked to make questions involving 'wh-extraction' and to judge the grammaticality of 60 examples of various 'wh-movement' structures, for example, 'What did the newspaper report the minister had said?' These grammatical features are difficult to acquire in English. 16 out of 45 participants, however, appeared to be native-like on various measures. White and Genesee argued that these results meant that some successful learners were able to achieve native-like levels despite starting the English language after puberty. Birdsong (1992) also studied the acquisition of French by 20 native English speakers who had been exposed to French after puberty, between the ages of 11 and 28 years. All participants had been residing in France for at least three years by the time the study was conducted. Birdsong found that six out of the 20 participants came within the native speaker range, thus suggesting that native or native-like performances in adult learners are not only possible but given the right circumstances, actually quite likely.

Based on the emerging evidence that the learners' environments matter more than their age alone, Bialystok and Hakuta (1999) question the existence of the critical period and they suggest that the evidence from ultimate attainment studies does not offer clear conclusions at all.

Quote 2.13   Casting doubt over the 'critical period'

Are young learners generally more successful than older ones when ultimate proficiency in a second language is assessed? Yes. Do younger and older learners approach the learning problem differently? Presumably. Are there neurological differences in the brains of younger and older learners? Probably. None of these statements, however, compels the conclusion that there is a critical period for second language acquisition.

(Bialystok and Hakuta 1999: 161)

Bialystok and Hakuta (1999) argue that in addition to age, cognitive factors are also crucially important in second language learning. In particular, literacy allows certain types of instruction that younger learners have no access to. Cognitive capacities such as memory and recall, both of which are crucial in language learning, deteriorate gradually across the lifespan, suggesting the same process for language abilities.

In order to find empirical evidence for the gradual deterioration theory, they conducted a study which was based on census data collected in 1990 in New York State. The data set included information about participants' home language background, length of residence in the USA, their age in 1990, their years of formal education and their self-reported English proficiency. The subjects had to rate their own performance in English by ticking one of the following options: (1) speak it not at all well, (2) not well, (3) well, (4) very well, (5) speak only English. The participants' length of residence was set at

ten years in view of the criticism levelled at some of the earlier studies that
some of the subjects who spent only five years in their target environment
may not have achieved their ultimate attainment. In a truly large-scale study,
overall, nearly 25,000 speakers of Chinese and 39,000 speakers of Spanish
were included. The results did not show any cut-off point around puberty or
the ages of 7, 12 or 15. In fact there appeared to be 'nothing special about
the age range before puberty'. The decline in proficiency remained constant
across the ages and it was similar for both Spanish and Chinese speakers.
Bialystok and Hakuta also found that schooling was found to be positively
related to proficiency. This is consistent with the suggestion that cognitive
processes play an important role.

In an attempt to explain younger learners' overall success, the authors
argue that younger learners typically enjoy special social support such as
the advantages of a nurturing environment, unlimited access to easy, simplified input, good educational opportunities and cooperative peers. All
these factors happen to help facilitate successful language acquisition at a
young age.

Indeed, the importance of social experiences has been confirmed by more
recent research, such as that by Jia and Aaronson (2003). In this longitudinal study, which lasted three years, the authors closely followed the progress
of ten Chinese-speaking immigrant children in the USA. The children's ages
ranged between 5 and 16. One group ranged between 5 and 9 years of age
(the younger group) and the other group ranged between 12 and 16 years of
age (the older group). The authors describe an interesting age-related preference for language use over time. While the younger children switched
mainly to English and cultivated close relationships with English-speaking
friends in a predominantly English-rich environment, the older group preferred to maintain their L1 by interacting with L1 Chinese-speaking friends
and thus limiting their access to English-speaking environments. The data in
this study are not based on just grammar tests but rather a range of sources
such as interviews with children and parents, surveys about languages spo
ken at home and at school, in the neighbourhood, reading practices in the
family and access to Chinese and English mass media.

Quote 2.14   On variability of acquisition rates among children

Taken together, L2 acquisition during the first 3 years of L2 immersion by these
10 children and adolescents of different ages was shaped by the dynamic interactions of multiple factors involved in language acquisition. Cognitive, social and
cultural variables interacted with each other and shaped the immigrant children's
and adolescents' language preferences and hence language environments. The
environmental differences in turn, at least partially, contributed to differential

---

Quote 2.14   (Continued)

language proficiency changes among immigrants, thus leading to the dominant language switch among younger arrivals and maintenance among older arrivals.

(Jia and Aaronson 2003: 156)

It seems that the longer and more systematically we study them, all L2 speakers will exhibit some unique linguistic features when compared to native speakers, whether they started learning the second language at a young age or later in life.

Quote 2.15   On post-pubertal and early beginners

It is true, as Hyltenstam and Abrahamsson (2000: 155) claim, that there is no case on record of a post-pubertal L2 beginner who has been demonstrated to behave in every last linguistic detail like a native speaker. However, it is also true, as Hyltenstam and Abrahamson recognise, that the more closely we study very early L2 beginners the more we realise that at the level of detail, they too differ from monoglot native speakers.

(Singleton 2003: 9–10)

2.4   Conclusion

There is no clear evidence for the existence of the critical period for L2 acquisition, but instead, social, environmental and individual factors help to explain many young children's success. Overall, there is a general decline in L2 learners' ability to acquire second languages across the whole of the life span. The decline is not sharp but continuous and linear. Marinova-Todd (2003) suggests that it is not age *per se* but the availability and access to good L2 input and instruction that will produce best outcomes for children of all ages. The main focus for language educators, therefore, should shift from providing early instruction to more quality-oriented instruction. Factors that contribute to success are complex, including an early start in an optimal environment, consistent, rich exposure, opportunities to practise, high motivation and some explicit instruction.

There are many methodological difficulties in the studies that attempted to look for evidence of the advantages of either younger or older learners. For example, a wide range of different participants are tested together, including younger and older children and adults in the same study. This makes selecting appropriate instruments to measure their abilities very difficult and generally young children's needs suffer. Most of these studies are also limited in that they use one-off testing measures rather than more longitudinal measures such as tracking participants' progress and performance over time. For example, it is relatively easy to read out a short text and concentrate on correct pronunciation. It is much harder to perform consistently well across different tasks, for a longer period of time. More studies are therefore needed to track learners longitudinally, drawing on a range of different data sources, and illustrating the complexities that lead to unique achievements in different contexts.

3
Contexts for Language Acquisition in Childhood

This chapter will

- introduce three different contexts: early infant bilingualism, second language acquisition in immersion/bilingual contexts and foreign language learning in primary schools
- compare different types of foreign and second language programmes in a variety of contexts worldwide
- consider relative benefits of different instructional programmes for language learning

3.1 Introduction

This chapter will consider the processes and benefits of learning second languages in childhood and becoming bilingual in a variety of contexts, including both home and school contexts, drawing on examples from different parts of the world. There are at least as many children growing up in bilingual or multilingual contexts as children in monolingual contexts, and this trend is certain to continue as a result of the ever-increasing mobility of people worldwide and the accelerated technological innovations in modern communication systems. In fact, bilingualism or multilingualism in childhood is the accepted norm in most parts of the world.

Different contexts will offer very different learning opportunities and challenges and will lead to different outcomes. Children who are born in families where parents have different mother tongues may become balanced bilinguals from birth. Then, they may learn additional languages at school. Many children naturally acquire a second language as a result of immigration (e.g. Suárez-Orozco, Suárez-Orozco and Baolian Qin 2005). Immigrant families will be using their L1 to a varying degree in the home and in their wider community. Children from these families will have varying access to their L1 in the L2 school system. Some of them may have the opportunity to maintain their L1 in their mainstream school (see e.g. Warriner 2007). Children in these contexts will be in the best position to develop bilingual and bicultural identities by using both their languages actively. Other children may be studying their L1 outside their mainstream schooling in so-called complementary schools, often operated by volunteer teachers in the L1 community (e.g. Creese and Martin 2003). There are also an increasing number of families that stay in a new country for a shorter period of time only, between one and five years, for business or study purposes. The children in these families may attend international schools (e.g. Murphy 2003; Grimshaw and Sears 2008) or local schools (e.g. Willet 1995; Mitchell and Lee 2008). Those children who are placed in local schools will have to cope with the new language often without much support. Finally, those children who are born into a monolingual family and who do not have the opportunity to travel in childhood often formally learn one foreign language as a timetabled subject at primary school (Johnstone 2002).

This chapter will consider typical contexts and will discuss the advantages, opportunities and challenges of these contexts. First, early balanced bilingual contexts, then second language learning contexts and finally foreign language contexts will be reviewed.

3.2   Early infant bilingualism

Very few people match the stringent definition of knowing and using two languages equally fluently in all situations which would describe 'balanced bilinguals'. Children who are born into families where two languages are heard, used and practised in a balanced way, can be considered early balanced bilinguals. For these infants, it is not possible to say which is their first or their second language because both languages are introduced at the same time. Continued bilingual exposure during the preschool years will generally lead to balanced bilingualism although the exact time frames are debated. De Houwer (1995: 222) refers to regular and continued exposure to more than one language that begins any time between birth and the age of just 2 years, McLaughlin proposes a time frame between birth and 3 years of age, whereas Genesee and Nicoladis (2007) allow for a period from birth to about 4 years of age.

3.2.1   Processes of early infant bilingualism

How are infant bilinguals different from monolingual children? Are the processes of language acquisition similar or different for monolingual and early simultaneous bilingual learners? Early examples of bilingual acquisition were described by Ronjat (1913) and Leopold (1949), who both analysed the bilingual development of their own children. Based in particular on Leopold's influential work, it was proposed that infant bilinguals all exhibited an early monolingual stage of development when they were not yet able to separate or differentiate their two languages (also referred to as the 'Unitary Language System Hypothesis'). This view was also held by Volterra and Taeschner (1978).

Quote 3.1   On the initial monolingual state in infant bilinguals

In the first stage the child has one lexical system which includes words from both languages...in this stage the language development of the bilingual child seems to be like the language development of the monolingual child...In the second stage, the child distinguishes two different lexicons but applies the same syntactic rules in both languages. In the third stage the child speaks two languages differentiated both in lexicon and syntax.

(Volterra and Taeschner 1978: 132)

Contrary to the claim of the Unitary Language System Hypothesis, i.e. that bilinguals go through a monolingual stage, more recent research indicates that bilinguals acquire separate language-specific properties early on (e.g. De Houwer 1995; Paradis and Genesee 1996). For example, Bosch and Sabastián-Gallés (1997) showed that 4-month-old infants (just 129 days old, on average) could already discriminate between their two languages, Catalan and Spanish. Infants at an early age can also tell the difference between languages that are familiar and those that are not.

Quote 3.2   On bilingual infants' abilities

The infant's ability to distinguish a familiar, previously heard language from an unfamiliar, foreign language implies that they have formed a neural representation of the familiar language which then acts as a template against which other test languages (familiar or unfamiliar) can be compared.

(Genesee 2003: 208)

Even though separation of languages does seem to take place very early on, some studies show that specific aspects of development may be interdependent. Grosjean (1994) suggests that an integrated model involving both independence and interdependence between the two language systems describes reality best. For example, Paradis (2001) with French–English bilingual children of 2–3 years of age, reports that the structural overlap between the two languages and the perceived ambiguity in the input play a role in language transfer. This transfer however is temporary and it affects only specific areas. Other areas of grammar seem intact in both languages.

Bilingual children begin to produce their first words the same time as monolingual children, around the age of 12–13 months (Patterson and Pearson 2004). The rate of vocabulary development is the same as for monolinguals as long as their combined bilingual lexicon is considered. Bilingual children produce translation equivalents from the time they begin to speak (Pearson, Fernandez and Oller 1993). By the age of 1.5 years, the percentage of translation equivalents in bilingual children's vocabulary increases sharply, showing that from this age onwards they definitely operate two distinct lexical systems (e.g Nicoladis and Secco 2000; Lanvers 1999). Nicoladis and Genesee (1998) argue that hearing parents talking about the same content in two different languages may help children develop an early awareness of translation equivalents. Bilingual children exhibit the same rate of morphosyntactic development as monolinguals, at least in their dominant language. At the same time there is also evidence for transfer between the two languages in morphosyntactic development. For example, Döpke (2000) found that Australian children learning English and German simultaneously used VO word order much more in all verbal clauses in their German than native monolingual German children.

Quote 3.3   On early bilingual acquisition

...although bilingual children are exposed to and must systematise two sets of language input, they appear to do so within the same general timeframe and approximately at the same ages as children learning only one language. Evidently, the challenges of bilingual acquisition can be accommodated within the same temporal parameters as monolingual acquisition and do not burden the child's mental capacities, leading to delays in development.

(Genesee 2003: 212)

Many researchers have studied infant bilingual code-mixing and confirmed that early code-mixing is grammatically constrained (i.e. the two grammatical systems are not violated in mixing). Some important studies include:

French and German (Meisel 1994)
French and English (Paradis, Nicoladis and Genesee 2000)
English and Norwegian (Lanza 1997)
English and Estonian (Vihman 1998)
Inuktitut and English (Allen *et al.* 2002)

Bilingual children use code-mixing to fill both lexical and grammatical gaps (Nicoladis and Secco 2000), especially in their weaker languages (Genesee, Nicoladis and Paradis 1995). Code-mixing is context-dependent and therefore children use it in some contexts more than others. For example, Vihman (1998) reported that the presence of the parents and the tape recorder changed the children's code-mixing behaviour in her study. Pan (1995) reported that identity functions were also associated with code-mixing. In this study, the children tended to switch back from Mandarin to English more than their parents, and they were more likely to maintain this switch than the parents. The author argues that these differences in the children's and parents' switching patterns is linked to concepts of self-identity, i.e. the children were aligning themselves closer to the wider community and English.

Children have also been reported to be experts at switching between their languages to accommodate different interlocutors. The amount of code-switching that occurs between languages seems to be related to the parents' and other interlocutors' own language choices and code-switching behaviours. Some parents may adopt bilingual discourse strategies, i.e. they tolerate and even encourage code-mixing, whereas other parents may discourage it and insist on the use of a single language at a time. For example, Lanza reported that an English-Norwegian 2-year-old mixed her languages more with her Norwegian-speaking father who used bilingual strategies than with her English-speaking mother who often pretended she did not understand Norwegian. In this way, language socialisation in families influences the children's code-mixing practices. Not only are young children expert at adjusting to their parents' strategies, they also have an ability to adjust to the code-mixing practices of unfamiliar interlocutors. Comeau, Genesee and Lapaquette (2003) found that whenever children were talking with an unfamiliar person, they matched closely the rate of mixing produced by that person.

3.2.2   Early infant bilingual contexts

While the expression 'balanced bilinguals' indicates that children acquire both languages to the same level, this is not in fact the case in reality. The great majority of speakers end up having a dominant language, because it is not possible to have the exact same input in the exact same circumstances in both languages over a longer period of time. Other factors also intervene. A child may have contact with speakers of one of the languages regularly but not with speakers of the other language. According to Baker (2006) a great deal of variety exists among simultaneous bilinguals, depending on the following variables:

- What language(s) do the parents speak as their mother tongue (s)?
- What language(s) do the parents speak to the child?
- What language(s) do other family members speak to the child?
- What language(s) does the child experience in the wider community?

Romaine (1995) categorises early bilingual/multilingual contexts according to the influences related to the languages used in the society, the home and each individual parent:

Type 1: one person–one language context

In this context the two parents have different native languages. One of these languages is also the dominant language of the community where the family lives. The parents will typically each have some degree of competence in the other's native language but both parents decide to speak their own language to the child. A strict 'one parent–one language' policy in the home will mean that the child (or children) will get used to interacting in a specific language with a specific parent. Many studies indicate that this policy can work well, but only if both parents are disciplined and consistent about their language choice.

Example study 3.1   Takeuchi (2006)

This study surveyed Japanese/English families in Australia. Japanese mothers and English-speaking fathers in Australia were using the one person–one language policy to raise their children bilingually. The study set out to discover what factors led to successful maintenance of Japanese in these families. The data showed that consistency in the mothers' language choice, their insistence that their child should speak only Japanese to them and their commitment to regular interactions seemed to have strong correlations with the children's Japanese competence. Early formal education in English (kindergarten and school) was seen as one of the biggest obstacles in the struggle to maintain Japanese. Those mothers who reported being less consistent with their Japanese use noticed that their children understood Japanese but did not speak it fluently.

Type 2: non-dominant home language/one language–one context

In this case, as in Type 1, parents have different native languages and one of the parents is from the dominant language background. However, at home the non-dominant language is used with both parents all the time and the child is exposed to the dominant language only outside the home. This presupposes that the parent who is from the dominant language background has high competence in the non-dominant language.

Example study 3.2   Caldas (2006)

This study documented the practices of a family where a Canadian French-speaking mother and a French/English bilingual father attempted to raise their children bilingually in the predominantly monolingual USA. The study documents the practical decisions the family had to take in order to achieve this goal. In their home (monolingual English-speaking Louisiana) an exclusively monolingual French environment was adhered to by cutting off English television, allowing only French books and using French exclusively for communication at all times. The children were exposed to English only outside their home. In the summer the children were always immersed in a monolingual French summer camp in Quebec. This provided authentic opportunities to interact with monolingual French-speaking peers. The study clearly indicates that bilingual and bicultural competence is achievable in monolingual contexts but only with consistent efforts on the part of the parents.

Type 3: non-dominant home language without community support

In this case parents share the same non-dominant language but the dominant language of the society is not the first language of either parent. The family speak the non-dominant language at home and they often have limited competence in the dominant language. This is often the case with immigrant families in their new environment. Children in families like this often struggle to maintain an equal competence in both languages.

Example study 3.3   Tannenbaum and Howie (2002)

This study focusses on Chinese/English bilingual families in Australia where parents aim to maintain Chinese. The Chinese immigrant parents in this study are not fully competent in English whereas the children are more competent in English than in Chinese. The study explores what factors contribute to the maintenance of Chinese in an English-dominant society. Interestingly, this study reports that family structures and parent–child relationships seemed to exert an important influence on the children's Chinese language maintenance. The use of Chinese by the children was associated with positive relationships they maintained with their parents and the secure family attachment patterns they enjoyed. In families where parents forced their children to speak Chinese and the parent–child relationships were problematic, the children associated the use of Chinese with a lack of choice and an imposed duty. This led to a great deal of resistance against the parents' L1 and a lack of maintenance of Chinese.

Type 4: double non-dominant home language without community support

In this category the parents have different native languages and the dominant language in the society is yet again different from both of these. The parents each speak their own language to the child from birth, and the child learns a third language outside the home.

Example study 3.4   Wang (2008)

This is a longitudinal study reporting on the results of a ten-year-long observation of two children acquiring three languages: English, French and Chinese, from birth. Two parents from very different cultures (Chinese mother and Swiss French-speaking father) attempted to raise their two sons trilingually in the USA. They both used their own heritage language with the children at home while the children encountered English in the community. The study documents ten years of trilingual interactions in a family setting. Many interesting observations are made about the process, such as how the acquisition of English and French facilitated one another. The parents noticed that their boys developed advanced metalinguistic abilities very early. There is also an interesting observation about the fact that the quality of the multilingual input compensates for the quantity of the input. The author's aim is to encourage other similar families to raise their children trilingually and specific advice is offered about family language practices.

Type 5: non-native parents

In this case parents share the same native language and the dominant language in the society is the same as the parents' but one parent decides to use another language (which is not his or her own) with the child/children. This is probably the most artificial of situations and it is certainly the most challenging to keep to. Typically this happens when a parent has a background in language studies and has a strong interest and motivation to teach a new language to their children.

Example study 3.5   Saunders (1982)

This study describes the acquisition of German as a second language by three Australian children, Thomas, Frank and Katrina from 'birth to teens'. The parents are both native English speakers. The children were growing up speaking English with their mother and everybody else in the wider community but they were speaking German with their father. The father had a degree in German and was a confident speaker of the language. The observations describe the family's strategies to adhere to this linguistic arrangement. They stayed in Australia for the whole time of the study except for one visit to Germany lasting six months. The book contains bilingual extracts from the children which illustrate that without any formal teaching, over time the children were able to acquire German with no expense to their English competence. This publication is also aimed at parents with specific advice about how to make the most of a bilingual family situation and how to overcome commonly experienced difficulties.

Type 6: mixed languages

In this case both parents are bilingual and they inhabit sectors of the community which may also be bilingual, with the consequence that parents code-switch and mix languages depending on the micro-contexts of interaction within that community.

Example study 3.6   Ledesma and Morris (2005)

The study explores the everyday use of two languages in the Philippines: English and Filipino. In this society these two languages take different functional roles and the purpose of this study was to find out the patterns of language use in school aged children. The study shows that English is used for the teaching of mathematics and science at school and Filipino is used for the rest of the curriculum. In most families Filipino is used in everyday social interactions with family and friends and English is used for formal occasions with a great deal of natural code-mixing. English, the language with high status, may also be used exclusively in the homes of middle-class and upper-class families.

3.3   Additive bilingualism

In addition to infant bilingualism, the two most common ways of becoming bilingual in childhood is by immigration or by schooling. In the first case, when a family immigrate to a new country, the children become L1 minority L2 learners. In the second case, when the parents decide to raise their children bilingually by schooling, they send them to a school where they can be educated partially or completely immersed in another language. These children become L1 majority L2 learners.

There is a sharp contrast between L1 majority L2 learners and L1 minority L2 learners and this distinction points to two very different types of bilingual experience. Generally, positive effects of bilingualism are associated with programmes for L1 majority L2 children. In these programmes both languages (L1 and L2) are highly valued and the children certainly learn an L2 without losing their L1. On the other hand, often negative effects are associated with programmes where children are 'forced' to learn the majority language of a new society, as a result of the family's immigration or relocation. In these programmes children are not always encouraged to continue developing their mother tongue.

Positive bilingualism refers to the process whereby children add another language to their developing first language, in other words 'additive bilingualism', while negative bilingualism may result in losing children's first language, i.e. 'subtractive' bilingualism' (Baker 2006).

Concept box: 3.1   Additive and subtractive bilingualism

These are two opposite categories. *Additive bilingualism* is a positive term suggesting that the learner is unlikely to replace or threaten his or her first language while learning a second one. He or she will simply 'add' another language to the first one. In contrast to this, if the first language and/or culture of the learner is undermined during the process of learning a second language, this leads to rather negative outcomes in that the L1 may be replaced, or *'subtracted'*.

Baker (2006: 74)

In the most serious case, when children's first languages are neglected and their second languages are not developed sufficiently they may be described as 'limited bilinguals' (Chin and Wigglesworth 2007: 9).

3.3.1   Processes of child second language acquisition

Most research to date has targeted immigrant bilingual children who have been observed by teachers, parents and researchers. Tabors (1997) described the process of early second language development, based on observing minority children in English-speaking preschools in the United Sates. Young children during the first few months in the new country simply continue to use their home language and then go through a non-verbal period or 'silent period' when they just listen actively but do not seem to talk much. Next, they will begin to use some formulaic language ('telegraphic period') and finally, they begin to produce language creatively. An interesting study describing the development of a Polish 7-year-old child in the United States (Winitz, Gillispie and Starcev 1995) documents the shift from the first period to the second, showing how the silent period was followed by a period when the child began to use two- or three-word sentences with his peers.

Children who start a new language when their first language is well-established and when they have already experienced academic tasks and school demands in another language come to language learning with many advantages. They can transfer learning strategies from L1 to L2 and they can begin to map the patterns of their new language against their L1 knowledge. Having a language already established and being more cognitively mature accelerates the development of L2 (see Chapter 2).

Quote 3.4   On cognitive maturity and L2 word learning

L2 lexical learning differs from L1 in that the child is more cognitively mature when the process starts, and also has an existing lexicon in their L1 to draw upon

> ## Quote 3.4   (Continued)
>
> for insight into conceptual-lexical mappings; therefore it is possible that child L2 learners accumulate vocabulary faster than younger L1 learners for the same target language.
>
> (Paradis 2007: 390)

Overall, it takes about five to seven years for immigrant children to catch up with their monolingual peers in terms of academic verbal skills (Cummins 2000) and this is not an automatic achievement at all. For example, Eilers, Pearson and Cobo-Lewis (2006) show that Spanish children in English-medium schools in Miami consistently score below monolingual English children on standardised tests for productive and receptive vocabulary throughout elementary school. At the same time, striking individual differences prevail even in similar instructional circumstances and after similar amounts of exposure (Paradis 2005; Wong Fillmore 1983). Many different individual variables may play a role, although Paradis argues that affective variables are less important than in the case of adults because of the universally accepted desire of young children to fit into their new context.

> ## Quote 3.5   On the cognitive gain of older learners
>
> ...it is possible that attitudinal variables are less likely to predict outcomes in younger children because they may not have a developed view of the intergroup and cultural differences (Genesee and Hamayan 1980). Furthermore, motivation is less of a concern for L1 minority children who, generally speaking, demonstrate a strong desire to assimilate to the new language and culture.
>
> (Paradis 2007: 395)

Two variables seem to be important: aptitude and personality. Harley and Hart (1997) found that memory-based aptitude skills better predicted the performance of early immersion children whereas the language-analytic aptitude skills better predicted the L2 proficiency of late immersion students. Personality types also seem to be important. For example, in a seminal study Wong Fillmore (1983) described two types of successful learners: those who were outgoing and social, who sought opportunities to practise L2 with their peers, and the shy ones, who had high cognitive abilities and a keen attentiveness.

There have been developments in studies measuring bilinguality. Up until the 1960s traditional IQ-based testing consistently showed that bilinguals were inferior compared to monolinguals on a range of verbal measures. These tests were conducted in contexts where L1 minority children were immersed in L2 majority languages (e.g. Spanish L1 minority in English L2 contexts in the USA).

Concept 3.2   Defining and measuring intelligence: IQ testing

Originally intelligence testing was developed to determine average intelligence performances for different age groups of children and to identify those children who needed remedial treatment. IQ represents the ratio of one's mental age versus one's chronological age. If a child performs exactly as expected, they will score 100. IQ tasks typically consist of verbal and logical tasks. Early versions of IQ tests reflected the view that intelligence was a fundamental, *general* human faculty rather than consisting of separate faculties (e.g. Binet and Simon 1916). More recent interpretations of intelligence suggest that it may not be a unitary entity (e.g. Gardner, 1983) but instead, consists of different 'intelligences' such as verbal, musical or spatial intelligences. Traditional intelligence tests have been reported to be culturally biased and they may disadvantage second language children.

The first study that showed significant benefits in terms of bilinguals' cognitive gains was conducted by Peal and Lambert in 1962 in Canada. In this study 110 English/French bilingual children from middle-class French schools were compared with their monolingual peers. For the first time, findings showed that bilinguals significantly outperformed their monolingual peers on most questions of an IQ test. Peal and Lambert argued that bilingualism was therefore associated with specific cognitive gains rather than deficiencies. These gains included greater mental flexibility, an ability to think more abstractly, superior concept formation, and an ability to think independently of words. These were very encouraging results for introducing and promoting bilingual education in Canada and elsewhere. It is, however, important to add that the children who participated in this study were from a middle-class background with special advantages. They were also specially selected as balanced bilinguals from among a larger group of children. Nevertheless, these positive findings in Canada inspired the first immersion education programmes for L1 majority L2 children and a great deal of research which now focussed on establishing the positive benefits of bilingual growth.

It seems that the relationship between L1 and L2 competence in bilingual children is crucial and will determine the benefits. Overall, those children who acquire second languages in contexts where their L1 is developed systematically and where their heritage culture is valued, do much better. In an attempt to explore and understand bilingual children's L2 proficiency, Cummins (1984) suggested that there is an important distinction between children's surface fluency in the second language and their academically related fluency (originally based on Skutnabb-Kangas and Toukomaa 1976). Children seem to be able to acquire surface fluency fast and effortlessly but may take a much longer period of time to acquire more academic aspects of the L2. Based on this distinction, Cummins proposed two concepts: BICS (Basic Interpersonal Communicative Skills) and CALP (Cognitive Academic Language Proficiency).

Quote 3.6   On BICS and CALP

The major points embodied in the BICS/CALP distinction are that some heretofore neglected aspects of language proficiency are considerably more relevant for students' cognitive and academic progress than are the surface manifestations of proficiency frequently focussed on by educators, and that educators' failure to appreciate these differences can have particularly unfortunate consequences for minority students.

(Cummins 1984: 137–8)

Cummins conceptualised L2 proficiency along two continua. The first continuum represents the contextual support available for expressing or receiving messages in L2. The extremes of this continuum would be described as 'context-embedded' versus 'context-reduced' situations. The context-embedded situation makes it possible for participants to negotiate meanings in face-to-face situations where the interaction is supported by paralinguistic and situational clues. This is more typical of situations outside formal classrooms, i.e. in playgrounds or during casual conversations between friends. In these contexts it is easy to guess what the other person is saying from the situational clues and the person's body language. Even if misunderstanding occurs, it often does not matter, in that the consequences of these breakdowns are not serious. Context-reduced situations, on the other hand, require that the learner relies on linguistic clues primarily. This is a more typical demand inside classrooms, where the exact meaning and the precise wording of messages is important and any misunderstanding may have serious consequences.

These two context types then interact with the cognitive demands of the task. The cognitive continuum ranges from 'cognitively undemanding' to 'cognitively demanding' tasks. Taking these two aspects of difficulty and imagining them as two axes, a grid of four sections can be drawn.

Cognitively demanding/ Context-reduced	Cognitively demanding/ Context-embedded
Cognitively undemanding/ Context-independent	Cognitively undemanding/ Context-dependent

Persuading someone of your own point of view, for example, would be a cognitively demanding task although still context-embedded in the sense that the conversation would be face-to-face and supported by paralinguistic clues, such as gestures. Writing an essay would be classified as a cognitively demanding task to be carried out in a context-reduced environment where the learner is dependent on solitary analysis of print materials. This is one of the hardest tasks to master.

Cummins (2000) described the differences between interpersonal and academic demands in particular as they apply to acquiring reading skills in the second language:

Quote 3.7　On interpersonal and academic demands

...considerably less knowledge of language itself is usually required to function appropriately in interpersonal communicative situations than is required in academic situations. The social expectations of the learner and sensitivity to contextual and interpersonal cues (e.g. eye contact, facial expression, intonation etc) greatly facilitate communication of meaning. These social cues are largely absent in most academic situations that depend on knowledge of the language itself for successful task completion. In comparison to interpersonal conversation, the language of text usually involves much more low frequency vocabulary, complex grammatical structures and greater demands on memory, analysis and other cognitive processes.

(Cummins 2000: 39–40)

Cummins further suggested that there was an important relationship between L1 and L2 proficiency and cognitively demanding skills could transfer between L1 and L2. In this way, a well-developed L1 could facilitate the development of academic skills in L2. This relationship was described as the Common Underlying Proficiency principle (CUP). The CUP assumes that irrespective of which language the child operates in, he or she is able to generate thoughts using the central underlying 'engine'. Thus information processing, thinking and learning should be equally possible in both/either languages. An important consequence of this model is that an insufficiently developed L2 will inhibit children from fully understanding the cognitive content, so that their successful functioning in the classroom will be impaired.

> ## Quote 3.8   On the transfer across L1 and L2 academic skills
>
> ...at more advanced stages there is transfer across languages in academic and liter-acy skills such as knowing how to distinguish the main idea from the supporting details of a written passage or story, identifying cause and effect, distinguishing fact from opinion, and mapping out the sequence of events in a story or historical account.
>
> (Cummins 2003: 63)

In this way, the level of development in the child's L1 is a strong predictor of L2 development and consequently L1 promotion at school helps with L2 development. Teachers should not be worried about spending time learning things in L1 as this does not hurt the development of the L2. The nego-tiation of bilingual and bicultural children's identity is a crucial factor in minority children's academic success. Yet in reality, L1 minority L2 children may feel under pressure to 'switch' to the L2 completely when they discover how powerful and important the L2 is compared to their L1. Writing about Korean families in the United States, Shin (2005: 28) reports that children themselves may decide to put effort into developing their L2 and neglect the L1 and parents face an uphill struggle to try and maintain Korean.

3.3.2   Immersion education

One of the best-known and well-researched bilingual programmes is the 'immersion programme' that originates from Canada. This programme was launched in the French-speaking province of Quebec, following the initiative of a group of Anglophone parents in the 1960s who wanted to provide bet-ter French education for their children than was available at local schools. Having consulted with specialists in bilingualism, they proposed a radical programme which involved their English-speaking children being placed in classrooms where they heard French all day and where in effect they began their education entirely in French. A consequence of this programme was that the children learnt to read and write in French before they did so in English. English was not introduced until grade 3. Such a programme became known as 'early total immersion' and varieties of it quickly spread to other parts of Canada and to many parts of the rest of the world.

According to Johnson and Swain (1997), the characteristics of immersion programmes can be summarised as follows:

- It is always the L2 that is used as the medium of instruction.
- The immersion curriculum parallels the local L1 curriculum.
- Overt support exists for the L1.
- Attitudes in the community are positive to both L1 and L2.

- The aim of the programme is to achieve additive bilingualism, with high levels of proficiency in both L2 and L1.
- In immersion programmes L2 is largely confined to the classroom.
- Children enter with similar (limited) levels of proficiency and from the very beginning instructional procedures, materials and curriculum can be tailored to the needs of the target group.
- Teachers are bilingual, able to communicate with students in L1, if necessary.
- The classroom culture is that of the local L1 community rather than the target language culture.

Immersion programmes may be full or partial.

Concept 3.3   Full or partial immersion

Full immersion implies that children follow the entire curriculum in the second language (90–100% of the time), whereas partial immersion implies that only some of the curriculum is taught in the second language. This arrangement leaves other subjects still to be taught in the first language (often this is a ratio of 60:40 or 50:50). Maths and science are often covered in the second language and arts and social sciences in the first language.

Early research into immersion education in Canada focussed largely on outcomes and compared the immersion children's language and content knowledge with monolingual children's knowledge to show that there were no disadvantages to being educated in immersion classrooms. Studies showed that immersion children's L1 development (English) did not suffer compared to their non-immersion peers (e.g. Genesee 1983; Harley, Hart and Lapkin 1986). Other studies showed that the immersion children's content knowledge was also as solid as their peers' knowledge in non-immersion contexts (e.g. Swain 1985; Genesee 1987). In terms of their proficiency, immersion students were compared with core French students who only learnt French as a school subject and the results predictably showed that they were more proficient, especially in terms of their receptive skills (e.g. Genesee *et al.* 1985). Comparisons between early and late immersion students indicated that early immersion was more effective, although some late immersion students also achieved comparable proficiency in the end (e.g. Day and Shapson 1996). More recent research has begun to highlight some of the problems in immersion education. Overall, little attention has been paid to grammar teaching and as Swain and Lapkin (1989) pointed out, this lack of attention to language forms was not conducive to learning. Other studies showed that learners had little opportunity for sustained talk in class and thus students' receptive skills were better than their productive skills. In particular, they struggled with the need to use complex grammatical constructions and precise vocabulary. According to Swain (2000), naturalistic immersion in the language is necessary but not sufficient for achieving native-like competence in an L2. Swain and her colleagues argue that immersion students need regular practice with language tasks that push them beyond their comfort zone and encourage them to engage in syntactic rather than semantic language processing. Such tasks include collaborative writing tasks, where students need to work together to solve grammatical problems. Tasks like these encourage students to focus on 'form' in their writing or speaking, thus developing areas of grammatical, syntactical knowledge which are hard to acquire from naturally occurring conversation in immersion environments.

There are many different types of immersion programmes. Cummins in Cummins and Corson (1997: xii) distinguishes five: (1) immersion in indigenous languages and native languages (e.g. Maori in New Zealand); (2) immersion in national minority languages which sometimes have official status (e.g. Gaelic in Ireland or Basque and Catalan in Spain); (3) immersion in international minority languages (relatively recent immigrants to a host country, e.g. Spanish in the USA); (4) immersion in a particular linguistic or cultural minority (e.g. deaf and the hard of hearing); and (5) bilingual and biliterate programmes intended for dominant and majority groups (e.g. Canadian French immersion).

3.3.3   Immersion contexts

Example source 3.7   Björklund (1997): immersion in a high-status language – Swedish in Finland

Swedish is a high-status official language in Finland and every child starts learning it in grade 3, at the age of 9. For the Swedish minority children the second language is Finnish and they start it at the same age. The Swedish immersion programme was launched in 1987 in Vaasa. The programme covers the age range from kindergarten to grade 6 in the comprehensive school and it follows the Canadian early immersion in broad outline. This programme is rapidly developing and expanding despite the fact that English as a global language is also popular. Most children learn to speak at least three languages: Finnish, Swedish and English.

Example source 3.8   Lindholm (1997): two-way immersion – Spanish/English programme in the USA

A two-way programme caters for minority Spanish-speaking children but at the same time offers a second language learning opportunity to English-speaking majority children. Ideally, equal numbers of L1 Spanish and L1 English speakers are put in a classroom for maximum linguistic benefit to everyone. At kindergarten and in the first grade 90 per cent of the instruction is in Spanish and English is used to develop oral language proficiency in the remaining 10 per cent of the instruction only. Children learn to read and write in Spanish first. By second grade students receive 80 per cent of their day in the target language and 20 per cent in English. By fifth grade, the instructional time is balanced between 50 per cent Spanish and 50 per cent English.

Example source 3.9   Knell *et al.* (2007): immersion in a high-status foreign language – English in China

English immersion for children in major cities in China is very popular because English has become a high priority in the educational system. This study describes a programme in a primary school affiliated with Shaanxi Normal University in Xi'an. This is a partial immersion programme (50 per cent English and 50 per cent Chinese) where students learn half of the subjects through English (e.g. arts, music and science) and half of the subjects through Mandarin Chinese (maths and Chinese). Comparisons of immersion and non-immersion students indicate that the immersion students develop their English proficiency to higher levels than the non-immersion students and their Chinese competence does not suffer at all. These results are achieved despite problems, such as a very high student–teacher ratio in classrooms, a general lack of English materials and teachers' relatively low competence in English.

Teacher preparation seems to be one of the biggest challenges in running immersion programmes. Teachers need to be equally proficient in two languages and they need to understand about the challenges of bilingual acquisition. In addition, as the quotation below illustrates, they may experience a transformation of their cultural identity:

Quote 3.9   On bilingual teachers' concerns

. . . . . as a recent article demonstrates (de Mejía and Tejada 2002) several teachers in a school which was in the process of becoming bilingual 'felt threatened' by what they perceived as a loss of cultural identity. They feared that in the development of the project, the national culture would be displaced or substituted by Anglo-Saxon culture (de Mejía and Tejada 2002: 111)

(de Mejía 2005: 61)

One of the most beneficial programmes seems to be the 'two-way immersion programme' because it aims to place equal numbers of students in each class with each language as an L1, and because of the clear aims to actively promote both languages and children's bicultural identity. Benefits of this kind of programme have been reported (Lindholm-Leary 2001; Thomas and Collier 2003) as children develop biliteracy, bilingualism, biculturalism and grade-level academic competence comparable to mainstream schools. Recent evidence, however, suggests that it is a struggle to maintain children's L1. Eilers, Pearson and Cobo-Lewis (2006: 87) warn that even two-way schools in Miami offer little if any threat to English and there is evidence of weakness in Spanish. Despite the cultural desire for Spanish, its use seems to be progressively weakened by the dominance of English.

3.4　Processes of multilingual acquisition

In many contexts, children learn a third language. For example, a Malaysian child will use Malay with her friends during playtime and in some lessons, but will use English during science and maths classes and use Arabic when practising reading the Koran. In the African and Indian continents children learn to speak a local vernacular language at home and an official regional language at school and finally an international/global language at around age 10 at school. In Zaire, for example, children learn a local vernacular at home and then Lingala or Kikongo, which are regional official languages, and then study French as a foreign language from the beginning of secondary school (e.g. Kachru 1992).

How is multilingualism different from bilingualism? According to Cenoz (2000), multilingualism presents more diversity and more complexity, with different possible acquisition orders among the three languages. There is more variation within each individual about which language might become dominant, what processes of transfer take place and what eventual proficiency levels are achieved (Cenoz and Genesee 1998). Generally, it is harder to maintain three languages than two languages and it is less likely that balanced levels of proficiency will be achieved.

Bilinguals enjoy advantages as opposed to monolinguals when it comes to learning a third language. These advantages include perceptual discrimination (Cohen, Tucker and Lambert 1967; Davine, Tucker and Lambert 1971; Enomoto 1994) and listening comprehension (Edwards *et al.* 1977; Wightman 1981). Also, according to Klein (1995), bilinguals have an advantage in lexical and syntactic learning measured by means of grammaticality judgment and correction tasks. Building on Cummins's Interdependence Hypothesis, which states that there is a positive and significant relationship between L1 development and L2 development (Cummins 1981), a similar relationship is likely to hold true for a third language (Muñoz 2000; Lasagabaster 2000). Muñoz (2000), in a study specially focussed on the effect of the third language, compared the linguistic competence of children in Catalan, Spanish and English through a series of language tests at ages 10,

12, and 17. The hypothesis was that high levels of competence in L1 and L2 would correlate with high levels of competence in L3. This was indeed confirmed in that the correlations among performances in all three languages were high. Similarly, in the Basque country, in Spanish/Basque bilingual programmes, Lasagabaster (2000) found that learning an L2 or an L3 did not have any negative effects on the development of L1 (whether this was the majority language Spanish or the minority language Basque) and that balanced bilinguals were able to take advantage of their bilingualism in relation to learning a third language, i.e. English.

Nation and McLaughlin (1986), McLaughlin and Nayak (1989) and Nayak *et al.* (1990) all found that multilinguals demonstrated greater flexibility in switching strategies for rule-discovery tasks and this superiority was explained by their experience as language learners. Lasagabaster (1997) reported that bilinguals learning a third language had a more highly developed metalinguistic awareness than monolinguals. When the languages are more similar there is evidence for transfer (Möhle 1989; Singleton 1987). Typological similarity seems to be more important for determining transfer as compared to which language is the speaker's L2 or L1.

3.4.1 Multilingual contexts

Example source 3.10   Muñoz (2000): Catalan/Spanish bilingual children learning English in Spain

In the Spanish/Catalan bilingual programme, children are immersed in Catalan in preschool and then start Spanish alongside Catalan in the primary school. At the age of 8 the first foreign language, English, is introduced for 2.5 hours a week. English is introduced as a timetabled subject and children have no access to it outside school. Later, at the age of 10, a second foreign language may be introduced, which is often French.

Example source 3.11   Broom (2004): South African children learning national languages and English

There are approximately 28 local languages in South Africa with 11 officially recognised languages. Afrikaans is one of the most widely spoken national languages but English enjoys a privileged status as a language of political, economic and intellectual power. Most children whose L1 is not a national language will be immersed in an L2 as soon as they start school. However, parents want their children to learn English above all, and as a result, some children may switch to English immersion by grade 3, age 8. Primary English teachers often do not speak the children's L1, which makes the language shift very difficult.

Example source 3.12   Hoffman (1998): children learning Luxemburgisch, French and German in Luxembourg

Luxembourg has developed a unique pattern of trilingualism. The native language is Luxemburgisch for most children. French represents power and prestige and German is seen as the language of convenience. Children speak Luxemburgisch at home and in preschool. In the primary school, they are taught both German and French. German is introduced as a subject in the first grade of primary school in 8–9 periods a week and it becomes the medium of instruction progressively by the end of the first year. French is introduced in the second half of the second grade, progressively increasing in hours of instruction per week. By secondary school French becomes the medium of instruction. Most pupils also learn English. It is not uncommon for an individual to speak four or five languages. The model enjoys the support of the population although it is acknowledged that the burden on primary children may be too high with progressive language switches.

3.5   Learning foreign languages

In many contexts, schools and policy makers do not aim for bilingual competence or for language immersion but instead they simply offer opportunities for children to experience a new language in a limited way. For those children who are born in monolingual families and stay in the same monolingual language environment for at least the first decade of their lives, the first encounter with another language usually happens in primary school. Typically, due to the unprecedented popularity of English as a language of international communication, more and more countries opt for introducing English as a first foreign language at school. Children start a foreign language at the age of 8–9 in such schools but sometimes even earlier, at the age of 6–7 (Kubanek-German 1998; Legutke *et al.* 2009). In some countries it is not uncommon to provide formal English language programmes for children as young as 3 years of age. This is the case, for example, in many private schools in Japan, Thailand and Taiwan.

When a foreign language is introduced in the primary school, often only a small number of teaching hours are devoted to it in the weekly timetable and there is virtually no access or very limited access to the target language outside the classroom. These contexts are referred to as 'low input level' contexts. By contrast, in 'higher input level' contexts children learn a second language integrated into the curriculum rather than as a separate subject. As a consequence of the integration, they may be exposed to the target language for longer periods of time during the week.

Table 5 shows the differences between foreign and second language contexts, although it is recognised that the differences are not always clear-cut. For example, due to the availability of the internet it is becoming increasingly possible for foreign language learners to have contact with

Table 5 Contrasting foreign and second language contexts

Foreign language	Second language
Low level of input: typically 1–3 hours a week timetabled lessons	High(er) level input: more than just a timetabled lesson
No/restricted opportunities outside class to use the target language	Regular opportunities to use the target language outside class
Focus is on language as a formal system and as a subject	Focus is on content and language integrated across the curriculum

native-speaking children at least in virtual environments and the internet also offers a huge variety of different authentic materials to access outside classrooms.

There is an enormous variety of primary-level modern foreign language programmes around the world: see recent reviews by Nikolov and Curtain (2000), Rixon (2000) and Edelenbos, Johnstone and Kubanek (2006). In the primary and pre-primary sectors, foreign language learning is considered preparatory for more serious secondary-level study and therefore there is less emphasis on linguistic and proficiency outcomes. Typically, the aims of such foreign language programmes are a combination of the following:

- Developing basic communication abilities
- Fostering motivation by making initial language learning experiences fun
- Encouraging early familiarisation with a new culture
- Developing cognitive, metacognitive and metalinguistic skills through an initial contact with a foreign language system

According to Edelenbos, Johnstone and Kubanek (2006), four main types of programmes exist:

- roughly one hour per week
- one hour per week but with some flexibility
- language awareness model
- bilingual or partial immersion

Quote 3.10   On the four models of language teaching

Four main models of language education which seem to be in operation: (i) roughly one hour per week for teaching a particular language, mainly based on a given course book and other material; (ii) as for (i) but with a more flexible

---

Quote 3.10 (Continued)

syllabus based to some extent on relating the modern language to other aspects of the curriculum, e.g. science or geography, but still within limited time provision; (iii) a language awareness model, not dealing with one additional language alone but instead giving access to a number of languages and cultures, in order to develop underlying qualities such as meta-linguistic awareness and intercultural sensitivity; (iv) provision of increased time and intensity in the form of bilingual or partial immersion education. Model (iv) yields the highest level of target language proficiency but is unlikely to be generally applicable. It seems highly desirable that ways should be found of combining the unique advantages of models (ii) and (iii) in particular.

(Edelenbos, Johnstone and Kubanek 2006: 5)

The most commonly encountered model in primary schools is encompassed in the subject teaching approach. The foreign language lesson is typically taught in 1–2 hours a week by either a specialist subject teacher (in many contexts imported from a secondary school) or the class teacher in the primary school who also covers the rest of the curriculum with the children.

In some contexts, a language awareness model may be incorporated into the foreign language lesson. This approach is largely inspired by the work of Hawkins (1984) and it generally focusses on basic comparisons between the children's L1 and the target language. The underlying aim is to develop the children's understanding of the concept of language, rather than learning a new language *per se*. Young and Helot (2003), for example, advocate this approach for contexts where various languages are already present in a school, such as minority languages in the UK.

Another possible approach is 'embedding', which means integrating the target language into the primary curriculum. This happens by incorporating meaningful activities from other curricular areas into the language lesson. Integrating language and content is useful in that this approach embraces holistic learning which is consistent with the learning needs of young children (e.g. Jantscher and Landsiedler 2000; Sundin 2000). This type of embedding can be quite minimal and ad hoc, or it can be more long-term and systematic. Different levels of embedding exist and when such embedding is consistent, the programmes are often referred to as CBI programmes (Content Based Instruction) or theme-based programmes.

Integration between content and language is an important principle which is actually shared by many language programmes, including immersion and content-based programmes, and even foreign language programmes may attempt to include at least elements of this. To illustrate how content can be integrated with language, Derrick (1977) describes one main principle in relation to a project which was aimed at helping immigrant children in the UK to learn English:

Quote 3.11   On the process of language selection

We have tried to devise a scheme that provides a series of language items with relevance to the children's language-needing activity, in school and outside. In the process of language selection we therefore start by identifying high priority activities...Items learnt can be continually reinforced by real use.

(Derrick 1977: 17)

In this way children learn to use their English for an increasingly wide range of functions in real life. This approach requires that teachers understand these needs and can proactively match new language to needs that arise naturally (Candlin and Derrick 1973).

Integrating language and content generally produces much better results than isolated language classes. One study reporting on a successful embedding programme in a typical foreign language situation in Turkey was conducted by Alptekin, Ercetin and Bayyurt (2007).

Example source 3.13   Alptekin, Ercetin and Bayyurt (2007): a type of embedded modern foreign language programme – English as a foreign language in Turkey

In this study a theme-based syllabus was designed which paralleled the content of the subject areas (e.g. geography and science) in the curriculum set by the Turkish Ministry of Education. The students studied wildlife in their science lesson in Turkish and then the English teacher presented the same information in the English class. After two years of instruction, the study showed that this embedded English programme led to superior English language proficiency compared to that of another group of children who followed a largely grammar-based traditional English syllabus. These advantages were remarkable because the actual lessons devoted to English were the same for both groups (theme-based and traditional), all students started as beginners and were from low SES (socio-economic status) groups.

Although the linguistic outcomes of different primary-level programmes are not very well defined and not very well understood, in some countries where there is a strong examination-oriented tradition, parents want to see evidence of progress translated into test scores. Internationally recognised exams such as the 'Cambridge Young Learners' examination are very popular around the world. In 2003, Cameron estimated that about 150,000 children sat the University of Cambridge Examination for Young Learners.

Concept 3.4   Cambridge Young Learners Examination

Young Learners English (YLE) is a reliable and consistent measure of how well your child is doing in the skills of listening, speaking and reading and writing. Tests are designed to make learning fun and children are encouraged by working towards certificates and earning the shields that record their progress. There are three levels for children to work through, Starters, Movers and Flyers.

(From the Cambridge ESOL website: http://www.cambridgeesol.org/exams/young-learners/yle.html)

3.5.1   Benefits of learning foreign languages in childhood

Is it beneficial at all to start learning a modern foreign language in primary school? Is it cost-effective and in any way advantageous or should it be left to secondary school to tackle language teaching, since it has already been demonstrated in naturalistic studies that older learners progress faster (see Chapter 2). The answers to these questions depend on how the benefits are measured.

On the whole, according to Johnstone (1999), there is no clear evidence that primary-school foreign language learning will necessarily lead to better attainments in secondary school. Some studies have demonstrated very modest advantages for learners who started a foreign language in earlier grades than their peers who started it later. For example, a research study in Slovakia suggests that children who started earlier and had six years of German outperformed those who started later and had only four years of German instruction (e.g. Garajova 2001). In 1997, the Braunschweig Project (Doyé 1995) indicated that early learners of English could become superior to pupils who started later, after primary school, but only if the teaching was appropriate, if teachers were fully qualified, and if there was continuity between primary and secondary provision. Also, the independent evaluation of the Scottish Pilot project (Low *et al.* 1995) confirmed a slight advantage for project pupils as compared with non-project late starters. Advantages in pronunciation, patterns of intonation, length of utterance, complexity of structure and use of communication strategies were evident. Yet other studies, such as a series of studies in Garcia Mayo and Garcia Lecumberri (2003), fail to document advantages for younger learners. These authors found that older learners performed better in phonetic perception and language production regarding fluency, accuracy and complexity. Studies in the Barcelona Project also indicated a clear advantage for the older learners.

If, however, linguistic outcomes are not considered as the main measures of success, many would argue that foreign language learning in primary schools is beneficial because it helps children to learn about other cultures (Brunzel 2002; Likata 2003), develops positive attitudes about languages and motivation (Nikolov 1999b; Kennedy *et al.* 2000) and promotes language awareness (Genelot and Tupin 2001).

Currently, very little is known about the actual processes of foreign language learning and what children can achieve at what stage. In fact, a common experience of foreign language programmes in many countries is that children are not exposed to the target language sufficiently to learn to participate in meaningful communication. They may learn songs and rhymes, some basic vocabulary and carefully rehearsed dialogues, but they rarely progress further, and typically they are unable to express their own meanings spontaneously. There is also a lack of continuity between primary and secondary schools, which has the effect that many children who start a language in the primary school need to start it all over again when they get to secondary level. This is detrimental to motivation levels and indirectly sends out a negative message about the value of language learning in primary schools to both children and parents. Parents, often dissatisfied with the general level of language teaching in state schools, send their children to private schools to learn more English (e.g. 'cram schools' in Taiwan, 'frontisteria' in Greece). Children in these schools follow parallel courses that often overlap a great deal in content with those in the state sector. Generally, there is no communication between these different school systems and programmes with the consequence that learning the language is wasteful and de-motivating to learners.

Another problem is the uneven provision of professional development for teachers. Schools, especially in remote areas, often employ teachers who are not fully qualified and/or whose own foreign language competence is not satisfactory. An interesting study by Butler (2004) conducted in Asia surveyed primary English teachers' perceptions of their own competences with regard to teaching English as a foreign language. The results indicated that the majority of these teachers in Japan, Korea and Taiwan did not think that they were adequately prepared for teaching English in primary classrooms. They identified the development of their own English language competence, including oral fluency and pronunciation as the most urgent areas in need of updating and development (see the summary in Chapter 4).

3.6 Conclusion

There is enormous variety in the circumstances in which children may be learning second or third languages. In families, balanced bilingualism can only be achieved if parents invest discipline, consistency and patience into orchestrating language practices. In preschool and school contexts, where children are immersed in a second language, it is important to continue cultivating the first language so that children can achieve effective bilingual competence and positive bilingual identities. In foreign language contexts, the restrictions are often too large to make real progress but high-quality language input, intensity and integration between language and content are likely to achieve positive results. Continuity of good-quality instruction from primary to secondary and high standards of teacher competence are both essential in all contexts.

From an individual child's point of view, there are many different pathways to success. Those children who are exposed to two or three languages from birth have a huge advantage but this is not the only way to succeed. Many children who are not exposed to second languages until much later (12 or even 14 years of age), may still achieve bilingual competence if they are learning under favourable circumstances and if they have the opportunity to be exposed to the target language by studying or working abroad for at least a temporary period of time. There are no two pathways that are the same, as every language learner is unique. Those children who miss out on early opportunities must also be encouraged to learn and must be made aware of how to extend their language learning opportunities despite the restrictions in their current contexts.

Part II
Overview of Research Studies

4
Child SLA and Pedagogy: A Broad Overview of Approaches to Research

This chapter will

- establish links with language learning contexts previously discussed in Chapter 3 and with the case studies in the next chapter
- provide a sample of studies (including SLA and pedagogy, focussing on both learners and teachers) to give the reader insights into the types of research that have been undertaken within the wider field of child SLA and classroom pedagogy
- highlight inherent benefits and limitations of dominant approaches and methodologies in these studies and discuss some of the implications between research and practice
- identify key areas for future research

This chapter together with Chapter 5 constitute a new section in this book. After reviewing some background to research and practice in the field of child second language learning and pedagogy, these two chapters take a close look at currently popular research approaches and processes to explore what applications arise for practitioners. Chapter 4 takes a macro-perspective via navigating through a broad range of research according to different methodological traditions, while Chapter 5 takes a micro-perspective, focussing on a handful of key case studies associated with the different traditions discussed in Chapter 4. Each study in Chapter 5 is described fully, including research procedures, research questions, outcomes, limitations and practical implications.

4.1 Introduction

Chapter 3 has already identified a wide range of different contexts where children are learning languages, either formally or informally. In order to continue to embrace all these contexts and appeal to researchers and teachers as widely as possible, this chapter will take some example studies from immersion, second and foreign language contexts, including some with temporary or permanent immigrant children engaged in language learning at home or at school.

Much research in developmental linguistics is rather theoretical in nature with an underlying aim to understand second language acquisition processes *per se* but without any real intention to apply the findings to classroom practice. In this chapter, we are concerned more with work that is applied, where authors themselves clearly point to pedagogical implications in relation to their findings. In terms of the content areas, the review aims to be wide in focus. There will be studies reviewed that tap into the learning and teaching of the four skills, grammar or lexis, language learning strategies, individual variables, identity development, and instructional materials and approaches such as syllabus or test types or reading schemes. The last group of studies will focus on the needs, perceptions and practices of language *teachers* in primary schools.

Although effort has been made to achieve an international appeal, it must be noted that the majority of studies in this chapter are concerned with children learning English as a second/third/foreign language rather than other languages. This is related to the current role of English globally but also to the type of literature reviewed, i.e. literature published in English. Despite English as a second language being dominant, an attempt has nonetheless been made here to report studies where children were learning languages other than English, such as German, French, Swedish and Dutch.

In terms of the geographical spread, a great many studies refer to programmes in the USA, Canada, Australia and the UK, where immigrant children have been studied extensively. Europe emerges as another well-represented area with English as the main language being studied, as in Spain, Greece, Hungary, Norway, Sweden, the Netherlands and Croatia. The third area of research activity is focussed on South-East Asia, with many studies conducted with Chinese-, Taiwanese-, Korean-, Indonesian- and Japanese-speaking children learning English. However, a clear gap emerges, in that other parts of the world such as Central and South America, India, the Middle East and Africa seem to be much less represented in the English-medium literature.

Table 6 lists the studies discussed here with information about the age of the children involved, the L2 or L3 learnt, the content area of the research and the background/L1 of the participants. Where the focus is on teachers, the age of the participants is not included (n/a).

Table 6 Overview of studies in Chapter 4

Type of study: approach/ method/ tradition	Name of authors and year of publication	Age of participants	Content focus	L2 or L3	L1 and context
Large-scale testing and correlation	Alexiou 2009	5–9 years of age	Aptitude testing	L2 English	Greek
	Butler and Lee 2006	4th–6th grade 10–12 years of age	Assessment	L2 English	Korean
Classroom experiments	Harley 1998	Grade 2 6–7 years of age	Focus on form instruction	L2 French immersion in Canada	English
	Simard 2004	10–11 years of age	Metalinguistic awareness	L2 English in Canada	French
	Peñate Cabrera and Bazo Martínez 2001	10 years of age	Story comprehension	L2 English as FL	Spanish
	Goh and Taib 2006	11–12 years of age	Metacognition in listening	L2 English	Singapore English and Chinese
Comparing two treatments	Drew 2009	Grades 3 and 4 8–9 years of age	A literacy programme	L2 English	Norway
	Kim 2008	5 and 6 years of age	Early literacy	L2 English	Korean and Chinese in the US
	Shak and Gardner 2008	Grade 5 11–12 years of age	Focus on form tasks	L2 English	Brunei (Malay and Chinese)

Table 6 (Continued)

Type of study: approach/method/tradition	Name of authors and year of publication	Age of participants	Content focus	L2 or L3	L1 and context
Comparing age groups	Leseman 2000	3–4 years of age	Vocabulary development	L2 Dutch	Turkish
	Shrubshall 1997	5–12 years of age	Storytelling	L2 English	Portuguese in London
	Bae 2007	Grades 1 and 2 6 years of age	Early literacy/writing	L2 English	Korean/English two-way immersion in the USA
	Tagoilelagi-Leota et al. 2005	4–6 years of age	Literacy development	L2 English	Samoan and Togan in New Zealand
	Mackey, Oliver and Leeman 2003	8–10 years of age	Feedback and tasks	L2 English	Different backgrounds in Australia
	Garcia Mayo 2003	11–17 years of age	Pro-drop parameter in grammaticality judgment tasks	L2 English	Catalan with Spanish as L2
	Heining-Boynton and Haitema 2007	All grades in primary	Language learning motivation and attitudes	L2 French L2 Spanish	English in the USA
Focus on individuals and small groups	Nassaji and Cumming 2000	6 years of age	Journal writing	L2 English	Farsi in Canada
	Dagenais, Day and Toohey 2006	12 years of age	Multilingual identity construction	L2/L3 French immersion in Canada	Chinese and L2/L3 English

	Cekaite 2007	7 years of age	Multiparty talk and participation	L2 Swedish	Kurdish in Sweden
	Hawkins 2005	4–5 years of age	Early literacy and separate academic and social development	L2 English	Spanish (Peruvian) and Korean in Canada
	Mitchell and Lee 2008	6–9 years of age	Documenting learning in the home/family context	L2 English	Korean in the UK
Children's views	Victori and Tragant 2003	10–18 years of age	Language learning strategies	L3 English	Catalan and Spanish as L2
	Papapavlou 1999	Grades 4–6 9–13 years of age	Language preference, socialisation and adjustment	L2 Greek	Different backgrounds in Geek Cyprus
	Lamb 2003	11–12 years of age	Language learning motivation	L2 English	Bahasa Indonesia
	Gu, Hu and Zhang 2005	Grades 1 and 3 7 and 9 years of age	Language learning strategies	L2 English	Malay, Tamil and Chinese in Singapore
	Gardner and Yaacob 2007	6–8 years of age	Role play	L2 English	Malay in Malaysia and the UK
Primary language teachers	De Courcy 2007	n/a	Pre-service teacher education, ESL awareness	L2 English	Australia

Table 6 (Continued)

Type of study: approach/ method/ tradition	Name of authors and year of publication	Age of participants	Content focus	L2 or L3	L1 and context
	Butler 2004	n/a	Primary language teachers' self-reported competencies	L2 English	Taiwan, Japan and Korea
	Tang and Nesi 2003	12 years of age	Teachers' approaches to lexis	L2 English	China and Hong Kong
	Lundberg 2007	n/a	Impact of in-service action research projects	L2 English	Swedish
	Carless 2006	n/a	NS/NNS language teacher collaboration	L2 English	Chinese in Hong Kong
	Lightbown and Spada 1994	n/a	Evaluation of an intensive ESL programme in Quebec	L2 English	French in Canada

4.2 Experimental studies: treatments in the classroom

A great deal of research involving child language learners is experimental in nature. In such studies researchers may design a set of teaching materials or tests to try out in classrooms, speculating that these new materials will lead to better learning outcomes. These types of studies often start with stating the researcher's hypotheses of the expected outcomes and the aim of the study is to confirm or refute these. In order to make claims about the effectiveness of a suggested treatment, researchers randomly assign their participants to an experimental group and a control group. Many studies follow a classic pre-test /post-test design. Here, two sets of tests (pre- and post-tests) are administered to both the experimental group and the control group. If the pre-test confirms that the two groups are comparable, the experimental group's better performance on the post-test will be taken as evidence that the intervention worked, and it was the intervention/treatment (and not anything else) that caused the positive changes. Some studies include delayed post-tests as well, to measure the performance of the experimental group after a longer period of time to see if the positive changes were carried forward. The experimental design is not specific at all to child research – it is widespread in adult research as well.

It is important to remember that it is difficult, if not impossible, to control all the variables in classrooms that might influence the outcomes. There may be many differences between control and experimental classes, such as the experience and the personality of the teacher, the background of the students, their motivation and anxiety levels, their personalities, or their learning styles. Any combination of these factors may influence the outcome of the research rather than just the treatment. In order to compensate for this problem, researchers often triangulate their experimental findings with additional data. For example, in addition to the student's scores on the post-test, they also gather interview or observational data to confirm the advantages of the treatment.

In this first section, we will explore six examples, all of which represent a variation of the classic experimental design: Alexiou (2009), Butler and Lee (2006), Harley (1998), Simard (2004), Goh and Taib (2006) and Drew (2009). The first two studies attempt to establish a statistically significant relationship between two variables. Alexiou's study (2009) confirms correlations between 5–9-year-old Greek children's L2 aptitude test scores and their ability to learn L2 vocabulary. Butler and Lee's study (2006) establishes correlations between young Korean learners' self-assessment scores and a range of different aspects of their L2 learning such as their L2 proficiency, motivation, personality and attitude. Both studies administered a set of tests and tasks to the children.

The rest of the studies have all proposed a new, innovative instructional approach or learning materials. Each study, however, is slightly different in the way the experiment is designed. Harley's study investigated learners in six classes and half of these children were in a control group while the other half were in the experimental group. The treatment was a set of materials designed to draw young children's attention to grammatical form in game-like activities. The researcher was interested to find out whether this intervention would have a lasting effect on the children's ability to use French gender correctly.

The next two studies focus on experiments developing children's metalinguistic awareness. Simard's study is about implementing diaries for reflection with French-speaking children (aged 10–11) learning English as a second language. She used two experimental groups and only one control group, while Goh and Taib's study (2006) did not use a control group at all. They worked with only one group of learners and simply measured their ability at the beginning of the treatment and at the end. Goh and Taib (2006) designed eight lessons with special input which were administered to a small group of only ten children. Finally, Drew (2009) used both control and experimental groups but here the two control groups were deliberately quite different from the experimental group. The author's point was that if the treatment is effective, those learners who are weaker and less proficient in the experimental group will still do better in the end as a result of the overwhelming effect of the treatment. The treatment in this study is a particular reading programme based on a structured scheme of graded readers.

Summaries of the studies

Example study 4.1   Alexiou (2009)

This study focusses on the correlation between young Greek learners' aptitudes and vocabulary learning. The aim of the study was to understand language aptitude in young learners.

The participants were 220 learners of English in Greece between the ages of 5 and 9. All the tests were administered on a one-to-one basis in Greek and they were presented as games. The children were tested twice a year (in January and June). On the second occasion a vocabulary test was also administered.

Aptitude is expected to contain memory, analytic and phonetic elements, so the following tasks/games were designed:

The first set of games were memory tasks (memory component):

- *Kim's game* (short-term immediate memory for pictures).
- *Picture shapes* (associative short-term memory): matched sets of cards are mixed up and the child is asked to match them again; measures the capacity to retain shape pairs.
- *Recognising shapes* (semantic integration): children are given a list of four shapes, then they are asked to look at a picture which contains some of these but not all and some new ones; they are asked to say which ones are the same, which ones are missing and which ones are new; this measures ability to recognise the presence or absence of significant information.

The next set of tasks were analytic tasks (analytic components of aptitude):

- *Colours game* (inductive learning ability): in this game the children are told that each colour represents a different category (e.g. green for animals and red for clothes); progressively more categories and more colours are introduced and the child has to drag each item to the correct colour).
- *Spot the difference* (visual perception): measures the ability to recognise the absence, presence and/or a change in information.
- *Story sequencing* (reasoning ability): four jumbled pictures are shown and the child is asked to make a story that makes sense; the aim is to measure reasoning ability, relying on situational clues, to be able to see the whole from the parts.
- *Jigsaw puzzle* (spatial ability): analysis by synthesis; looking for missing jigsaw puzzle pieces to fit in the picture; it measures the ability to make sense of limited information.

In addition to these tests, the learners were also tested with two vocabulary tests to look for correlations. Vocabulary test 1: receptive vocabulary test where items appeared on the screen and the researcher asked the child to point to the one that was being named. Vocabulary test 2: productive test where the learners had to name different items. Both tests included items that the learners had been taught during the academic year.

The relationship between all aptitude tasks and the vocabulary tests showed significant correlation.

Example study 4.2   Butler and Lee (2006)

The aim of the project was to examine the validity of two types of self-assessment procedures among fourth graders (70 students) and sixth graders (81 students) (age range from 10 to 12) with regard to two types of self-assessment: off-task assessments which are more general and require students to make judgments about their learning in a de contextualised manner, and on-task instruments where students need to reflect on their performance directly related to a particular task after completing it.

The questions that the researchers asked in this paper were:

(1) Are there differences between the two types of self-assessment when compared with teacher assessment and general proficiency tests such as the well-known and widely used Cambridge Young Learners' test?
(2) Do age, proficiency levels, attitudes and personality factors influence students' performance on self-assessment tasks?

In order to answer these questions, five research tools were used: off-task and on-task self-assessment, teachers' assessment, the Cambridge Young Learners'

Example study 4.2   (Continued)

English Examination and a questionnaire to assess personality and attitude factors. In order to construct this questionnaire the authors identified five different constructs that they believed influenced young learners' self-assessment performance. These included motivation, sociability, social interdependency, anxiety and confidence. There were five items for each of these categories in the questionnaire.

The discussion of the findings indicated that students evaluated their performance differently on the two types of assessment tasks. It was also found that motivation, anxiety and confidence were highly correlated with test scores in both classes. In fact, confidence was the strongest predictor for the off-task self-assessment (SA) for both grade levels. Oral proficiency was the best predictor for the on-task SA for sixth grade levels and also for the teachers' assessment. On-task assessment predicted teacher assessment and Cambridge scores better than off-task assessment for both grade levels. Fourth graders' results were less clear than sixth graders' results and there was an age effect for general ability to self-assess. The generally low correlations between self-assessment and the teachers' assessment/Cambridge Test among the fourth graders in the present study may suggest that administering self-assessments to students younger than those at the fourth grade level (or possibly the fifth grade level) may indeed present a problem (Butler and Lee 2006: 514). An additional finding was that whilst students' on-task assessment was best predicted by their proficiency levels, personality and attitude correlated more with the off-task type of self-assessment.

Example study 4.3   Harley (1998)

In this study two hypotheses were established: grade 2 French immersion children will assign French gender more accurately than their peers after a 'focus on form' instruction programme; and they will they be able to generalise this new knowledge to unfamiliar words.

Six French immersion classes in the Toronto area were selected for the experiment. The control groups were six grade 2 classes who did not receive the experimental treatment. The experimental treatment comprised instructional packages to be used for 20 minutes a day. The intervention lasted for five weeks and it focussed on a new approach to grammar. These instructional materials included a variety of games designed to get the French gender right; e.g. in *Simon says* they had to perform contrasting actions according to the gender of the noun they heard. Other games included: *I spy*, *Bingo* and *My aunt's suitcase*. Different testing instruments were also prepared for the pre-test, the post-test and the delayed post-test. The results showed that the experimental students became better at assigning the correct gender to familiar nouns in the post-tests; however they were unable to extend this to unknown nouns.

Example study 4.4   Simard (2004)

In this study the focus is on diaries in which learners were asked to verbalise their reflections about their own language learning processes. The research question of the study was about the potential of diaries as metalinguistic reflection tools to promote SLA among elementary school French-speaking learners of English.

The participants were 81 grade 6 ESL learners in Quebec who were all French L1 speakers. They were divided into two groups: the first comprised two 'convenience' experimental groups (one regular and one 'enriched' group with slightly more learning time and with more motivated learners), and the second was a control group.

A pre-test was administered a month before the study. The study itself lasted for two months. The first post-test was administered immediately after the treatment and a second delayed post-test was administered a month after the first post-test. Both experimental groups received the same training about how to use diaries. During the treatment at the end of every English lesson they were asked to (1) to write down things they had learnt and (2) to write down differences noticed between French and English.

Naturally, these reflections were written in French. The tests were composed of five different tasks measuring students' language proficiency and metalinguistic ability. In addition, questionnaires were used to find out about the students' linguistic background (e.g. whether their parents spoke and used English at home or not) and the ESL teacher's evaluation of the students was also taken into account. Research assistants were present during the treatment, who also kept a diary. This helped with the analysis and the interpretation of the data.

Results showed that all students tended to report more about vocabulary than any other category of language. The enriched group tended to write more than the regular group for all categories. The regular groups reported more about lesson content and focussed less on metalinguistic reflection. In terms of the students' ability to report, there were no large differences between the groups. The enriched group verbalised more than the control and regular groups, but the control group reported more information about the target language than the regular group in the post-test. By the time the delayed post-test was administered all students' ability to report about the target language decreased, which may be explained by the fact that they got bored with the task.

Example study 4.5   Goh and Taib (2006)

The aim of this study was to elicit and identify primary school pupils' metacognitive knowledge about listening in English.

(1) How well do these children manage to articulate their metacognitive knowledge?
(2) How useful can a process-based instructional approach be?

Example study 4.5   (Continued)

Metacognition and its key features are defined as (1) person knowledge, (2) task knowledge and (3) strategy knowledge. In the study two types of knowledge are focussed on: task knowledge and strategy knowledge.

The participants were ten children (11–12 years old, five girls and five boys) who were preparing for an end-of-year listening examination, all in their final year of primary school in Singapore. Half of them were considered to have average or poor listening ability in English. English was not their dominant language although they did interact with one another using a local variety.

As part of the treatment, eight process-based listening lessons were conducted. The lessons followed a three-stage sequence: (1) listen and answer, (2) reflect, (3) report and discuss. The first stage was the same as their usual examination task. The second stage asked students to reflect individually on how they had completed the listening task. During this phase they were guided by questions written on the board to help the process of reflection. The final stage was facilitated by the teacher. Pupils took turns reading out their reflections and the class discussed these.

A great many factors were reported to have influenced their listening, such as vocabulary, text length, topic familiarity, memory limitations and the density of information in the texts. They did not manage to report many strategies however. The most commonly reported strategy was inferencing (i.e. using contextual clues such as key words) to make sense of texts. This was reported three times more than anything else. Planning by way of previewing comprehension questions was also frequently done. Strategies for monitoring and evaluating were not reported at all. Affective strategies such as motivating themselves were also barely mentioned.

In conclusion, they had limited knowledge of comprehension strategies; however it was discovered that they knew quite a bit about test-taking strategies (e.g. using logical deduction and elimination).

At the end of the eighth lesson the researchers evaluated the process. They asked the students to write a reflective piece entitled: *What I think about my listening ability at the end of the eighth lesson.* This was preceded by some discussion in pairs. The authors also compared the children's listening scores before and after the intervention.

Overall, there seemed to be two benefits: (1) pupils reported in their reflective writing an increased level of confidence and metacognitive knowledge, and (2) there was an indication that the metacognitive instruction contributed to the pupils' improvement in two sets of listening test scores. Final reflections revealed that they were now aware of a greater range of useful strategies. In the 'before' and 'after' test comparisons all but one student increased their scores. Those who scored the lowest at the beginning showed the biggest improvement.

Example study 4.6   Drew (2009)

This study sets out to investigate the challenges, advantages and effectiveness of an originally L1 literacy programme adopted in an L2 context. An innovative literacy programme (EYLP programme) in third and fourth grade EFL classrooms in Norwegian primary schools was designed. The author is interested in the measurable effects of this programme compared to 'normal' literacy classrooms.

Three classes, altogether 75 third grade pupils, participated in the study. In addition to the experimental class, two control schools for comparison (with 35 and 23 pupils) were used. Both of these control schools had pupils from high socioeconomic status families. The experimental class followed the new approach, using the readers in their literacy classes. The children were divided into homogeneous ability groups and the classroom was organised into learning centres or 'stations'. One of these stations was led by the teachers while in the others the students worked autonomously. Pupils rotated between stations every 10–15 minutes. The teacher's station was devoted to monitoring pupils' reading. The Cambridge Young Learners Starters Test was administered to all learners as a pre-test (with a 20-minute listening component, a 20-minute reading and writing component and a five-minute oral component) in spring 2006. At this point the experimental students scored lowest.

By the second test (autumn 2006), all the children in the experimental school scored higher on the Cambridge test than those in the other two schools (control schools) even though initially the experimental pupils' scores were lowest. Their rate of progress was highest especially in listening and oral tests. In addition to the test scores, other data were also collected showing the benefits of the new approach. Classroom observations and teacher interviews were also conducted. Two teachers from the experimental school and one teacher from each control school were interviewed. They were asked about literacy materials, classroom organisation, time spent on skills, typical classroom activities, and successful and less successful aspects of teaching literacy.

The teachers in the experimental group generally expressed satisfaction with the learning centres approach although they pointed out how demanding it was to prepare these materials and how frustrating it was not being able to leave the monitoring centre. They considered a flexible approach incorporating some other elements into the 'learning stations' approach as best practice.

Observations in the school confirmed that the experimental school was rich in environmental print, they had a rich supply of books and computers while the control schools had fewer books and less environmental print.

There was an interesting but somewhat unexpected finding about the experimental children's high oral test scores in the tests. The author speculates that the substantial amount of reading may have helped children with their oral skills. The experimental learners' scores in reading and writing did not increase that much although they were still higher than the scores in the other two schools.

Comments

All studies argue that children are able to benefit from experimental treatments. Alexiou (2009) showed that even young children (age 5) coped with the experimental tasks/games. Butler and Lee (2006) showed that children were able to assess themselves, although the differences between the younger and older children indicate that this ability increases sharply after the age of 10. Children were also able to focus on form and derive benefits from an approach that focusses on grammar (Harley 1998). Children are able to reflect on their language learning processes especially if they are encouraged to do so, for example, with the use of diaries in Simard (2004). Goh and Taib (2006) showed that 11–12-year-olds can benefit from metacognitive training and, as a result, their listening improves. Goh and Taib also point to a crucially important outcome in the study, which is the fact that in addition to the development of metacogonitive skills, the materials helped to raise children's level of confidence. Sometimes unexpected benefits can also occur. In Drew's study (2009), the experimental children were found to have improved their oral test scores after participating in the reading programme.

However, these studies also illustrate that test materials can be problematic in experimental research. For example, Alexiou (2009) administered a range of tests/games on a one-to-one basis but there is no discussion about the children's reaction to these unknown tests. It would be interesting to know what the children actually did and which games they enjoyed more and why. The test materials were somewhat problematic in Harley's study. The teachers reported that the vocabulary input in the planned activities was too high and the sheer variety of the tasks was overwhelming. As a consequence, not all tasks were integrated with the curriculum, which led to teachers abandoning some of the tasks, especially by the end of the intervention. In Simard's study (2004), where the children were asked to use a reflective diary, the author comments that the children may have got bored with the diary task and this may be the reason why they decided to write less about their reflections in the later stages. In other words, the diary was perhaps not sufficient on its own to elicit the children's reflections.

In experimental studies the researchers need to decide how long they want to carry on with the treatment. In reality, many have to opt for a shorter than ideal period due to practical difficulties, such as restricted access to classes or lack of permission to interfere with the set curriculum. In Harley's study (1998), it is suggested that five weeks was perhaps not sufficiently long to measure the children's full potential to learn from the new approach. In Simard's study (2004), this same question comes up and the author wonders whether a longer duration of the experimental treatment might have provided more insights and might have led to more reflection on the children's part. Drew's study (2009) is at the opposite end of the scale in terms of timing. Here, the treatment lasted for a whole academic year, but because of this it could not be a tightly controlled experiment. It only resembled the classical experimental design in its basic interest to contrast groups of learners with or without the experience of the treatment.

What can researchers do to counteract the limitations of the classic experimental design and the time constraints? As is clear from these studies, researchers can gain further data and additional evidence to strengthen the numerical outcomes of scores and test results. For example, in Drew's study (2009), in addition to the numerical data gained from the test scores of the experimental and the control groups, other evidence, i.e. interviews with teachers and in-class observation by researchers, are also presented. In fact, it is the teacher interviews that reveal most clearly that the approach, although clearly superior to the traditional approach, does have its own shortcomings, which must not be ignored if the decision is made to implement the new approach in other schools. In Simard's study, although the results were encouraging, they were not as clear-cut regarding the differences between the experimental groups and the control group as the researcher would have liked. However, further evidence about the treatment was gained from research assistants' diaries and additional child questionnaires. The research assistants' notes also helped to make sense of the children's diary entries. Goh and Taib (2006), to compensate for the lack of a control group in their study, collected evidence from the learners in the form of some reflective writing at the end, and they paid a great deal of attention to the actual process, describing both the learners' strategies and their own (researchers') insights during the intervention. This combined evidence makes a convincing case in favour of the new approach, although it is important to note that the researchers only make careful, measured claims.

In some of these studies, the researcher was an outsider to the classroom, in other studies the researcher was the regular teacher, and in yet others several people collaborated, including both teachers and outsiders. In the first two studies de-contextualised tests were used by outsiders. In Harley's study (1998), six different teachers were asked to carry out the interventions in different classes and it is therefore reasonable to assume that these teachers may have taught the materials slightly differently. Similarly, in Drew's study (2009), different teachers were teaching the new reading scheme in different classrooms so there may have been individual differences that played a part. Another, perhaps a more important, question also arises here about the project teachers. Were they better trained, better motivated and generally more committed because of the project? It is often highly skilled, committed teachers who can make the difference rather than the instructional approach *per se*. In Goh and Taib's (2006) study and in Simard's (2004) study the teacher and the researcher were the same person. While this is advantageous in terms of the already existing rapport with the children, the double identity of teacher-researcher may lead to conflicts, as the teacher needs to constantly switch between the two roles. This further underlines the difficulty of eliminating all variables in a classic experimental design.

4.3 Comparing different treatments

This group of studies represents a variation on the classic experiments. In these studies, two or more competing treatments are compared. In these types of experiments the researchers need to take special care avoid the effect of a particular order of administering the treatments. Three studies are reviewed here: Peñate Cabrera and Bazo Martínez (2001), Kim (2008) and Shak and Gardner (2008).

Peñate Cabrera and Bazo Martínez's (2001) study is with English as a foreign language learners in Spain. In this study the learners are randomly assigned to two groups for two relatively short 'treatments'. Both groups experience both treatments. The children listen to two stories delivered in two different ways to find out which of the two conditions will lead to better story comprehension. The second study (Kim 2008) also attempts to compare two different treatments but here the researcher is working with just two individual subjects. Kim (2008) is interested to find out which type of treatment will lead to better learning outcomes, the one where the learners are only receiving oral input or the one where they receive a combined oral and written input. Finally, Shak and Gardner (2008) compare four instructional tasks with 10-year-old children in Brunei. All four tasks were genuinely believed to be beneficial but the researchers wanted to find out how they would be received and rated by the learners.

Summaries of the studies

Example study 4.7   Peñate Cabrera and Bazo Martínez (2001)

The aim of this study was to find out whether 10-year-old children would find it easier to understand a story when it was told with linguistic modifications only, which meant using simplified language (condition 1), or by combining both linguistic and interactional adjustments, including repetitions, comprehension checks and gestures (condition 2).

The study was conducted in the Canary Islands, Spain, with 60 learners from different classes in a state primary school. The children had been learning English for two years and they were in the fourth grade. Two versions of the two stories were prepared: one version with linguistic modifications and one version with interactional adjustments. The pupils from the three classes were randomly assigned to one of two groups. Each group listened to both stories, alternating the two conditions. The two stories selected were Tale A: *The Long Nose* and Tale B: *The Princess and the Pea*. Both groups listened to both stories. The same male teacher delivered all storytelling sessions. After the sessions, all children completed a listening test based on the stories.

The test scores did not show any significant differences between the two student groups but when the two conditions were compared, results clearly showed that the second condition, which incorporated the interactional adjustments, led to significantly higher levels of understanding. Pupils also consistently rated the second condition as much easier.

Example study 4.8   Kim (2008)

This study aimed to find out how to effectively support beginning-level ESL children's academic English. The author claims that although young children often communicate quite well after spending just one year in their new L2 environment, they do not automatically develop a wide range of linguistic skills.

The participants of the study were two ESL students (one Chinese and one Korean) living in the USA. Yang was 6 years old, from China and Yun was 5 years old, from Korea. Neither child had any formal schooling in their home countries.

The researcher was interested in the effects of markedly different instructional approaches to help these children progress with their L2 development. To this end, two treatments were designed: a set of instructional sessions based on oral–written integrated input and another set based on just oral language input. Both treatments lasted 12 hours and both were administered but were counterbalanced between the students. The primary objective was to expand the students' vocabulary. The treatments continued for ten weeks. Four themes were selected and treatments were administered like this:

Places we live/Clothing: Yang (integrated) and Yun (oral)
Food/Transportation: Yun (integrated) and Yang (oral)

The integrated lesson followed four steps: (1) teacher read story, (2) the student wrote in the journal, (3) activities around the journal, and (4) review of sentence structures. The oral version followed these steps: (1) teacher read story, (2) student listened to teacher's explanation of words, (3) oral language games were played, (4) oral review of what happened in the session was conducted.

Oral measures were taken before and after the treatment. A picture description task was used for assessment to measure treatment effects. Scoring was based on total number of words, semantic acceptability, syntactic acceptability, the absence of prompting, and fluency, which was calculated as the mean length of comprehensible utterances (MLCU).

Although both students made progress in learning English oral language skills during the research period, the integrated language-based intervention led to greater gains in their oral language development than did the oral language-based intervention.

(Kim 2008: 443)

Example study 4.9   Shak and Gardner (2008)

This paper reports on administering 'focus on form' tasks with young learners of English in Brunei schools. Recent studies show positive effects of focus on form instruction but learners' views on these have rarely been the point of interest. The aim is to find out how the children rate the different treatment tasks and what task features influence their preferences.

The four tasks were: a consciousness-raising task, a dictogloss, a grammar interpretation task and a grammaring task. A consciousness-raising task is defined as

---

Example study 4.9   (Continued)

provision of data to learners that illustrates the linguistic form. On the basis of this, learners are asked to verbalise the language rule. A dictogloss is when learners listen to a short text and then reconstruct their version of the original text in pairs. A grammar interpretation task is where learners make salient distinctions in meaning and use between related forms (e.g. in this study between active and passive past forms). Finally, a grammaring task is when learners extend the use of grammatical structures to attain communicative clarity and appropriacy.

A total of 78 grade 5 children participated (three classes from three different schools). The teachers were provided with materials and lesson plans. The instructional treatment was conducted over four weeks and each week the children were introduced to a new 'focus on form' task. In addition to the four tasks, an attitude questionnaire was used (asking the children to reflect on their perceived task enjoyment, ease, performance and motivation). Also, a group interview explored which activities the children enjoyed and why and which ones were more difficult and why. These interviews were administered by the teachers.

The result showed that children generally enjoyed all the tasks and their attitudes were positive. Familiarity with the task demands over the two-day periods led to an increase in positive perceptions. The children reported a decrease in positive attitudes over the two days for the grammar interpretation task because of the writing element.

Comments

Peñate Cabrera and Bazo Martínez (2001) demonstrate that teacher language use in the L2 classroom is an important learning source, especially if it is accompanied with effective interactive adjustment. Shak and Gardner (2008) show that 10-year-old children are interested in working with focus on form tasks and Kim's study highlights the importance of early literacy in L2. Practising with writing tasks helps children to develop better L2 proficiency even in the case of young children who have not experienced literacy at school in their mother tongue.

As was discussed in relation to the previous set of studies, in order to supplement the primary data based on numerical results, other data are added to triangulate the results. In Peñate Cabrera and Bazo Martínez (2001), in addition to the numerical scores the researchers also elicited the children's opinions in order to confirm the primary findings. In Shak and Gardner's study (2008) teachers were interviewed about their views and this additional information was also taken into account in addition to the scores children gave each task.

When making a claim that one approach or treatment is more beneficial than another, it is important that researchers scrutinise their materials very carefully. In Peñate Cabrera and Bazo Martínez's study (2001) the results are not surprising in that intuitively we know that gestures, repetitions, frequent comprehension checks and reformulations will enhance children's understanding. It is not quite clear, however, which one of the interactional adjustments made the difference. Was it gestures or was it repetition? Or was it a particular combination of both? An interesting question also arises about the choice of stories in the same study. One of the stories, *The Princess and the Pea* is a very popular story and the children may have been familiar with its content in Spanish. If this was the case, the children's familiarity with one story but not with the other could have influenced the results. In Shak and Gardner's (2008) study, there may have been a strong 'novelty effect'. The children may have responded to the tasks positively because they were new and exciting, and different from their routine tasks. Had the learners and the teachers worked with these tasks for a whole term, their attitudes might have changed over time.

Similarly to Harley's study discussed earlier, in Shak and Gardner's study (2008), the researchers designed the materials and these were then handed over to teachers to incorporate into their normal classes. This decision always carries the risk that the researchers' original intentions may be altered. In addition, in order to please their teachers, the children may exaggerate their positive responses. When interviewed by the class teacher, the children may be hesitant to voice negative feelings. In Kim's study (2008), the children had the teacher/researcher's undivided attention for the whole of the sessions for ten weeks. This special one-to-one relationship may have contributed to the positive results.

4.4 Comparing age groups, adults and children, and bilingual/monolingual children

The interest in comparative research approaches is often related to the debate around the 'age factor'. Researchers continue to try to tease out differences between adult and child second language learning processes. Some studies focus on the comparison of different age groups and others focus on the comparison of those who started learning a second language early or relatively late in childhood. Comparisons are also made between bilingual children and their monolingual peers, as well as between individual children's L1 and L2 abilities.

Seven studies are included here illustrating a range of different comparative perspectives: Leseman (2000), Shrubshall (1997), Bae (2007), Tagoilelagi-Leota *et al.* (2005), Mackey, Oliver and Leeman (2003), Garcia Mayo (2003) and Heining-Boynton and Haitema (2007).

The first two studies compare L1 majority children (NS) and L2 minority children in two contexts, the Netherlands and the UK. Leseman (2000) compares very young (between the ages of 3.2 and 4.2) Turkish immigrant children's vocabulary development with the development of monolingual Dutch children who are of similar ages. The comparison is justified by teachers' overwhelming experience that Turkish children tend to fall behind their monolingual Dutch counterparts at school. Shrubshall (1997) also compares monolingual (L1 majority) and bilingual (L2 minority) children's competence in a London school. All these children are L2 English speakers with Portuguese as their L1. The author is focussing on the children's storytelling ability. Both these studies (Leseman and Shrubshall) refer to Cummins's work about academic proficiency (discussed in Chapter 3). The third study (Bae 2007) compares children with different backgrounds in a two-way Korean-English bilingual programme in the USA. Half of the children are Korean-proficient with English as an L2, and the rest of the children are English-proficient (although not necessarily with English as an L1), learning Korean as an L2. The researcher was interested in assessing the children's English competence through exploring their story-writing ability. These types of comparison are carried out to reassure teachers, parents and policy makers that the two-way bilingual education does not hurt the children's English language development. In the fourth study the comparisons are made between the L1 and L2 competences of the same children. Tagoilelagi-Leota *et al.* (2005) explore a heritage language under threat in New Zealand, and by comparing young children's spoken competence in their L1 and L2 they point to a very real danger that their L1 will be lost. Mackey, Oliver and Leeman's study (2003) makes comparisons between L2 adults and L2 children in Australia. The researchers investigated NNS/NS versus NNS/NNS adult and child dyads interacting using language tasks. The last two studies are longitudinal in design. Garcia Mayo (2003) compared age-related differences with Spanish/Basque bilinguals learning English as an L3, focussing on grammaticality judgment tasks. They tested the same two groups of learners after four and six years of study. Finally, Heining-Boynton and Haitema (2007) compared the same subjects' views and responses about second language learning in primary schools and ten years later in young adulthood. The aim of the study was to show the extent to which children's primary school language learning experiences may be of relevance in later life.

Summaries of the studies

Example study 4.10   Leseman (2000)

The study compared 31 Turkish immigrant preschool children in their vocabulary development with 77 same-age Dutch children. The children's vocabulary development was measured three times between the ages of 3.2 and 4.2.

The children were subjected to some receptive and productive vocabulary tests and some cognitive tests which tapped into both their non-verbal intelligence and their logico-mathematical concept knowledge. The researchers had an extensive interview with the children's mothers at home. The researchers also took note of which language(s) were used in the home and whether the children were receiving high-level language interactions in the home, what the families' socioeconomic status was and whether the children were receiving child care services.

Results indicated that the Turkish children's vocabulary in Turkish as well as in Dutch was below or far below the level of comparison groups of Dutch low socioeconomic status (SES) and Dutch high SES groups upon introduction to kindergarten.

Example study 4.11   Shrubshall (1997)

This study aimed to explore whether in the context of Cummins's academic proficiency measure, storytelling might also be an important academic skill for L2 speakers to acquire.

The author compared the storytelling performances of both monolingual and L2 children of different ages with respect to those features of oral storytelling which are related to academic discourse (e.g. episode structuring, evaluation of the narrative and temporal sequences).

Two inner London primary schools were used. All bilingual participants were Portuguese speakers and had spent about 2–3 years in the UK by the time the study was undertaken. Three age groups were included: children from year groups 1–6, aged between 5 and 11.

First of all a story was selected (*Come away from the water, Shirley*) and read to the children. They were encouraged to comment on the pictures. Afterwards they were asked to imagine being Shirley, and to tell the story in the first person. The story was about Shirley's parents falling asleep on the beach and Shirley taking off to have exciting adventures involving pirates and treasures. After some preparation time, the pictures were taken away and the children were all asked to tell a good story individually. The resulting stories were recorded and analysed according to how the narrator evaluated the events and how the events were moulded into episodes.

With regards to evaluation, monolinguals were twice as evaluative as bilinguals and the differences were biggest with 3–4 year group students. With regard to episodic structure, in the case of the youngest children (year 1–2) the number of episodes was so low that it was difficult to draw conclusions. Greatest differences for episodic structures emerged in 3–4 year students between monolinguals and bilinguals while the differences were much less obvious with the 5–6 year group. Overall, bilingual speakers' stories were less sophisticated in terms of episodic features.

Example study 4.12   Bae (2007)

The aim of this study was to explore Korean–English bilingual children's writing development. A performance-based narrative task was selected and three aspects of writing, i.e. coherence, grammar and content were focussed on.

For all children in the programme, from kindergarten onwards, the majority of instruction was given in Korean and only 30 per cent of instruction was

Example study 4.12   (Continued)

conducted in English. The English instructions gradually increased to 50 per cent by grade 2 and in the rest of the primary school this 50-50 per cent was to be maintained.

A total of 192 students participated in the study, 97 first- and 95 second-graders in two groups: English-proficient and Korean-proficient. With regard to the participants, one group in each class was Korean-American, and the non-Koreans were of Hispanic, Anglo-Saxon, Filipino, Arab or Chinese ancestry. The non-Koreans had all to be proficient in English to be admitted into the programme. These children were contrasted with regular classes where 100 per cent of instruction was in English.

The writing prompt was a series of pictures depicting a story. Each child wrote a story towards the end of their school year (either grade 1 or 2). The author argues that this story-writing task is a useful prompt to observe language development beyond sentence level. Accordingly, the following aspects of the writing were evaluated: coherence, grammar and content.

The results indicated that there were no significant differences between Korean-proficient and English-proficient students in any of the areas (coherence, content and grammar) and this was the case for both first- and second-graders. This means that both groups within the programme were doing equally well in English. There was a significant improvement for both groups from grade 1 to grade 2. When compared to the monolingual class, immersion students scored equally well.

Example study 4.13   Tagoilelagi-Leota *et al.* (2005)

This study focussed on the comparison of young children's indigenous L1 and L2 proficiency and literacy levels during their transition between L1 immersion preschools and L2 primary schools in New Zealand.

As part of a larger study, in this paper the authors report on the comparisons between the L1 and L2 abilities of 23 Samoan and 26 Tongan children who had been attending early childhood centres that offered immersion education in the heritage L1. From these centres the children progressed to English mainstream classrooms.

The children were tested four times between the ages of 4.6 and 6.0, using a variety of literacy measures in both their heritage language (L1) and English (L2). The measurements included levels of language proficiency just a few weeks into starting school (around age 5) and a year later at the age of 6.

The measures used in the tests included:

- Language measures: 'Tell me' a listening test which involved listening to an unfamiliar story and re-telling it with the help of the book. Sentence complexity, vocabulary, general organisation, expression and content were scored.
- The Peabody Picture Vocabulary test (see Chapter 8).

- Literacy measures: concepts about print, ability to identify letters, ability to recognise words, and ability to write words.

The researchers all spoke the children's L1 and English (L2).

Up to the beginning of primary school the children were growing steadily more proficient in both languages. Having spent one year at school the children dropped their language measures for L1 while their English continued to develop. This was the case for both the storytelling and the vocabulary tests. Similar results emerged for the literacy measures.

The results also show that there was great variability among the children and only about half of them had high levels of both L1 and L2. Levels of English tended to be correlated with English literacy measures but not with home language literacy measures. This suggests a degree of separation between literacy development in the two languages. A few weeks into school children's L2 development was gaining dramatically. In particular, between the ages of 5 and 6 a rapid growth of literacy and comprehension knowledge in English was evidenced.

Example study 4.14   Mackey, Oliver and Leeman (2003)

This study explored differences between the amount and the nature of the feedback provided during communication tasks and the opportunities that arose to utilise this feedback. The comparisons were made between adult and child NS/NNS and NNS/NNS.

Altogether 96 participants (half adult and half children, both groups from a variety of backgrounds) were selected. The adults were university students and the children were 8 to 12 years old. Two tasks were used, a 'one-way' and a 'two-way' task (one way: describe and draw, two-way: complete a picture together). The 96 participants were randomly matched with a partner, producing 12 NS/NNS and 12 NNS/NNS adult and 12 NS/NNS and 12 NNS/NNS child pairs.

Both tasks were administered to all dyads and the first 100 utterances in each task were transcribed for analysis. First of all target-like and non target-like utterances were identified, then feedback in relation to non target-like utterances was marked. Then the researchers looked at whether there was an opportunity at all for the interlocutor to produce modified output and whether or not the original source of ungrammaticality was corrected.

Results indicated that:

(1) NS in both groups provided more feedback than NNS – but this was only significant for adults.
(2) For adults, feedback provided by NNS was significantly more likely to offer opportunities to produce modified output.
(3) In child dyads, learners produced significantly more modified output when interacting with a NNS rather than a NS.
(4) There was no significant difference in the amount of feedback provided in adult and child dyads.
(5) There was a significant age-related difference in NNS/NNS dyads.

Example study 4.14   (Continued)

The authors state that 'although adult interlocutors seemed to provide differ-ent amounts and types of feedback, the type of interlocutor seemed to have no effect on the immediate output learners produced in response to that feedback. In contrast, however, in child dyads there were no significant differences between NS/NNS and NNS/NNS dyads in either amount or nature of feedback provided, but there was significantly more modified output (in response to feedback) in NNS/NNS dyads than in NS/NNS dyads'.

(Mackey, Oliver and Leeman 2003: 55)

Example study 4.15   Garcia Mayo (2003)

This study directly addressed the effect of age on the acquisition of English as an L3 in the Basque Country (Spain) where children already speak two languages (Spanish and Basque) when they start English.

The main issue of interest is whether the age at which a student is first exposed to a second or foreign language will have an effect on the L3 acquisition process. The methodology used was a specific test called the 'grammaticality judgment test' focussing on structures related to the so-called pro-drop parameter (Jaeggli and Safir 1989). Grammaticality judgments are reflections of a learner's compe-tence in the target language. The learner's intuition about whether a structure or sentence is correct or incorrect reflects the development of his/her interlanguage knowledge.

Basque and Spanish both belong to the so-called 'pro-drop languages' and thus are very different from English. Pro-drop languages exhibit certain characteristics such as: (1) they can have missing subjects (literally: We will be late for school if don't take this bus) (2) they can have free subject–verb inversion (Slept the baby for three hours) and (3) they can exhibit the 'that-trace' effect (Who did you say that arrived late?).

The subjects of the study were two groups of bilinguals who were matched for number of hours of exposure to English and type of instruction but who differed in the age of first exposure to English (8–9 years of age as opposed to 11–12 years of age). Both groups were tested twice, first after four years of learning and then after six years of learning. The only difference was that Group A started learning English at an earlier age.

A GJ (grammaticality judgment task) was designed with 17 sentences related to the pro-drop parameter and 13 distractors. The test contained six ungrammatical sentences with missing subjects, five ungrammatical sentences with subject–verb inversion and six sentences relevant to the 'that-trace' effect. Two of these were ungrammatical and four were grammatical. Students were given instructions in Basque and were asked to rate whether the sentences were correct or not.

The results show that length of exposure seems to have a positive effect in the target-like performance of these subjects. The longer the exposure the better the learners became. In other words, both groups did better on the GJ test after six years of exposure.

Example study 4.16   Heining-Boynton and Haitema (2007)

The aim of this study was to document the changes in attitude to foreign language learning in North Carolina in two school districts. A survey (FLES programme evaluation inventory) was conducted to track the children's attitudes to learning a foreign language at school (either Spanish or French). They were administered a questionnaire at the end of the school year. Altogether many thousands of students participated throughout the primary school grades.

The results from the survey indicated that, first of all, girls scored higher than boys for every question. Student attitudes changed over time, largely in a downward direction. This was characteristic of both boys and girls. The data also showed that girls had more desire to continue their foreign language studies than boys and this result was statistically significant. Girls also had a more positive attitude to their linguistic development over time. Overall, students seem to lose interest in a foreign language as they move up the grades and the same downward pattern occurs in both cohorts. Still, despite the decline girls were still positive while boys became neutral.

The high school study was conducted as a follow-up to find out how early foreign language learning impacts on high school years. Ten years after the original study, 13 high school students were interviewed (five males and eight females, who were also participants in the previous study and were in their 11th or 12th grade, between the ages of 16 and 18). They were volunteers. Overall, ten students' responses (7 females and 3 males) were classified as sympathetic while three students' responses (1 female and 2 males) were classified as indifferent/neutral. Seven respondents felt that that study of foreign languages was in itself valuable while the other six viewed it as a means to an end.

Nine out of 13 of these participants felt that their primary language learning experiences had helped them to maintain a positive attitude to language learning. Nine out of 13 students had also positively commented on the relationship between early foreign language learning and their appreciation of other cultures. Seven reported that thanks to their early language learning, they viewed foreign language learning as a valuable exercise for its own sake rather than as a means to an end.

Comments:

Both Leseman (2000) and Shrubshall (1997) show convincingly that the L1 minority L2 children were not able to perform at the level of their native speaker counterparts; see Chapter 3. In contrast to the first two studies, Bae (2007) reports inspiring findings regarding bilingualism in a two-way immersion context. This example highlights the characteristics of 'elite' bilingual programmes, where the children, the parents and the teachers are all dedicated, motivated and well-prepared for the challenges bilingual education may present. Mackey, Oliver and Leeman (2003) also focussed on immigrant children in Australia but here the focus was on the comparison with adults rather than their NS peers.

Tagoilelagi-Leota *et al.*'s study (2005) shows that in contexts where heritage languages are learnt at home and children switch to English (L2) in their first year of primary school, it is very difficult to maintain the L1. In fact, at a very young age languages can be lost completely.

The last two studies are in EFL contexts. Garcia Mayo (2003) suggests that the length of exposure does matter when it comes to the acquisition of grammatical knowledge in English as an L3. Heining-Boynton and Haitema (2007) show that in the case of some learners at least, initial language learning experiences in childhood will influence their language learning trajectories in adulthood. The study also reminds us that girls seem to have more positive experiences and more positive attitudes in relation to language learning than do boys.

Many studies that rely on a comparative design also resemble experiments discussed in the previous section in that the primary data is often difficult to interpret in its own right. In Leseman (2000), for example, while the numerical data are convincing in terms of highlighting the general trend, a particular question about the testing materials arises in relation to the age of the children. It is difficult to see how some of the complicated cognitive and mathematical tests could be administered to such young children. In fact, the paper skates over the details of these tests. Questions about the actual instruments and materials also arise in the other studies. In Shrubshall (2007), a question might arise about how relevant, motivating and attractive the same story may have been to the different groups of learners, given that children from quite a wide age range were included (from 6 to 11 years). In Bae's study (2007), the researcher selected a story-writing task to measure the children's English ability. However, it is clear from the contextual description that these children practised this type of task a great deal. In view of this, perhaps it would have been a good idea to include some other tasks as well. Bae describes the school as a very positive environment where teachers are well-grounded in theories of bilingualism and immersion. They use cooperative working methods and the interactions in class are of high quality. The teachers are also described as dedicated and excellent in providing writing instruction. In fact, these students were getting extra tutoring of five hours a week in Korean and in English so it is quite likely that both children and parents were highly motivated and prepared to put in a great deal of extra effort and work. It may be that the high-quality teaching and the high levels of motivation can explain the results. In Garcia Mayo's study (2003) the task is very restrictive. Again, additional instruments tapping into the learners' grammatical knowledge could have been used to complement these results.

In Heining-Boynton and Haitema's study (2007), the questionnaire was piloted and validated and it was administered to many thousands of students. The sheer volume of data makes the findings likely to be robust but an interesting question arises about the interviews. Is it really possible to reflect back on experiences that happened ten years earlier? The participants will find it difficult to evaluate their experiences from such a distance. In fact, many other important influences may have occurred that would have also shaped participants' current views, perhaps much more than what happened at primary school.

4.5 Individual cases of children and small groups

This section focusses on studies that explore cases of individual children or small groups, or in some cases, families. This focus contrasts with the above studies interested in generalisable findings in that the emphasis is on the unique characteristics of language learners, and the underlying idea is that we can learn just as much from individual trajectories and the longitudinal tracking of learners. In case studies researchers want to understand the complexities of a particular learning situation and there is a need to observe and explore the situation for a longer time to account for the dynamic nature of changes, trends and emerging patterns. Studies in this section use a wide variety of different methods and tools in combination, such as diaries, in-depth interviews, field-notes and different types of observation. Learners are studied in their natural environments and there is less focus on their performance in relation to tests and tasks. The studies in this category should be seen as complementing the studies in the previous section.

There are five example studies included here: Nassaji and Cumming (2000), Dagenais, Day and Toohey (2006), Cekaite (2007), Hawkins (2005) and Mitchell and Lee (2008).

Individual learners are in focus in the first two studies (Nassaji and Cumming 2000 and Cekaite 2007). The first study explores a single learner's writing development, while the second study tracks oral development. In Nassaji and Cumming's study (2000), Ali, a 6-year-old Iranian boy, and Ellen, his ESL teacher, are engaged in a journal-writing dialogue. Using a Vygotskian framework, the aim of the paper is to describe how one of the Vygotskian concepts, the zone of proximal development (ZPD) (see Chapter 1) actually works in practice. In Cekaite (2007), Fusi, a 7-year-old Kurdish girl's spoken contributions in play activities are described during her first year in a Swedish kindergarten. Cekaite (2007: 46) claims that that 'focussing on how novices negotiate access to a variety of classroom activities, as well as on what skills and competencies are cultivated and recognised as valued, is central to our understanding of classroom learning.' Over the year, Fusi's identity in the classroom changes through the various opportunities she has to participate in classroom discourse.

The next two papers (Dagenais, Day and Toohey 2006 and Hawkins 2005) both focus on learner identity development through the examination of individual learners over time. In Dagenais, Day and Toohey's project, the authors studied a 12-year-old multilingual learner (Chinese L1, in French immersion in Canada where English is another official language). The study lasted for five years. The authors' intention in the paper is to uncover how Sarah's identity was constructed collaboratively, by herself, her peers and her teachers at school. Interestingly, her teachers had surprisingly contrasting opinions of her progress and future educational prospects. Hawkins's (2005) study contrasts two learners (4–5 years old) in a US kindergarten. Here the researcher and the regular class teacher collaborated in conducting a joint research project. The class teacher knows the children and their parents, their family circumstances while the researcher brings a fresh eye, some research skills and expertise that will also benefit the process. Based on the two boys' contrasting trajectories, which were different from the researchers' original expectations, the author suggests that negotiating particular identities in the classroom can afford or deny access to language learning practices at school. The final study in this section (Mitchell and Lee 2008) is conducted in a home context where informal language learning takes place (see Chapter 3). In this case, the researcher is a parent with a strong interest and professional background in language learning. This family ethnography focusses on the language learning opportunities three Korean children created collaboratively while playing together at home.

Summary of the studies

Example study 4.17   Nassaji and Cumming (2000)

The aim of the paper is to understand and document how the ZPD is negotiated by exploring the joint journal-writing process between a young Iranian child in his L2 (English) and his teacher.

The authors analysed 95 exchanges in the interactive dialogue journals written over ten months, shared between Ali, a 6-year-old Farsi-speaking child from Iran, and his Canadian teacher, Ellen. The analysis is focussed on the intricate patterns of teacher scaffolding.

The journals were written every few days, as part of Ali's routine classroom activity. Ellen told students to initiate topics of their own interest. Then she replied to students and extended the range of language functions every few weeks. Two salient characteristics of the ZPD were noticed, based on the joint journal: sustained intersubjectivity and complementary, asymmetrical scaffolding.

Both Ali and Ellen used these regular written interactions to understand and appreciate one another. A fundamental asymmetry in the language functions between learner and teacher was noticed: Ali mainly reported personal facts, opinions, or general facts and although Ellen used the reporting function too, she requested information and clarification; she also evaluated, predicted and gave directions. The teacher pitched her discourse to match Ali's basic reporting function. Ellen gradually moved from simple questions to queries, requiring fuller, deeper responses. She also modelled the spelling and the syntax of phrases. Ali picked up these question patterns and began to ask Ellen about things that interested him. On occasions where Ali wrote shorter entries, Ellen wrote more, to encourage him to do the same. Conversely, where Ali wrote a great deal, Ellen often replied with a brief response. Backing off allows the learner greater expression and this is an important element of the ZPD, permitting the scaffolding to be contingent. The more Ali reported opinions, the less Ellen asked for them. Ali often spontaneously added a third element to the interaction request for information – an answer and acknowledgement, as in 'I like your answer'.

Example study 4.18   Dagenais, Day and Toohey (2006)

The aim of the paper is to illustrate how a multilingual child called Sarah is variously constructed/represented by teachers and peers socially, materially and linguistically. The authors argue that this informs educational practitioners concerned with multilingual children.

Sarah was one of the 12 multilingual French immersion students observed over five years during a longitudinal ethnographic study. As part of this, between 1999 and 2001 Sarah's participation was recorded in classroom activities, in field-notes, in audiotapes twice-monthly over one year, and monthly over the second year. Her classrooms were videotaped and relevant documents such as instructional materials and examples of student work were also used and analysed. During this period Sarah and her teachers participated in individual semi-structured interviews.

At the end of the fieldwork Sarah was 12 years old and was able to speak and write in French, English and Chinese. In this paper the data selection and data analysis focusses on two themes: (1) to show how her teachers constructed her very differently and (2) to show how her own behaviour was very different depending on whether it was a small-group task or a public whole-class task that she was expected to participate in.

In small group activities Sarah participated confidently but in public oral presentations and whole-class discussion she was much less confident. Her teachers reinforced this contrast. In French immersion, reluctance to perform in oral presentations signals a problem: that is why one of the teachers has given Sarah an 'at risk' identity. The authors argue that these are institutional practices with hidden meanings. The unspoken assumption is that high-performing students are verbal, display knowledge publicly, and seek support from teachers. However the authors argue that Sarah was not *always* quiet. She shared her cultural and linguistic knowledge with her peers, displayed her identity as a literate multilingual and invited her classmates to explore her cultural heritage.

Some conclusions and recommendations for teachers working with multilingual children:

1. Multilingual children need to work with peers; and teachers need to think of creative ways of encouraging this type of interactions.
2. Multilingual children need to be able to draw on all their linguistic resources; sharing linguistic and cultural resources with all.
3. Multilingual children need to be able to claim desirable identities at school including identities of expertise.
4. Multilingual children need to participate in classrooms in meaningful ways, whatever their proficiency might be.

Example study 4.19   Cekaite (2007)

This ethnographic case study offers a detailed longitudinal analysis of the relationship between participation and L2 learning.

The researcher examined Fusi, a 7-year-old Kurdish girl's development in terms of her interactional competence during her first year in Sweden. When the recordings began Fusi had been in this class for just two months. Fusi's ability to join in conversations with her peers and the teacher is analysed at three distinct points in time: the beginning of the year, the middle of the year and the end of the school year.

A microanalytical approach relying on techniques in conversation analysis is used by the researcher to tap into Fusi's interactional competence in multiparty conversational activities. The researcher describes her changing identity as evidenced by her linguistic and turn-taking choices and the consequences of these in her participation in classroom interactions. The findings of the research point to an interesting curve of development.

The first phase: In the first phase of data collection it was evident that Fusi was generally silent and often appeared to be uninterested in teacher-fronted activities. Fusi was often on her own in the playground and in the classroom as well. She complained that she did not want to live in Sweden and she was quite unhappy. During this first phase her meaning making was heavily embedded in visual activities. When she initiated talk it was more often dyadic rather than multiparty.

The second phase: By the middle of the year Fusi became more visible both in the classroom and in the playground. She became loud and disruptive even, often leaving her desk in the classroom without permission, creating disturbance. She tried to position herself as a successful student and wanted to become part of the group of Arabic children, without much success. She was often assigned the least favourable tasks and roles by her peers. In her talk with the teacher she relied heavily on repetition and on interactional routines picked up in the classroom. It was noticeable that her contributions were often ignored and judged as irrelevant or even disruptive in the classroom.

The third phase: In sharp contrast to the first two phases, by the end of the school year Fusi became a competent participant in the classroom. She learnt to actively demonstrate her academic knowledge and had now abandoned her loud assertive tone. Her ability to defend a standpoint developed a great deal and this seemed to secure the teacher's attention and positive responses. She also learnt to participate in spontaneously evolving whole-group conversations. Her contributions were phrased in such a way that they indicated their newsworthiness to the others. In a nutshell, she became a successful student who fully participated in the multiparty interactions in class.

The researcher draws important implications from these findings:

'Learning and participation cannot be seen as a unilinear development toward full participation nor as a unidirectional development of one unified learner identity. Over time, one and the same L2 learner can position himself or herself very differently within the classroom community, depending in part on his or her interactional skills.'

(Cekaite 2007: 59)

Example study 4.20   Hawkins (2005)

The aim of the study was to uncover what factors play a role in shaping very young children's academic success at school. The participants were kindergarten children (aged 4–5) with kindergarten teacher Lynn. There were 14 learners in the class. Four children were from a language background other than English and in this paper the focus is on two children: Anton from Peru and William from Korea.

The methodology aims to combine children's different experiences inside and outside the school and to elicit their views and opinions in addition to adults' opinions about them.

- Home visits: to observe language practices and interactional practices of the family; to listen to stories of parents about their own children.
- Interviews with focal children twice, in September and in April, to elicit their understanding of school, definitions of play and school.
- Interviews with parents about their children, to elicit parents' interpretations of their children's school life.
- Observations: twice a year in October and May the children were followed around all day and recorded; the observer would take note of what was happening every 15 minutes, who the child interacted with and what they were saying, how they were behaving; snapshots of social interactions, behaviours and language use.
- Sociograms: each child is the class was also interviewed; they were asked to think about questions such as 'If you could choose someone in a science experiment to work with, who would it be (in class)'? Or 'If someone could come to your house to play,who would it be?'

Anton

Anton, the Peruvian child, was exposed to school experiences through his older sister and used effective strategies to observe and analyse what others in the school environment valued. Frequently he chose one of the most popular boys in class to interact with. Through these interactions he gained both language practice and access to social interactions. This way he gained access to language needed for science work. He liked new challenges, displayed himself as confident and considered himself as a good learner. Several other children named him as someone they would like to work with on a science project; however none of the children mentioned him as someone they would like to play with outside school.

William

William was already well-equipped with language and behaviours needed for school from home and preschool. Yet, he never seemed comfortable in an activity where he was positioned subordinately. As soon as someone else took control, he rejected activities and thus denied himself opportunities to interact and learn from others. He opted out when the others did not comply. Others named him frequently as someone to play with outside school but no one chose him as a partner for a science project. He had high social status but no academic status in the class.

Example study 4.20   (Continued)

At the end of the academic year Anton's academic language was around the 88th percentile while William's was in the 47th. This is an interesting outcome considering their predicted chances at the beginning.

In conclusion the author states that social status and language and literacy development were distinct. Not having high social status did not inhibit Anton's access to academic literacies. William's social interactions provided access to and acquisition of language (English) but not acquisition of the forms of language or the discourses aligned with academic literacies. Play and work practices were clearly different.

Example study 4.21   Mitchell and Lee (2008)

The aim of this study was to document the children's spoken language development over time in the home context.

The family in question lived in England for two years only. The mother was studying and looking after the children. The children, Susan aged 9 and Amy aged 6, were enrolled in regular classes in a primary school in the UK. At the weekends they also attended Korean school through the social network of the local Korean church. Five months into their stay Diana (age 8) joined the family from Korea. She was the children's cousin. They also had a Korean-speaking grandmother with them and this offered opportunities for the children to discuss their school experiences in Korean, too.

Data collection started at three months after arrival and continued for nine months. There were different instruments used:

- Repeated picture descriptions measuring the children's ESL proficiency
- Informal comments, notes and reports from the class teacher
- Writings in English produced by the children
- Detailed research journal kept by the children's mother
- Audio- and video-recordings made in home settings documenting both L1 and L2 conversational, literacy and play activities (main data set: over a 100 separate recordings). The recorder was operated by the mother or Susan. This recorded data has three components: (1) various home activities such as reading aloud, language games, storytelling, role play, (2) interviews with children about current activities (reading, writing and playing) and pre- and post-assessments to investigate spoken language development and change of learning strategies over time.

From this enormous data set, two key events were selected for this paper: home reading and home play. Six episodes were selected with Amy as the central participant.

The paper contains long bilingual extracts where the children play together and read together and the analysis focusses on the language development in the following areas:

- developing L2 word knowledge
- developing global understanding
- managing L2 interactions
- fluency development
- collaboration and scaffolding each other
- changing patterns of playing school

This study identifies important dimensions of home L2 use and the motivations that underlie it.

Comments

Ethnographic case studies are able to shed light on aspects of language learning that remain invisible in experimental studies. For example, Nassaji and Cumming (2000) point out the importance of emotional development for young children. A great deal of Ali's writing revolved around emotional matters like how much he loved his family and how much he loved Ellen, his teacher. The teacher gave him plenty of reassurance that she reciprocated his feelings. This emotional connection seemed to be an important prerequisite of language learning. Cekaite's study (2007) reminds us that individual children's language learning is not linear, but instead cyclical with natural ups and downs. Fusi's development would have been evaluated very differently had the researcher only considered observations for a few weeks or months. It was the longitudinal design that uncovered the route leading to positive identity construction. Hawkins (2005) shows that traditional risk factors that teachers often recognise do not necessarily diagnose correctly children's social and academic trajectories. A child that is popular and happy in the playground and has many friends, may not be successful and actively involved in academic contexts. Hawkins (2005) argues that the teacher's role is not simply designing effective lessons but designing ecologies where all children have opportunities to access vital academic skills.

Dagenais, Day and Toohey's (2006) research underscores the importance of trust and affect in collaborative work in classrooms and the value of close friendships with trusted peers. In terms of its implications for classrooms all over the world, it is important for teachers to appreciate the particular needs of multilingual children.

Typically, in case studies data are collected over a long period of time, using a variety of different methods and research tools. Some studies last for years and the researchers accumulate a vast amount of data. For example, in Dagenais, Day and Toohey's study, the data collection continued for five years and the final data set contained fieldnotes, video- and audio-recordings, interviews with Sarah, her peers and teachers and observations of her classes. This variety of data helps to build a convincing picture of Sarah's changing identity. In Cekaite's study (2007), even though the researcher focusses on just three phases in the learner's development, the study is still based on a total of 95 recorded hours of talk. Hawkins (2005) also draws on a range of different data sources. There are home visits, child and adult interviews, observation schedules, and children's views are elicited using sociograms. With such complex methodologies and with large amounts of data, when it comes to analysis and interpretation questions arise about criteria for data selection. One of the most important challenges of ethnographic research is how to select data for analysis. What themes are important? Which details are necessary?

Another question in these studies is about how typical or unusual these selected learners are. Is Sarah (in Dagenais, Day and Toohey 2006) just a regular learner, or is she in fact a motivated and especially talented learner? Similarly, in Nassaji and Cumming's (2000) study, a special relationship developed between Ali and his teacher and Ali benefited from this joint journal writing a great deal. However, it would have been interesting to know what this teacher's experience was with the rest of the class. Was Ali, in fact, quite a special boy who was motivated, enthusiastic, well-supported and received a great deal of positive emotion and attention from the teacher? Similarly, were William and Anton two special cases (Hawkins 2005)?

Researchers who follow children closely in ethnographic studies face special challenges due to the intensity of the relationship between the researcher and the participants. For example, it is possible that participating in the study had given Sarah a special status among her peers, which in itself may have improved her attitudes, motivation and willingness to try harder at school and become more aware of her multilingual identity. Even shorter interventions may influence children and thus modify their behaviour. It is difficult to know to what extent the outcomes can be explained by the effect of the project itself. In Hawkins's study (2005) the two children were observed very closely for about 15 minutes every day and the observer recorded everything about who they talked to and where they went. Such close observation may in fact alter the child's natural behaviour.

Parent-researchers face other challenges, such as to what extent they may allow the research project to penetrate family life and at what point they may need to protect the children's privacy (Mitchell and Lee 2008).

4.6   Children's perceptions, views and opinions

Although many studies in previous sections have included a supplementary focus on learners' views and opinions, the studies in this section make this the primary goal. Many of the studies that explore children's views and opinions use traditional questionnaires, which often present special challenges. These will be discussed in some detail in Chapter 6, where we will look at differences between approaches to researching adults and children. Other studies have used different types of interviews, in particular group or pair interviews. Yet other studies have used creative, less conventional methods to elicit children's views and opinions. These methods are especially important in the case of younger children, who are less able to articulate their opinions in questionnaires and interviews.

Five example studies will be discussed here: Victori and Tragant (2003), Papapavlou (1999), Lamb (2003), Gu, Hu and Zhang (2005), and Gardner and Yaacob (2007).

In three of these studies, questionnaires were used (Victori and Tragant 2003, Papapavlou 1999 and Lamb 2003). These three studies were conducted with children aged 9 or older. In Victori and Tragant's study, questionnaires were used with a range of different age groups to elicit children's language learning strategy use in English as an L3 (Catalan L1 and Spanish L2). A large number of students were surveyed and the study combined both cross-sectional and longitudinal data. In addition to the questionnaires, the researchers also tracked a group of learners over a period of two years. Papapavlou administered a questionnaire to 9–13-year-old immigrant bilingual children (with different L1 backgrounds and Greek as an L2). They were asked to report on their socialisation and cultural adjustment, and perceived success in their languages (both L2 and L1). In Lamb's study, the questionnaires are supplemented with focus group interviews to gain deeper insights about the children's views. This study explored Indonesian 11–12-year-old learners' attitudes and motivation to learn English.

In the last two studies, the participants are much younger. In Gu, Hu and Zhang's study (2005) a 'think aloud protocol', and in Gardner and Yaacob's study (2007) a role play, are used to elicit views. The role play is particularly successful at eliciting spontaneous reactions from younger children.

Summary of the studies

Example study 4.22   Victori and Tragant (2003)

The aim of the study was to compare language learning strategies of different age groups. Six primary schools and seven high schools in Barcelona were involved, with students who were Catalan/Spanish bilinguals learning English as a third language. Two sets of data were collected. (1) cross-sectional data was collected from 766 students from three age groups: 10, 14 and 18 years old; and (2) longitudinal data involved 38 students tracked over a period of two years (from 12 to 14 years of age). The cross-sectional subjects differed in the number of hours completed (in English) and also in their grade level.

In the analysis of the cross-sectional data, significant differences between age groups in the reported strategy use were found. The results indicated that the strategies reported by the youngest group varied significantly from the other two groups, who both reported using a greater number of strategies. However, no significant differences were found between the 14- and 17-year-olds. As students'

Example study 4.22   (Continued)

age increased so did the reported use of cognitively complex strategies such as mnemonic techniques and classification. The increased use of these strategies is linked to cognitive maturation. Older learners also reported a greater number of other strategies: this shows that with increasing age reporting gets better. Social strategies decrease with age. In 35 per cent of the cases the use of specific strategies was kept constant between the ages of 10 and 14 and a marked change happened at 17. In 25 per cent of the cases a specific strategy was constant across ages 14–17 and it either increased or decreased with the younger group: e.g. analysis of word meaning, some memorisation strategies.

In the longitudinal data, stages of development were observed. *Stage 1*: reliance on external help; *stage 2*: mention of written or oral repetition to learn words, spelling or pronunciation; *stage 3*: elaborate memorisation techniques; *stage 4*: higher degree of elaboration or association on the part of the learner.

The authors acknowledge that there is a great deal of individual variation but equally there is evidence of developmental change between ages 12 and 14.

Example study 4.23   Papapavlou (1999)

The aim of this study was to gain insights into a range of issues related to bilingual children's languages:

- their L1 background
- their other languages
- degree of code–switching
- which language they preferred
- their feelings of loyalty toward their languages
- whether they face problems of socialisation, adjustment
- degree of success in other languages (Greek)

The questionnaire was administered in Greek. The participants were 39 primary school children in Greek-speaking Cyprus, aged between 9 and 13 (grades 4–6) from a variety of L1 backgrounds: Russian, Arabic, Rumanian, Filipino and others. All children had already spent at least two academic years in Cyprus. In addition to the questionnaire results class teachers were asked to provide the students' final grades for Greek and Maths.

The bilingual children's academic results were compared with the results of another group of 210 monolingual children and no significant differences were found. The author also conducted some correlation calculations based on the questionnaire data and found that there was a significant correlation between the bilingual children's willingness to take up new ideas and their ability to mix well with the monolingual children.

The results were very positive in that immigrant children claimed that they were well-accepted by the majority of children, and they did not face problems in mastering spoken and written Greek (although the percentages are interesting:

55 per cent said 'no problems', 26 per cent had no opinion and 19 per cent reported difficulties).

L2 children clearly saw themselves as different from their monolingual peers but they performed as well as monolingual children in their academic achievements and their proficiency in Greek.

Example study 4.24   Lamb (2003)

The aim of this study was to uncover general patterns of attitude and motivation related to learning English among 11- and 12-year-old Indonesian children.

219 students filled in a questionnaire reflecting on issues related to their English language motivation. This was followed by focus group interviews conducted with 12 selected learners to get deeper insights about findings that emerged from the questionnaire data. Observations and teacher interviews as additional insights were also used but the paper does not discuss these.

The questionnaires contained simple three-point Likert scale items on the following issues: (1) how satisfied the students felt with their progress in English; (2) how confident they were of their own abilities to learn well; (3) how much they liked learning English; (4) how important English was to them; and (5) how important English was compared to other subjects. In addition, two further items asked them to rank the importance of five possible reasons to learn English and to state when and what type of activities outside school required that they used English. Finally, some open items were added to ask students to give reasons why they liked English. Interviews were conducted about their feelings and their friends' feelings and attitudes. Interviews were started in English but switched to the children's L1: Bahasa Indonesian.

The questionnaire responses showed that all these learners had studied English in the primary school and/or outside the school system, and in general the children indicated that they used English frequently to watch TV, read or use computer programs. All children stated that English was either important or very important to them. Some even believe that English is more important than other school subjects. In analysing the reasons given, the author states that both integrative and instrumental reasons were important to these learners.

When the researcher tried to pin down their ideas of integrative motivation in the interviews, it was found that instrumental and integrative orientations were often blended in their comments and it was not possible to differentiate between the two in this context.

Example study 4.25   Gu, Hu and Zhang (2005)

The aim of the study was to find out about lower primary students' language learning strategies but also to discover to what extent this research method was feasible.

The participants were 18 lower primary pupils (nine were 7 years of age in grade 1, and nine were grade 3 pupils aged 9) in a multilingual, multicultural

Example study 4.25   (Continued)

primary school in Singapore. The children were all bilingual pupils of L1 Malay, Tamil and Chinese and they were selected as representatives of the top, middle and bottom stream of their class according to their latest English examination results.

The main elicitation method was the 'think-aloud', or a 'probed introspective verbal report'. Altogether four tasks were used for the children to try think-aloud: (1) a listening comprehension based on a taped fairytale; (2) a reading task based on a passage *The Ant with a Secret* from a coursebook no longer in use; (3) a writing task based on a set of four pictures presented in a scrambled order; and (4) a writing task which asked pupils to select one topic out of three and write about it. All these were typical classroom tasks for these children.

Warm-up and think-aloud training was provided. The training was provided in the big group while the actual research was conducted on a one-to-one basis with individual learners left alone with just the researcher. Pupils were both audio- and video-recorded and they were using mainly English. Some of the training 'games' simply did not work as the children refused to respond and did not find the games interesting to play.

During the actual research project it was found that the children were not able to verbalise their strategies and the researchers had to help with some probing. The researchers felt that there was a great danger of putting their own strategies into the children's mouths. Despite all these difficulties, in terms of the strategies that emerged, the results were showing clear differences between the two age groups. Older children did much better. Primary 3 pupils reported a wider range of strategies. Students in the top category used more effective strategies than students in the lower categories within both age groups.

Example study 4.26   Gardner and Yaacob (2007)

The aim of the study was to gain data from children to gauge the 6- to 7-year-olds' perceptions of literacy practices in their English classrooms. To this end, researcher-initiated role plays were used alongside other methods: classroom observations in nine schools, and child and teacher interviews. The role plays were video-taped and then transcribed.

Two groups of children (one group in the UK and one in Malaysia) were involved. The first group was a natural friendship group and the second group was volunteers selected by the teacher. The children were asked to pretend that some nursery school children were coming to their class to see what it was like to be in Year 1. This was set up so that the researchers could gain access to the children's views and opinions about what it meant to be studying literacy in English.

These were the actual instructions given out: 'Role Play situation (page 12)'

'Let's pretend that some nursery children are coming to your class to see what it is like to be in Year 1. They don't know how to read so you have to teach them. One of you will pretend to be the teacher. Role play what happens in your English classroom.'

Each role play lasted about 15–20 minutes. The discourse that emerged contained elements of both school and play. The children acted out vivid episodes from their literacy classes. The two groups (UK and Malaysia) perceived literacy practices very differently. The UK group's role play centred around a story book while the Malaysian role play was all about the use of their English textbook. Valuable insights into what is right and what are the proper ways of doing things in the classrooms emerged in both cases. A clear understanding of teacher and learner roles was evident and explicit comments were made about acceptable practices. In terms of merging school and play, children were slipping in and out of their performances naturally. Both groups used code-mixing, although in a different way. The freedom of language choice provided insights into their language preferences but it also helped to maintain the dialogue.

The role plays were found to mitigate against the researcher's paradox by creating a space between the observed and the unobserved. There was evidence of classroom behaviour directly copied from their ordinary literacy classes that teachers might not want observers to see.

Comments

Overall it is clear from all the survey-based studies that questionnaires need to be constructed with care and that they are not ideal instruments for children. Younger children find it difficult to verbalise their thought processes even in oral interviews, let alone through questionnaires. Lamb's (2003) study also shows that there can be substantial differences between what children reveal in interviews and how they tick boxes in questionnaires. Children get better at reporting their views, experiences and thought processes as they grow older. With regard to reporting strategy development, Victori and Tragant (2003) suggest that as the learners get older and become more proficient in English they become more resourceful as language learners. They use strategies that are more complex, and they become more autonomous in their language learning. The authors also note that both the ability to report and the repertoire of strategies students use, improve, and the combination of these two developments means that the older learners emerge as more effective.

All the studies using questionnaires have brought some problems to the surface. In Victori and Tragant's study (2003) the questionnaires worked quite well, but even here, the authors reported that the younger group (10-year-olds) experienced problems with the instrument. When the authors describe significant differences between the reported strategies of 14-year-olds and 10-year-olds, we do not know to what extent this difference was also influenced by the younger children's problems with the actual instrument. It is also important to remember that what learners/children report is not necessarily what they actually do. Their reports may present a more favourable picture than is actually the case. Papapavlou's study raises these kinds of questions. Sensitive subjects are notoriously difficult to research because children may not be willing to reflect on their negative experiences. Here the researcher claimed that the children's responses were largely positive. However, when 55 per cent of the children ticked 'yes', 29 per cent ticked 'don't know' and 19 per cent ticked 'no' to a sensitive question, can we say that the responses were generally positive? Some questions in the instrument may have been difficult to respond to truthfully. For example: 'Are you accepted by your class mates?' or 'Was it difficult for you to make friends?' Children often hide their true feelings, especially if these are negative, to save face and to protect themselves. It is easier, more comfortable and safer to put 'Yes, I am accepted' and 'Yes, I made friends easily'.

In Lamb's study (2003), the interviews were used to triangulate children's questionnaire responses and to get deeper insights about their views. Interestingly, but not surprisingly at all, some of the interview data directly contradicted the results from the questionnaires. For example, the questionnaires overwhelmingly indicated a positive response regarding liking English, but in the interviews many of the children reported that some of their friends were not interested in learning English and in fact half of the class did not like English nor wanted to learn it. Contradictions like this often signal that children could not or did not want to respond to the questions in the questionnaire.

While there are many inherent problems in questionnaires, one advantage is that they can be administered relatively easily and without a concern for building a relationship between the researcher and the children. When questionnaires are administered by teachers, the children may well say what they think the teacher wants to hear.

Interviews and other alternative ways of collecting data that tap into children's opinions and views will yet again bring problems about the researcher–child relationship to the surface. Lamb emphasises the importance of explicitly acknowledging the researcher/participant relationship in interviews after he raises question marks about his data gained from the interviews as he reflects on his own role as the researcher. He admits that he may have been the first native speaker these children had ever met and this must have influenced the outcome of the interviews.

When the researcher is working in a one-to-one situation with the children, as in Gu, Hu and Zhang's study (2005), we may be reminded of the experimental studies where such a set up was deemed problematic. Being recorded in the company of an outsider/researcher may lead to young children clamping up and saying nothing at all. The 'think-aloud' protocols did not seem to work for the 7-year-old children and there is some doubt as to how the 9-year-old children's data can be interpreted. Gu, Hu and Zhang are fully aware of these issues and they devote some space in the (2005) paper to discussing their methodology. Their account is particularly refreshing in its honesty regarding the problems that the researchers faced while attempting to use this method of data collection with children.

Another issue is the language of the instruments. In both Gu, Hu and Zhang's (2005) study and in Papapavlou's (1999) study, the children's L2 was used. Having to use the L2 (rather than their L1) may have presented an additional burden to these children.

4.7   Primary-level language teachers

The last section of this chapter aims to review some studies where the focus is on teachers, rather than on learners and learning processes. Research/practice cycles in classrooms cannot be complete without exploring what teachers think and do, and why, how they handle their classrooms, how they develop as professionals over time, and what aspects of the classroom reality they find important, problematic or worthy of investigation. Research focussed on primary-level language teachers will enable us to develop a better understanding between learning and teaching.

In this section some studies are concerned with pre-service teacher education and some with in-service teacher education. Some studies will focus on large-scale surveys to understand trends and patterns in teacher behaviour, or to indicate needs and concerns of teachers. Some studies will focus on just one teacher or two focal participants, and others focus on teachers themselves undertaking explorations in their own classrooms (i.e. exploratory practice or action research). Some studies will have an evaluative focus, e.g. exploring the impact of a teacher collaboration scheme or evaluating the impact of an innovation in primary language teaching.

This last section contains six studies: Butler (2004), Tang and Nesi (2003), De Courcy (2007), Lundberg (2007), Carless (2006) and Lightbown and Spada (1994).

The first two studies focus on what primary language teachers know and want to know, and what they do in the classroom. Butler's study (2004) explores primary school language teachers' perceived needs in three Asian countries: Japan, Taiwan and Korea. These views were elicited by means of a questionnaire. The teachers were asked about their training needs and about the extent to which they felt that they were well-prepared for teaching English as an L2 in the primary classroom. Tang and Nesi's study (2003) explores how teachers use language in their classrooms by comparing two different contexts in China and Hong Kong. The aim is to compare the learning opportunities in these two classrooms as a result of the differences between the two teachers' language use. The particular focus is on the vocabulary learners can access in these classrooms.

The next three studies focus on developmental projects. De Courcy (2007), a trainer in a teacher training institute in Australia, explores her students' understanding about ESL issues. Pre-service primary teachers who are not language specialists are surveyed, and the paper discusses their views and offers a framework within which their awareness can be investigated and raised. Lundberg (2007) conducts an action research project with a group of teachers from Sweden. The author is exploring the learning opportunities offered by action research as an alternative to structured input-based in-service courses. The participants are qualified primary specialists but they have no background in teaching English. Carless (2006) evaluates a scheme which involved NS and NNS teachers team teaching in primary English classrooms in Hong Kong. This study is motivated by the debate around the relative benefits of NS versus NNS language teachers in children's language classrooms. In this particular research project in Hong Kong a scheme was initiated in primary schools which encouraged NS and NNS teachers to collaborate and thus maximise advantages from both sides. The aim was to explore whether this collaboration would lead to professional development for both parties.

In contrast, and finally, the last study is large-scale in its scope. Lightbown and Spada (1994) bring together a range of different methods, participants and research questions in an attempt to evaluate an innovative project.

Summary of the studies

Example study 4.27   Butler (2004)

The aim of this study was to explore how elementary school English teachers in Japan, Korea and Taiwan evaluate their own proficiency and what gaps they would identify in their own competences. The study was motivated by the concern that although all these countries in Asia had introduced English in primary school, teachers overall were not adequately prepared.

Questionnaires were used which were translated into the different languages (Chinese, Japanese, Korean). 204 copies were distributed in Korea, 206 in Taiwan and 112 in Japan. The response rate was over 70 per cent in each country. The assessment of language proficiency was oriented towards the four skills.

The results showed that 91.1 per cent of the surveyed elementary school teachers in Korea, 80.1 per cent in Taiwan, and 85.3 per cent in Japan believed that their current proficiency levels did not meet the necessary minimum levels.

Although there were some differences between the different groups of teachers (e.g. the Japanese data showed most variability), a gap existed between the teachers' actual and desired skills in all three countries.

Example study 4.28   Tang and Nesi (2003)

The aim of the study was to compare two English classrooms (Hong Kong and Guangzhou) by measuring both oral vocabulary input (from teachers and materials) and output (from students). Of particular interest to the researchers was how the incidental vocabulary learning compared in these two Chinese classroom environments.

The educational environment was similar in both contexts, such as the class size and the classroom organisation. The participants of the study were two English teachers (one from each context). They were both teaching in a similar type of school and shared a similar educational background. Both schools were considered among the best ones in their category in each context. All students in the two teachers' classes were aged 12.

In terms of data collection, all English lessons the teachers had with the selected class were audio-recorded for a full week. Both teachers were asked to list words they were intending to teach (i.e. the 'planned' words, see below) and at the end of the week they were also interviewed about their views of vocabulary teaching.

The teachers' talk was measured for lexical richness using a measure called the 'type/token ratio' (where types were defined as all the different words in the corpus and tokens as the total number of words). These word lists were compared to frequency lists. The actual words taught in the week were categorised according to input types such as unmodified (i.e. presented without explanation), premodified (where the teacher has prepared an explanation beforehand) and interactionally modified (where the students requested an explanation as the need arose).

According to the findings, lexical variation ratios were higher in Hong Kong than in Guangzhou. This finding suggests that the Hong Kong classroom is lexically richer than the Guangzhou classroom. Many more low-frequency words were used in Hong Kong than in Guangzhou while the Guangzhou classroom provided more explicit teaching of both planned and unplanned words. Unplanned words were regarded as less important in China than in Hong Kong.

Example study 4.29   De Courcy (2007)

The aim of the study was to explore what conceptions pre-service teacher education students had about ESL children and their needs in mainstream Australian classrooms. This was a small-scale action research project that was undertaken in a multicultural context in Australia, motivated by the author's observation that many ESL children in Australian schools are educated in mainstream classrooms by teachers who know little or nothing about ESL.

The participants of the study were all at the end of their first year at college and as part of their course they regularly had to write 'reading reflections' based on key articles assigned in class. For their last assignment their tutor (the author) assigned four articles which were all about ESL children, bilingualism, and cultural diversity. While reading the four articles, the students had to respond to the following key questions:

- What are the four most interesting issues related to this series of articles?
- What ideas and issues challenged your beliefs about learning/teaching literacy?

Example study 4.29   (Continued)

- What do you believe are the most significant or valuable issues applicable to you as a pre-service teacher?
- What unanswered questions have you still got about this topic? (The reflections must include direct references to your readings!)

This way the tutor collected 37 anonymous 'reading reflections'. There were two stages in the analysis: first a simple search for themes in the texts, such as challenges and unanswered questions; and second, a further search for comments by the students about ESL children.

The analysis revealed very low levels of awareness overall. Some students were surprised that dialects were actually language varieties rather than just bad English. They were also surprised that opportunities for ESL pupils to use and develop language had to be planned for. The realisation that certain cultural interpretations may not make sense to ESL children was also a great surprise to many.

After the analysis of emerging themes, a more fine-grained discourse analysis of the texts was carried out by the author. In this analysis it was discovered that trainees had a deficit view of ESL children and generally ESL children were portrayed as problematic. Students tended to focus on cultural diversity but not linguistic diversity. They consistently used contrasting language such as 'us' and 'them', and focussed on negative social and cultural differences.

Example study 4.30   Lundberg (2007)

The aim of the study was to implement an in-service primary language teacher education programme in Sweden.

The research questions were:

(1) What impact can action research have on the development of language teaching in the young learners' classroom?
(2) How do teachers and pupils view the changed educational practice?

The participants were 160 teachers in a pre-service programme at Umeå University. The teachers were free to choose their research questions within five themes which were: (1) an early start, (2) target language use, (3) strategies for teaching and learning, (4) motivation, and (5) documentation and language portfolio.

The action research projects incorporated a variety of data collection methods such as teacher diaries, field-notes, pupil diaries, interviews, surveys, digital photos, filming and evaluation of materials and activities. The participants had to produce a report which encouraged them to reflect on the processes of research in a meta-analysis.

All teachers completed their projects with enthusiasm and they all devoted much more time and effort to it than previously anticipated. They were empowered to make changes and enjoyed being 'in control' of their own development.

Example study 4.31   Carless (2006)

Based on earlier work which looked at NS and NNS collaboration in secondary schools, a new scheme of NS/NNS collaboration was launched for primary schools in Hong Kong.

Building on these results the primary scheme was launched with the following aims:

(1) to develop models of innovative teaching;
(2) to have a positive influence on pupils;
(3) to provide professional development opportunities for all teacher participants.

The aim of this study was to evaluate a collaborative EFL teaching scheme in Hong Kong primary schools. As part of a pilot scheme, trained native speaker teachers were invited to work in 40 Hong Kong primary schools.

The results show that the NS teachers' impact on students was very positive. The questionnaires indicated that the majority of the NNS teachers also appreciated the presence of the NS teachers. Some however, pointed out problems too, such as less able pupils being unable to understand the NS teachers.

In terms of innovative teaching the results are more mixed: no clear evidence was found that the presence of NS teachers led to the introduction of progressive ideas. Other NS teachers described their collaboration with local teachers as a tug of war. Local teachers were generally more positive than NS teachers. Most NS teachers did not report much professional development and local teachers painted a slightly more positive picture. There was evidence that team teaching led to reflection, but this cannot be equated with professional development.

Overall the collaboration between NS and NNS teachers was evaluated in positive terms and some further advice is offered to teachers wishing to collaborate like this in other contexts.

Example study 4.32   Lightbown and Spada (1994)

The aim of this article is to describe the main findings from research projects which were all built around an innovation in Quebec, Canada. Altogether data were collected from more than 50 classes and more than 1,500 students and their teachers.

An innovative ESL programme was launched which offered a so called 'language bath', immersing children in English for five months of the school year. Between 1976 and 1993 nearly 22,000 students had the opportunity to spend five months of a school year immersed in English.

The innovative programme emphasised meaning-based activities, pair and group work, oral fluency and comprehension and communication strategies to help learners cope with English in their everyday lives. Form-focussed activities and error correction were discouraged and positive experiences and confidence were underlined.

Example study 4.32   (Continued)

Observation (a modified version of the Communicative Orientation of Language Teaching scheme: COLT) was used to describe instruction in these classes. This confirmed that the instruction was based on oral/aural aspects and the teachers did not devote very much time or attention to reading and writing. Speaking and listening were the main skills focussed on and grammar was not explicitly taught. All form-focussed activities were contextualised. The materials were entertaining but not very challenging.

Learner language was also studied via comparing the listening comprehension abilities of those participating in regular ESL and innovative ESL courses. Learners' production abilities were measured. Comparisons between regular and intensive ESL students showed that the intensive course students outperformed their peers in the regular classes. The intensive ESL students were also more confident and fluent.

Contact with English was also investigated: again those in the intensive ESL programme were more favourably disposed to English than the students in the regular programmes. They also had more contact with English through watching more television.

Long-term effects were also investigated to find out whether learners would be able to maintain their advantage over a longer period of time. A specific study to investigate this was undertaken with 60 students from grade 11. This long-term effect analysis revealed that those who took part in the intensive ESL programmes in grade 5 or 6 still had significantly more contact with English outside the classroom; they were more likely to have English-speaking friends and part-time jobs which required English. They watched more English television programmes. Both groups, however, expressed dissatisfaction with their English proficiency. Several years on, their language in the interviews showed that the intensive students produced longer turns, and they were more accurate in some aspects. Overall, these findings showed that students from these ESL courses managed to maintain their superiority even after a couple of years of having been reintegrated into the regular ESL programmes.

Experimental studies on focus on form and error correction showed that learners who received instruction and corrective feedback on adverb placement and question formation did better than other groups that did not.

Comments

Given that in the globalised modern world, more and more primary teachers will have L2 learners in their classrooms, often on a temporary basis, pre-service teacher preparation needs to embrace issues related to L2 learning, so that mainstream primary teachers no longer see these children as 'problems' (De Courcy 2007).

Butler's study suggests that elementary school language teachers need a solid grounding in all areas related to child L2 learning and this should include the development of spoken proficiency, in particular, grammatical accuracy in speaking. In terms of implications for practice, it is clear that it is important to: (1) identify the level of proficiency for each language domain necessary for primary teachers in different contexts; (2) create appropriate guidelines for measurement in each context; and (3) provide systematic support to teachers.

What teachers actually do and say in classrooms needs to be captured and studied to understand processes of learning and teaching. Action research projects can have an empowering effect (Lundberg 2007). This type of teacher-initiated research is important because it can focus on local issues that seem most meaningful to teachers. Lundberg (2007) concluded that it was difficult to bring about change in the classrooms, although the action research format with its cyclical characteristics had a better chance of dealing with resistance than other input-based courses. On the whole, the participants in this study all reported that action research felt like a powerful form of professional development. The trainees reported that they felt they were 'in control' and they were key figures in initiating change and improvement in their own schools. The implications of this suggest that collaborative action research or exploratory practice initiated at the individual school level has the best chance of succeeding in bringing about educational changes.

Limitations related to the research instruments apply here as well. For example, in the study by Butler (2004), the results were based on the teachers' perceived, self-reported shortcomings in terms of their English language proficiency, rather than their actual performance as indicated by, for example, a standard proficiency test. It may be that some teachers lacked confidence and reported lower than actual levels of competence. On the other hand, given that the data sample came from major cities, we may suspect that teachers might be even less confident about their ability to teach English in rural areas where teaching and training resources are less available.

Both De Courcy's study (2007) and Lundberg's (2007) involved participants who were engaged in an assessed course of study while responding to their tutors' questions and instructions. It is possible that the trainees would have responded differently in informal interviews as opposed to these reflections, which formed part of their assessment on their course. A similar effect may have played a role in Lundberg's study (2007) in that participants felt they were 'obliged' to report positive feedback to their tutor.

Another issue arises in Tang and Nesi's study (2003). Working with just two teachers can be quite challenging in that it becomes difficult to avoid evaluative comparisons, such as whose classroom was 'better' or more 'effective'. Teachers may be sensitive to these issues and they may not feel happy about being exposed in this way. Similarly, sensitive issues may have interfered with the responses in Carless's study (2006). The NNS teachers may have reported more positive feelings than they actually felt. Even though the author makes it clear that the partnership factor was emphasised and thus the NNS teachers did not feel inferior, the NS teachers are still associated with techniques and approaches that are seen in this context as more progressive, innovative and above all, more authentic.

4.8　Conclusion

The studies above have been selected to illustrate the richness of the research activity in the broad field of child second language acquisition and pedagogy. It is difficult to draw definitive conclusions based on just a handful of illustrative studies, but it is perhaps possible to make some general remarks. What has been achieved to date and where should future research be directed?

Processes of language acquisition in childhood

A vast amount of research has addressed different aspects of the 'age factor' in second language acquisition. Different tests and tasks have been administered to mainly immigrant children of different ages to uncover younger children's advantages as compared to adults and older learners. Despite the fact that older learners initially progress faster in all contexts (e.g. Snow and Höfnagel-Höhle 1978 or Muñoz 2006), research shows that starting early in childhood can have advantages in the long run, at least in naturalistic contexts (e.g. Flege, Yeni-Komshian and Liu 1999 or Bialystok and Hakuta 1999). What exactly the source of this advantage may be, however, is not quite clear. In fact, it looks as though a combination of favourable social factors rather than just young age is responsible for most young children's success. Studies that have tracked different learners to explain the complex variables that interact in unique ways in the case of individual learners bring together both quantitative and qualitative methods over time (e.g. Jia and Aaronson, 2003). These studies show that in addition to attitudes, motivation, personality and identity, social networks and practice opportunities can all usefully contribute to children's success.

Important differences between younger and older children have been uncovered by research (e.g. Muñoz 2007; Nicholas and Lightbown 2008; Harley and Hart 1997). Some recent work also shows that adolescents are more similar to adults in their L2 acquisition processes whereas younger children follow a somewhat different order of acquisition, at least in some areas of grammar (e.g. Dimroth 2008a). Older learners rely on their cognitive and analytical abilities and more explicit learning methods while younger children rely more on imitation skills, repetition and implicit learning. Older children can use their memory strategies more effectively. Like adults, they are able to use fuzzy trace memory (Brainerd and Reyna 1990) while younger children need to rely on verbatim memory, which is less effective. In vocabulary learning, younger learners do not plan or rehearse, and even when they are taught these strategies, the training has little effect on their memory performance (Baker-Ward, Ornstein and Holden 1984) whereas older learners' efforts are accelerated by their increasingly effective use of memory strategies. Research suggests that older children (those above the age of 9 or 10 years of age) are increasingly able to reflect on their learning and assess their own performances (Butler and Lee 2006; Lan and Oxford 2003) while younger children are less able to reflect (e.g. Gu, Hu and Zhang 2005).Young, preschool children go through substantial silent periods and exhibit specific forms of language play that are not evident with older learners (Nicholas and Lightbown 2008). Preschool children are happy to play together even when they do not understand each other while older learners are much more aware of the need to join in with peer interactions and are much more conscious of their own lack of ability to contribute much (Wong Fillmore 1991).

Positive attitudes and motivation are very important for children and therefore the role of the teacher is crucial (e.g. Nikolov 1999b; Heining-Boynton and Haitema, 2007). Young learners' emotional needs are greater than older learners' (Nikolov 1999b; Nassaji and Cumming 2000), but for all learners their teachers represent powerful sources of influence. Children change quickly (e.g. Cekaite 2007) and they exhibit a great deal of individual variability not just in terms of their patterns of development but also in terms of their personality, motivation and interests (Wong Fillmore 1983). Individual variation is evident even when the age of the children and their circumstances are comparable (e.g. Paradis 2005; Jia and Fuse 2007; Wong Fillmore 1991). Two individual variables that seem particularly important, correlating highly with success, are aptitude (e.g. Kiss and Nikolov 2005; Alexiou 2009) and personality (e.g. Wong Fillmore 1983).

L2 learning is a complex process and for each child it is a unique interplay between developmental processes, L1 constraints and transfer, instructional input and special affordances in the immediate context (e.g. Lightbown and Spada 1999).

Contextual opportunities and restrictions

Children are exposed to second languages in naturalistic environments, in different types of schools, and at home, in a more informal context. These learning opportunities combine in unique ways for individual children. Early infant bilingual acquisition of two languages is an effortless process. As long as the parents are consistent and systematic about their language strategies, children acquire two or even three languages from birth (e.g. Döpke 2000; Wang 2008). After the preschool years, bilingualism is associated with largely positive effects when L1 majority children are immersed in L2 contexts (e.g. Harley 1986), while more negative effects are associated with L1 minority L2 learners (e.g. Leseman 2000; Verhallen and Schoonen 1993). When comparisons are made between L2 children and their monolingual peers in their target language performance – for example, in vocabulary learning – immigrant children generally compare less favourably than L1 majority L2 children. It is important for bilingual children in both of these contexts to develop both their languages, and for teachers to cultivate a positive image of bilingualism where both cultures and languages are highly valued (e.g. Cummins 2003).

Some children become immersed in a new L2 at the start of their formal schooling and this new language experience is so overwhelming that they gradually lose their L1. Parents of immigrant children often face a difficult dilemma about what kind of school they should put their children in, and how to maintain the L1. Shin (2005), for example, mentions that parents often receive misguided advice about bilingual education, and they encourage their children to opt for dropping their L1 altogether for fear of lack of adequate progress in their new L2. Formal schooling in L2 is also a turning point for children whose L1 is an endangered heritage language, because intensive exposure to L2 often cancels out a weak and unstable L1 (e.g. Tagoilelagi-Leota *et al.* 2005).

In immersion contexts and naturalistic environments, children learn from a variety of sources. In addition to teachers' influence, peer interaction has also been documented as a major source of learning (e.g. Dagenais, Day and Toohey 2006; Bongartz and Schneider 2003; Gregory, Long and Volk 2004; Mitchell and Lee 2008).

Child-friendly methodology

Widely accepted child-friendly methodologies have been challenged by research. For example, primary language teaching methodology traditionally suggested focussing on teaching vocabulary and unanalysed language chunks through stories, songs and rhymes, based on the understanding that children are not interested in grammar, and they do not benefit from 'form-focussed' instruction. However, research is beginning to show that children as young as 8 years of age are able to learn grammatical terminology to use for analysis and further learning (e.g. Bouffard and Sarkar 2008). Other studies that used focus on form techniques with children (e.g. Harley 1998; Shak and Gardner 2008) also suggest that children can cope with, enjoy, and above all, benefit from these approaches. Even in foreign language contexts such as exist in many European countries, research suggests that more challenges should be offered to young learners in addition to fun activities (Edelenbos, Johnstone and Kubanek 2006). Such challenges include teaching metalanguage and more focus on how the language works. Another example is L2 literacy. In many L2 contexts (both foreign and second language contexts) reading and writing are not taught at the beginning stages (e.g. in Japan or Korea). And yet according to research, it seems increasingly the case that in all contexts, literacy in L2 has an important role to play (Kim 2008; Bae 2007; Edelenbos, Johnstone and Kubanek 2006) and that children are interested and keen to use texts in reading and writing. Early literacy practices can accelerate the learning process. The specific challenge of exactly how to teach L2 literacy in different contexts is still very much open to debate and research. It is important to consider the characteristic features of the two languages, the complex processes of transfer between specific first and second languages (e.g. Geva and Wang 2001), and the children's L1 literacy experiences, if they have any. L2 literacy learning in one sense may be less effortful if the child is already able to transfer strategies from L1. On the other hand, L2 children often lack a solid spoken proficiency in the language, and one consequence of that is that they will be unable to recognise familiar words in print. There are development patterns across different languages and orthographies that seem universal, such as phonological processing skills. Advanced phonological skills in one language can predict reading abilities in another language (e.g. Durgunoğlu and Öney 1999).

4.9 Future directions for research

Research activity in the field of child SLA and pedagogy is already rich, combining many approaches and research traditions. There are, however, some gaps that will need to be addressed in future research.

More focus on different languages (other than English)

There is a great deal more research conducted, written up, and disseminated about children learning English as a second language than any other languages. There are some examples in this book where children are learning other languages, for example, a Kurdish child learning Swedish (Cekaite 2007), Turkish children learning Dutch (Leseman 2000), or American children learning German (Bongartz and Schneider 2003). On the whole, however, the dominant L2 is English, all over the world. Even though the global dominance of English is likely to continue, and as a consequence, the number of children learning English will further increase, it is clearly important for research to focus on other second languages in less well-researched contexts.

More focus on multilingual classrooms

As a result of global travel and migration, more and more classrooms that have been traditionally monolingual now have some L2 children, for either shorter or longer, more settled stays. These children receive varying levels of L2 language support, ranging from organised support classes to no support at all. Classrooms with only a handful of L2 students will require different strategies from the teacher as compared to classrooms where 80 per cent or more of the students are L2 users. More research targeting temporarily resident children is needed. Local schools need to take advantage of the multicultural learning opportunities, while the L2 children need specific support to settle down and join in with the rest of the class as soon as possible.

Many L2 children are actually multilingual and speak a third language at home. As we saw in Bae's study (2007), for example, many English-proficient speakers who were learning Korean as an L2 were in fact L1 speakers of other languages. The focal learner in Dagenais, Day and Toohey's (2006) study, Sarah, was a trilingual speaker (with Chinese, English and French) but her parental background suggests that at home she was exposed to Vietnamese and Mandarin as well as Cantonese. L2 teachers are rarely aware of these complexities in their classrooms. More research targeting multilingual learners is needed.

More focus on connecting formal and informal settings

Informal learning contexts and practices and their relationship with formal learning make up an important area, and this to date has not been explored a great deal. Studies that attempt to map out the learning opportunities of individuals are beginning to show the complexities of these processes (e.g. Jia and Aaronson 2003) but more studies connecting formal and informal learning processes are needed. In addition, many learners move from one context to another over time. For example, the Korean children in Mitchell and Lee's study (2008) started learning English in a typical foreign language context in just one or two lessons a week and then they came to the UK where the family were immersed in English. On completion of the mother's study programme, however, the children will return to Korea and may not again have opportunities to use their English. Moving from one type of learning context to another is not uncommon and the effects on learners' language development can be enormous.

The influence of home background and children's socioeconomic status determine the relative success of L2 development (e.g. Hakuta, Bialystok and Wiley 2003). More research that includes parents is needed so that relationships between home and school practices can be better understood. Effective home practices can then be developed in collaboration with schools, and these practices can be shared more widely. Children's behavioural patterns and responses may change drastically from context to context, such as home and school, and thus it would be enlightening to have more studies that consider children's language learning experiences in different contexts at the same time.

More focus on foreign language contexts

In comparison with second language contexts, there is much less research targeting foreign language contexts. One reason for this is that the typical circumstances of the foreign language contexts make some types of research really difficult to implement. Tracking learners' progress in negotiating their L2 identity, for example, would not be easily feasible as a study in a foreign language situation where children are exposed to the language only minimally, and where they may not develop an L2 identity at all. Rather, the children see the language as another timetabled school subject. The majority of the time in many foreign language classrooms is spent listening to the teacher or working on exercises from the textbook. Research in foreign language contexts, therefore, tends to be more focussed on testing skills, vocabulary or strategy use (e.g. Nikolov 2006; Butler and Lee 2006). In foreign language contexts, there seems to be much less consensus about the actual standards and linguistic skills that children may be able to achieve after learning different modern foreign languages in primary school contexts for given periods of time (e.g. Edelenbos, Johnstone and Kubanek 2006). What language skills and language functions should teachers cover and what level of proficiency is aimed for by the end of primary school are not at all clear. More research is needed to explore learning processes in foreign language contexts and studies that challenge traditional child-friendly methodologies and content are also needed.

The international market has been flooded with handbooks for teachers concerning child-friendly methodologies and activity packs with titles on how to do storytelling (Wright 1997; Ellis and Brewster 2002), how to teach through games, TPR (total physical response), drama or project work (e.g. Moon 2000; Slattery and Willis 2001; Scott and Ytreberg 1990; Halliwell 1992). And yet, little is known about the actual progress children make with these materials in contexts where they only encounter the foreign language once a week. There is very little research about child–child interactions in foreign language contexts (although see Nikolov 1999a). In fact, one major criticism that emerges from foreign language contexts is that the children often do not achieve fluency and cannot express their thoughts in a spontaneous way.

The most important question for foreign language programmes is how to maximise opportunities for learning when the overall time available is so severely limited. We know from research that elements of content-based instruction make learning immediately more meaningful and purposeful from the children's point of view (e.g. Alptekin, Ercetin and Bayyurt 2007; Mihaljević-Djigunović 2009). Some other variables that contribute to effectiveness seem to include the intensity of the instruction (i.e. break down two hours per week into several daily 20-minute input sessions – Curtain 2000), the level of teacher training and learning in small class sizes. Continuity between primary and secondary programmes is also crucial (Nikolov and Curtain 2000). Research that attempts to explore how some of these variables could be integrated into the restricted one or two lessons per week programme, would be extremely useful.

While the language exposure in foreign language learning contexts stays minimal (just one or two lessons a week), it becomes increasingly important and urgent to explore opportunities for teaching children strategies for using their L2 outside the classroom. The effectiveness of different approaches to developing learner autonomy and independent learning with children is therefore an important topic for future research in all contexts (e.g. Thomsen 2003; Dam 1995).

More research with learners as active participants

Many studies that have been reviewed here where children were asked their opinions and views about their own language learning processes (e.g. Shak and Gardner 2008; Papapavlou 1999) are still largely adult-dominated. There is a need to learn more about children's views and opinions, especially focussing on their perspectives. Children can give us first-hand information about what they experience, what they enjoy or struggle with, how they feel, what they would like to learn, and why. Children's views can sometimes be contradictory to what teachers and parents say or think, and this is another reason why we need to seek out their views. In this way, teachers' and learners' views can be brought closer together. In eliciting children's views, it is vital, however, that appropriate instruments and approaches are used and children are given the opportunity to take an active role in the process: see Chapter 6. More research that is participatory, and innovatively targeting all age groups, is urgently needed.

More research into teacher development and more teacher-led research

Many primary language teachers lack confidence in their own target language skills, especially their spoken fluency and pronunciation. For example, low levels of confidence were detected amongst primary teachers about their readiness to teach English in primary schools in Korea, Taiwan and Japan (Butler 2004). The debate about NNS versus NS teachers is also quite sensitive and relevant, as in many counties in the private sector NS teachers are employed exclusively. Employers believe that parents prefer native-speaker teachers at all costs because they can teach the 'real' language, whereas NNS teachers teach 'book language'. Research shows that both types of teachers have their advantages and disadvantages (Medgyes 1994) and research also shows that collaborative work between NS and NNS is a promising way forward (e.g. Carless 2006). More research is needed to explore the possible patterns and dynamics of collaboration by NS and NNS teachers, where this is possible. In general, more research will be needed to identify primary language teachers' pre-service and in-service needs in different contexts.

There is a gap to fill for classroom-based studies to be carried out by classroom teachers themselves. Such practitioner research leads to teachers taking control of the research agenda in their own classrooms (e.g. Lundberg 2007). It is also important for this research to be publicised widely so that experiences and good practice can be shared. Much informal work that is happening worldwide in primary language classrooms does not get published and disseminated effectively. There is also a gap in terms of truly collaborative projects between teachers and academics, such as the case reported in a study by Denos *et al.* (2009). More research into how primary language teachers develop via collaborative opportunities will be needed.

More research with longitudinal design

Research using a wide range of different approaches, small-scale and large-scale, ethnographic, experimental or comparative are all needed to continue developing our understanding about language learning in childhood. These studies complement one another, taking different social, cognitive and psycholinguistic perspectives to research. The renewed interest in young learners and their language learning is reflected in the vast variety of research that is already happening with children as second language learners in different contexts. While it is important to continue research using a variety of different methods and approaches, it seems that longitudinal studies are especially needed. Longitudinal studies that manage to track the development of a learner over time are in the best position to discover patterns of change. These longitudinal, larger-scale studies can combine different methods, utilising both quantitative and qualitative dimensions. They can cut across different contexts such as home and school, but also changes of context types over time, such as moving from a foreign language context to an immersion context.

More research taking advantage of current and future technologies

Our children are now growing up in an age of unprecedented technological development. Most of their everyday activities are dependent on digital technologies. Many children have computers, mobile phones, cameras and game consoles, and the opportunity to search the internet is becoming more readily available to everyone. Children take learning about new technologies in their stride; it is therefore important that research in second language learning in the future embraces this opportunity. For example, through the internet, it is now possible for a class of children to be in regular contact with children from other parts of the world, and this 'direct' contact can have uniquely important effects on children's motivation and willingness to learn another language through intercultural contacts (e.g. Kormos and Csiszér 2007). The computer also offers bilingual children and families the opportunity to stay in contact with the rest of their extended family and friends while they are in another country (either temporarily or permanently) and these opportunities will contribute to the development of bilingual and bicultural identities. Technology cannot however, replace teachers, and there is still an acute need for trained teachers who can help children navigate these ever-changing opportunities for learning.

5
Case Studies: Interactions between Research and Practice

This chapter will

- present and discuss eight selected case studies in terms of their research aims, participants, data collection tools, data analysis, results, and their implications for both future research and L2 language classroom practice
- present these studies as possible exemplars of what readers can do
- discuss cycles of research and practice emerging from these studies

5.1 Introduction

In this chapter we focus on a handful of additional studies that have been selected to exemplify the types of research discussed in Chapter 4. Each of the eight studies will be discussed in terms of what they achieved and what potential benefit/implications they bring for both future research and practice. We explore the studies in greater detail than was possible in Chapter 4, including a closer look at the research questions, the data analysis, some data extracts and outcomes. The studies are presented in pairs, two studies in the experimental/comparative tradition, two studies focussing on individual learners or small groups, two studies focussing on eliciting data from children about their views and opinions, and finally, two studies focussing on primary second language teachers.

Table 7 summarises the case studies according to the type of study, the context, the age of the learners, the languages involved and the content area.

5.2 Case studies

5.2.1 Case study 1 Philp, Oliver and Mackey (2006): experimental and comparative

Background

This article represents a very popular and rapidly expanding field of research with children, and also illustrates well both the inherent advantages and the

Table 7 Details of case studies

Type	Author(s)	Context	Age of learners	Languages	Content
Experimental/ comparative	Philp, Oliver and Mackey 2006	Australian primary school	6–7 and 11–12 years old	Range of L1, English as L2	Tasks and planning time
	Llinares Garcia 2007	Spanish primary school	5 years old	Spanish L1, English L2	L2 language functions
Focus on single learners	Bongartz and Schneider 2003	Germany, both at home and at school and preschool	5-year-old and 7-year-old siblings	English L1, German L2	L2 spoken development over the first year
	Swain and Lapkin 2003	Canadian French immersion primary school	12 years old	English L1 and French L2	Collaborative L2 writing
Eliciting children's views	Lan and Oxford 2003	Taiwanese primary schools	11 years old	Chinese L1 and English L2	Language learning strategy use
	Nagy 2009	Hungarian primary schools	10–11 years old	Hungarian L1 and English L2	Motivation and attitudes to L2
Focus on teachers	Peng and Zhang 2009	Chinese primary schools	n/a	Chinese L1 and English L2	Teacher language use
	Devlieger and Goossens 2007	Dutch -medium primary schools in Belgium	n/a	Dutch	Teacher assessment tool development

(e.g.

shortcomings of the experimental/comparative approach. Within the growing field of task-based research and task-based teaching, adult learners rather than children have been explored as participants. However, there is now a growing body of research concerning children's behaviours and approaches to communication tasks, mainly in second language learning contexts (e.g. Van den Branden 1997; Oliver 1998, 2002; Mackey, Oliver and Leeman 2003; Mackey, Kanganas and Oliver 2007). In this article, the authors combine two research approaches within task-based learning, i.e. the so-called 'interactional' approach and the 'production' aspects of task performances. They also want to explore the impact of planning for both of these aspects of task-related performances with immigrant children in Australian primary schools.

Within the pyscholinguistic tradition, one fertile area for research with adults has focussed on examining the effects of planning (both pre-task planning and on-line planning) on spoken output. This research shows that adult learners are assisted significantly by the opportunity to plan their speech both before they start the task and while they are engaged in the task (on-line). Adult learners typically use more complex and more fluent language in strategic planning conditions. The other popular area where tasks have been used as elicitation tools is interactional research. When communication breakdown occurs, learners negotiate meaning and give corrective feedback to each other, which in turn leads to new language learning through modified output.

Aim: research question

The aim of this study was to identify how planning time (pre-task planning) affects children's performances on language tasks. The following research question was formulated: What is the relationship between pre-task planning and linguistic production in children's ESL classrooms?

Concept 5.1   Pre-task planning

Pre-task planning: Time is given to the children to prepare what they are going to say. The researchers investigated whether the amount of time given to the children made any difference with regard to their language output. Three different planning conditions were used: 0 minutes, 2 minutes, and 5 minutes.

Concept 5.2   Feedback and modified output

Sample data (page 2):

A: How many girls can you see feeling?
B: What?
A: How many girls can you see feeling...fly...flying?

In this interaction, speaker A says something that does not make sense, so speaker B gives *feedback* in the form of a clarification request. As a result, A is able to *modify* her/his input from 'feeling' to 'flying'.

Concept: 5.3 Fluency, accuracy and complexity

Fluency is the naturalness of speech production without too much hesitation. In this study it is measured by counting the number of reformulations and false starts and word production per minute.

Accuracy is related to the extent to which this speech conforms to target language norms or not. In this study it was measured as percentage of correct, target-like 'c-units' (communication units, i.e. utterances that are meaningful though not complete).

The third aspect of measurement, *complexity*, refers to the relative syntactic complexity of the output and in this study it was measured as amount of subordination and coordination in children's speech.

Participants

In this study a total of 42 children participated. They were ESL learners in four intact classes and for the purpose of this study they were divided into two groups according to their age: two classes aged 6–7 and two classes aged 11–12. The children came from a variety of first language backgrounds, including Vietnamese, French, Arabic, Indian, Russian, Chinese, various African languages and Serbo-Croatian, and their English level was described as pre-intermediate. They were all ESL learners in pre-mainstream classes.

The elicitation tool (task)

Altogether three tasks were used. All tasks were two way information gap tasks.

Concept 5.4 Two-way information gap tasks

Two-way information gap tasks are communication tasks where two learners have a natural need to communicate with one another in order to complete the task. Both partners will need to ask for and receive information.

The tasks were developed in collaboration with the class teachers and were administered as part of the children's regular daily activities for a period of three weeks. Unfortunately, the actual picture images of the tasks are not attached to the paper – however, the authors give a detailed description of the tasks:

Quote 5.1   Describing the tasks

The language included mathematical terms related to shape and number, common vocabulary related to animals, body parts and colours as well as topic theme words. The themes of the tasks were designed to reinforce those topics covered in the classrooms concerned. For instance, animals and their body parts were associated with the forthcoming 'zoo' excursions, the athletics task was related to the forthcoming school athletics carnival, and the shape activity in a street scene related to both maths and language content covered in class. The three tasks were two-way, information gap activities requiring participants to describe the details of pictures about animals or people, and to compare them with a partner in order to fill in an information grid. The objects featured in the pictures were familiar to the children.

(Philp, Oliver and Mackey 2006: 552)

Research procedures and data analysis

The researchers aimed to compare children's linguistic output in three different planning conditions (no planning, 2 minutes' planning and 5 minutes' planning) using the same type of task every time, while the children were working with the same partners. In the planning condition the children were given paper and pencil to jot down any ideas in preparation for the task.

The design of the study

	Picture description A	Picture description B	Picture description C
6–7 yrs	No planning	2 mins 5 mins	5 mins 2 mins
11–12 yrs	No planning	2 mins 5 mins	5 mins 2 mins

All task interactions of all pairs were audio-recorded and transcribed. Then the data were coded to identify the interactional features (i.e. meaning negotiations, corrective feedback and modified output) as well as production features (i.e. fluency, accuracy and complexity).

Quote 5.2   Coding procedures in the study

The interactional data were coded as follows:

(1) Each participant's turn was coded as TL (target like) or NTL (non-target like),
(2) If NTL, turns were coded based on whether feedback was provided or not,
(3) If feedback was provided, it was categorized as: recast, clarification request, confirmation check, or explicit correction,
(4) Turns were coded according to whether or not there was an opportunity or no opportunity to use feedback,
(5) Turns were coded as modified output (more TL or not) or no modified output.

(Philp, Oliver and Mackey 2006: 553)

The results of the study are presented using inferential statistics. Chi square tests were used to analyse the interactional data and Friedman tests (non–parametric equivalents of ANOVAs) were used for the fluency, accuracy and complexity data. The alpha level was set at .016 after Bonferroni correction.

Reported results

The results indicated that children produced comparatively fewer non-target-like utterances when they were given 2 minutes of planning time (23%) than when they were given 5 minutes (32%) or no planning time at all (47%). The 2 minutes planning time condition led to more corrective feedback than the 5 minutes planning time and this difference was statistically significant. Older learners seemed to produce more non-target-like turns than younger learners when they were given planning time. In terms of feedback provision, the 'no planning time' condition was the most conducive with regard to modified output and there was a pattern of decreasing opportunities with increased planning time.

With regard to the children's production in terms of fluency, accuracy and complexity, the data indicate that fluency and accuracy were not impacted on by planning time. Fluency was consistently high for all conditions. The figures for accuracy did not produce any significant differences statistically although there seemed to be a trend for increasing levels of accuracy with more planning time. Complexity showed clear gains as a result of planning. Complexity gains were associated with the longest planning time, the 5 minute condition. Surprisingly, the younger children produced significantly more complex sentences in the no-planning condition. This outcome is counterintuitive as well as different from adult studies.

Sample data 5.1   Philp, Oliver and Mackey (2006: 561)

This dialogue extract illustrates the kind of talk that was produced while the children were carrying out this task in the 5 minutes planning condition:

A: How many boys you see jumping?
B: Jumping or skipping?
A: Jumping
B: I can see seven boys jumping. How many girls do you see jumping?
A: Two girls (later turn)
B: How many girls do you see are flying?
A: Two girls. How many boys do you see playing football?
B: Three boys. How many girls do you see when they kick?

In addition to the recorded task interactions, the researchers asked the teachers to reflect on the implementation of the tasks and the children's views were also sought. The researchers looked at how the children spent their planning time.

Sample data 5.2   Philp, Oliver and Mackey (2006: 562)

Children's use of planning time:
In the 2 min planning sessions, children often rehearsed the kinds of questions they were going to ask each other by writing the questions down, as shown in this example from the writing of one child:

Example 10
"Haw meny boys are runing. Haw meny girs are damping."
    When they had more time, in the 5 min planning condition, they sometimes rehearsed questions as with the 2 min tasks, but they also seemed to practice an order as we see in Omar's plans

Example 11
"I am going to say what is the snake doing, but first I am going to say do you have snake green snake and that I am going to say."
    Children also called out to one another "how do you spell..." "what's this..."
The children seemed to combine preparing for the task with rehearsing for the task and to do this in more depth with more time.

Conclusions

The authors conclude by bringing together the combined results in production and interaction:

Quote: 5.3   On the results

The results show that in terms of interaction, the children's provision of feedback to each other was greater when they did not have any time to plan (when they provided each other with feedback 23% of the time) or when they had a short amount of planning time (21%). When 5 min of planning time was given, they only provided feedback to each other 12% of the time. Children produced more speech overall (measured as words per turn) when they did not plan. In terms of fluency and accuracy, there were no significant differences according to planning time. Children's speech was significantly more complex after 5 min of planning, compared to no planning or 2 min planning.... In general then, it seems that providing children with planning time did not necessarily result in more learning opportunities for the children, at least in terms of feedback provision and use, and fluency and accuracy gains.

(Philp, Oliver and Mackey 2006: 557)

Discussion

This study might serve as a good model for you if you wish to conduct a comparative study between readily available groups. The experimental design using standard procedures involving recording the pair interactions, and coding the children's production to measure significant relationships, are straightforward to replicate in different contexts. The study can be completed within a few days or weeks and results can be produced quickly. Corresponding changes can also be implemented in your classroom relatively fast. At the same time this study also illustrates that the experimental design cannot always fully explain the reasons behind the outcomes.

The significance of the study is that it offers insights into how children use planning time in task-based interactions. Overall, it suggests that longish preparation/planning times are not effective, and children can and will provide feedback to one another without planning time. This is different from what we know about the relationships between planning time and task output in adult studies (e.g. Foster and Skehan 1996). One question that arises is about the possible reasons behind these surprising results. When children had less time to plan they provided more feedback to their partner. The authors suggest that this may be the case because planning prompted children to focus on what they wanted to say rather than paying attention to what their partner was saying. This is a plausible idea in that it makes sense in terms of young children's lack of readiness to be concerned with their partners (Chapter 2). However, could there be an alternative explanation? For example, it may that the children found the idea of being given explicit planning time with familiar tasks somewhat unusual, and they simply did not use the planning time because they did not think they needed it. In fact, it is noted in the study that some children did not use the pencil and paper for planning so it is possible that some of them did not really plan anything at all.

Some interesting differences emerged between the two age groups but these also seem somewhat difficult to explain. For example, the younger children produced significantly more complex sentences in the no-planning condition than the older learners, and they produced more target-like utterances than older learners when given planning time. It is hard to make sense of these findings, which overall suggest that the younger children managed the task better. More research, especially probing into these differences, would be needed. We also note that the tasks were interactional/dialogical tasks rather than monological (as opposed to the majority of tasks used in other planning studies). In the case of dialogical tasks, planning is only applicable in a limited way. When you plan some questions or ideas to talk about, you may not have a chance to put these into practice, because your partner's contributions may change the direction of the discussion. There is a spontaneity about dialogical tasks that makes planning more difficult and you simply might not get to say what you planned.

The results of this study are presented largely through statistics, combined with some excerpts from children's dialogues. The main measures are very clearly explained, and examples are provided. However, no mention is made of problematic or ambiguous data. For example, how were overlapping utterances coded? Were there any instances where it was difficult to decide what code to allocate to a fragmented utterance?

The authors themselves discuss the limitation of the single context and the use of just one type of task. It is indeed very hard to come to firm conclusions on the basis of data from only 42 children in one context. Many new questions arise and thus the authors argue that more research is needed with children of different age groups interacting on different language tasks if we are to gain further insights into the children's task interactions that are different from those produced by adults.

5.2.2   Case study 2 Llinares Garcia (2007): experimental and comparative

Background

This study was selected because it offers you a simple but replicable design to work with within the experimental tradition while keeping the statistical analysis to a minimum. The theoretical background of the study is concerned with language functions in teacher talk and how these affect learners' L2 production. The study uses the functional categories identified by Halliday (1975) and Painter (1999). In order to work with these functional categories, however, the authors first collected a large amount of spoken data from L2 immersion classrooms and examined the children's naturally occurring language in terms of most frequent functions. In this way six different functions were identified:

- Heuristic function: to ask for information about something
- Informative function: to inform somebody about something
- Personal function: to inform somebody about self
- Regulatory function: to demand action
- Instrumental function: to demand actions for personal benefit
- Interactional function: to interact socially with someone

Among these, the most common category was the personal function, i.e. when the children were talking about themselves, their friends, their families and pets and toys. This is explained by the age of the children (only 5 years old). However, the researcher felt that it would be possible to increase the use of the other language functions as well.

Aim: research question

The aim of the experiment was to increase the range of functions in young children's L2 production and thus investigate whether it was possible to approximate to the functionality evident in the children's L1.

Quote 5.3   Explaining the experiment

The experiment consisted of asking the teacher in the experimental group to perform some activities and role plays that promoted the pupils' discourse initiations in the L2 and to perform the same communicative functions as in the L1.

(Llinares Garcia 2003: 40–1)

The design of the experiment

There were two groups of learners, one experimental group and one control group. The teacher in the control group taught the class in the 'normal' way and the teacher in the experimental group was asked to use the following activities to foster the use of the selected functions:

- Instrumental: ask for a specific coloured ball
- Regulatory: children give teacher instructions how to put a jumper on

- Personal: children talk about objects they brought from home
- Heuristic: ask questions about a toy in the box
- Informative: describe and draw task
- Interactional: no specific suggestion

All sessions with both groups were based on oral tasks, given the age of the children. Data were collected from four sessions in each group, and all sessions were video-recorded and then transcribed. The first session in each group was recorded before the experiment began. The treatment therefore was only three sessions long.

The author proposed two hypotheses:

Quote 5.4   The two hypotheses

Hypothesis (1)
The learners' functional linguistic production (in terms of frequency of discourse initiations) in the experimental group will improve after practising activities aimed at the production of initiation functions by the children.

Hypothesis (2)
The learners' functional linguistic production (in terms of frequency of discourse initiations) will be higher than that of the control group after practising activities aimed at the production of initiation functions by children.

(Llinares Garcia 2007: 41)

Participants

The children were randomly distributed into two groups with two different teachers. Group A, the experimental group, consisted of 18 children (14 boys and 4 girls) while the control group, Group B, consisted of 17 children (6 boys and 11 girls). Although the size of the two groups was similar, the girl/boy ratio was very different.

Data analysis procedures

Although this is an experimental study, the data were analysed both quantitatively and qualitatively. As part of the qualitative analysis, activities which promoted the children's initiations were identified in the transcripts. The following example is from the experimental group where the children were encouraged to ask questions (use the heuristic language function). The data show that there was a clear need for the children to ask these questions and they were motivated to do so.

Sample data 5.3   Llinares Garcia (2007: 42)

124   VIC: It is big. (informative)
125   TCH: It's big.
126   VIC: Purple (informative)
127   TCH: It's purple.
128   VIC: Fat. (informative)
129   TCH: Very fat. And where does it live? In the ...
130   CH: Water
131   TCH: In the water.
132   CH: [Me]
133   CH: [Me]
134   TCH: Adrian.
135   ADR: Is it a fish? (heuristic)
136   TCH: No, it is not a fish.

Results

The quantitative analysis focussed on the functional production of the pupils in both groups before and after the treatment. The data analysis indicated that before the treatment the children produced very few initiations in either group although Group B (control group) used slightly more. Consequently, the treatment needed to have a sizeable effect for the 'less successful' group to overtake the initially 'more successful' group.

Statistical analysis (t-test) was used to determine whether there were significant differences between the two groups after the treatment in terms of the functions used and the children's initiations.

Concept 5.5   T-test

The *t-test* is a frequently used measurement in second language research when comparing mean scores for two groups or two sets of scores for the same group. T-test calculations can inform the researchers whether the differences between two measures are statistically significant or not. You may want to consult Brown and Rodgers (2002) for further examples of t-test calculations.

In Group A (experimental group) the total L2 initiations were 227 (95.31%) while in the control group (Group B) it was 192 (70.54%). This result was significant at the $p = 0.01$ level and established a clear effect for the treatment. Another interesting finding was that pupils in the experimental group used less L1 after the treatment because they could express themselves spontaneously using a variety of functions in L2.

Sample data 5.4   Llinares Garcia (2007: 44)

The table indicates how frequently each function was used either in L1 or L2 in the two groups

Functions	Group A		Group B	
	L2	L1	L2	L1
Personal	31	25	13	66
Informative	100	4	35	12
Heuristic	15	7	16	17
Instrumental	1	9	4	12
Interactional	3	0	9	0
Regulatory	77	9	115	35

The author comments that if not encouraged to use these functions in the L2, the children will use them in their L1. It is still the case that the most frequently used function remains the personal function.

Quote box 5.5   On the results

This present study shows that, in low immersion EFL contexts, very young children can communicate in the L2 if the teacher motivates them with activities that lead them to use the L2 for some purpose, in a similar way to their use of the L1. These activities should encourage the children to initiate interactions in the L2, and not simply respond to the teacher's queries.

Llinares Garcia (2007: 44)

Discussion

Some very clear implications arise here for materials design for young learners. It seems that children at this young age are able to diversify the language functions they use and this can lead to less reliance on their L1. These language functions simply emerged in the experimental group as a direct result of a range of communicative activities, so these kinds of activities could be incorporated into course-books and schemes of work intended for this age group. This study is also directly relevant to you if you wish to reflect on your own language use and use of functions in L2, and the long-term effects this may have on your learners' language use. The implications are thus relevant for all L2 classrooms of all ages.

We can see from the table above that the results are perhaps not quite as clear-cut as the researchers would have liked. In fact only two functions show higher frequency in the experimental group. There were several factors that could have influenced the results. One question that may arise is: Was the treatment sufficiently long? Is it really possible to achieve a lasting effect as a result of just three sessions? An additional issue concerns the base line data, i.e. the first session in each group. We might want to argue that a single session may not be enough to serve this purpose, because comparisons between just two sessions (one in each group) might distort real differences. Another issue is the meaning of the phrase 'normal practice'. Given that both groups were engaged in oral language practice and games, is it possible that there was some overlap between 'normal practice' and the 'experimental treatment'?

Even though the children were put in randomly organised groups, an interesting question may arise about the composition of the two groups. Will a group where the majority of the members are boys react differently to some of the activities as compared to the other group? The teachers were also different and so were their personalities, teaching styles and background experiences as well as the general rapport they had with the children. In sum, teacher factors and group factors may also have played a part. As a short, focussed experiment, it suffers from many of the shortcomings we discussed in Chapter 4, but despite these criticisms, this study offers a solid basis for possible replication. Teachers who work in schools where they have access to different classes or groups of learners may be in a position to conduct a study like this.

5.2.3   Case study 3 Bongartz and Schneider (2003): focus on individual learners

Background

This study highlights an interesting research opportunity for you if you want to work with your own children. Most projects that focus on just one or two learners longitudinally use qualitative methods, often an ethnographic approach. This paper combines both qualitative and quantitative approaches. It is a year-long study focussing on just two young learners who are brothers. The two boys (Perry, aged 5 and Martin, aged 7) are English L1 speakers acquiring German as a L2.

The motivation for this study was a family's temporary relocation from the USA to Germany for a period of one academic year. The mother, who is also one of the authors, decided to document her own boys' acquisition of German as evidenced in peer interactions. The researchers state that overall both boys successfully acquired German within the first year of their stay, but there also seemed to be important differences between them:

Quote 5.6   Explaining the differences between the boys

At the end of the year, both boys had succeeded in learning German, as measured by social and academic yardsticks: the ability to participate in everyday social interactions, develop and sustain friendships with peers that speak the target language, and, in the case of the older boy, Martin, the ability to complete school-based tasks that increasingly required literate skills. Defining the boys' success in learning German in terms of these criteria, however, masks real differences between them in both patterns of social interaction and linguistic development associated with these patterns.

(Bongartz and Schneider 2003: 13)

The aim of the study

The study aims to document the boys' language acquisition by combining two dominant paradigms in SLA research, cognitive/linguistic and socio-anthropological/ethnographic approaches. While both of these approaches are widely used in the field, it is rare to find studies that simultaneously rely on both approaches in both their data collection and data analysis. The two authors took responsibility for working with one of the approaches each. Schneider (the children's mother) focussed on the children's interactions in social contexts and this was a starting point for the analysis. Next, Bongartz analysed the boys' grammatical development. The aim of the paper is to bring these two lines of exploration together.

The social/ethnographic approach

The research questions were:

1. What patterns of social interaction are evident in the two young boys learning German as an L2?
2. What types of LP (language play) and other interactional sequences do these children use in the L2?
3. What evidence is there to suggest that the boys' use of LP and other interactional sequences contributed to their L2 acquisition?

In order to answer the above questions, a year-long ethnographic study was undertaken between August 1997 and August 1998. During this time the children were enrolled in a German school and a kindergarten where they were the only English L1 speakers. There were no L2 children at all in Martin's class and there were only a few Turkish- and Russian-speaking children in Perry's class. Prior to their experiences in Germany, Perry completed two years of preschool and Martin completed kindergarten in the USA. Martin aged 7 (brother 1) started German in grade 1 and since he could read English, he soon began to decode German in writing. He developed loose friendships with several children in his class. Perry aged 5 (brother 2) started in a kindergarten where he was exposed to oral German only. He did not develop friendships with many children but he had one best friend, a Turkish boy.

The authors emphasise the unique position of the mother/researcher in terms of her natural, unlimited access to the data and point to some problematic issues that this dual role entails.

Quote 5.7   Problems mother-researchers face

Schneider's role as mother and as participant observer allowed her to gain in-depth knowledge of the boys, both in school and out of school. In these twin roles, she not only had the opportunity to observe in both school and home settings, but could also compare the children's behaviours and interactions in these dual settings... Ethically, there is a tension between the researcher's right to know and the informants' right to privacy. These issues become undoubtedly problematic when children, and especially one's own children, become participants in a study.

(Bongartz and Schneider 2003: 17)

In order to overcome these problems, the boys' mother made every attempt to involve the children in making decisions about when to record and when not to, and whenever the children felt uncomfortable or uneasy, the recording machine was stopped.

The ethnographic data collection and analysis

As part of the social/ethnographic data collection, 25 audiotapes of interactive data were collected together with field-notes of different activities such as structured activities at Martin's school and unstructured activities at Perry's kindergarten, at home, and in the homes of Martin's and Perry's friends. Only five tapes were selected from each boy's collection and transcribed for the purposes of this paper. These tapes were transcribed and then Schneider identified preliminary categories that she felt characterised the children's interactional sequences.

Some findings from the ethnographic analysis

The most prevalent category that was immediately identified was language play (LP).

Concept 5.6   Language play

'At the formal level, there is play with sounds (or with letter shapes, though this is less common) to create patterns of rhyme, rhythm, assonance, consonance, alliteration, etc and play with grammatical structures to create parallelism and patterns (Jacobson 1960). At the semantic level there is play with units of meaning, combining them in ways which create worlds which do not exist: fictions.'

(Cook 2000: 228)

Different types of language play were identified which the researcher labelled as 'sound play' and 'word play', 'narrative construction' and finally, 'insults and tough guy talk'. Sound play emerged very early and the children continued to use it throughout the whole year. Word play also emerged early, especially with Perry. Word play is characterised by repetition of words and phrases, use of puns, often rhyming puns with the intention to amuse others. Word play uses routine phrases that are salient in the language the children are exposed to. Sometimes new nonsense words were coined indicating that the children understood the way German words were constructed. Extracts given here in the paper illustrating different types of sound and word play are quite difficult to follow because of the fragmented phrases embedded in only locally meaningful situations.For example, consider this extract:

Sample data 5.5   Bongartz and Schneider (2003: 18)

Melanie (Mel) with Martin (M) and Jacob (J) playing with glow-in-the-dark linking forms at home:

Mel: That glows in the dark, in der dunkel ['in the dark']
     XXX
  J: Ho, ho, hah, ha, ha
Mel: Show him how it__
  M: Ich weiss xxxxx ['I know xxx'] Ahh, (rustling movement)
  J: Ha!
  M: Ahh, Ya ha ha ha! (laughter)

Another category that emerged as a result of the analysis of the transcribed data was narrative co-construction. These narratives typically developed out of play situations and they contained events involving two or more characters. The two boys did not always occupy subordinate roles when interacting with native speakers and they were both observed actively co-constructing these narrative sequences with their friends. Another type of language play that seemed characteristic of the children's talk was 'tough guy talk' which is a form of verbal 'swaggering'. Trading insults directed to others strengthens solidarity between the boys. In the following extract, the two brothers and one of Martin's friends, Christian, launch into a 'Barbie-bashing talk' to create solidarity by attacking girly toys and mocking a Barbie TV advert.

Sample data 5.6   Bongartz and Schneider (2003: 21–2)

Perry (P), Martin (M) and Christian (Chr)

P: Du hasse. Ich hasse Barbie ['You hate. I hate Barbie']
M: Ich auch. ['Me too']
Chr: Ich hasse auch Barbie, den du das tolle Babe bist ['I hate Barbie too, because you're a cute babe']
M: Ha, du kannst so viel mit Barbie ['You can do so much with Barbie'] (Chr picking up on Barbie theme; sarcastically mimicking the Barbie TV ad)
Chr: Du kannst alles mit Barbie! Du kannst alles mit Karkerlake Barbie! ['You can do everything with Barbie! You can do everything with cockroach (insult) Barbie.']

In addition to language play, negotiations emerged as pervasive characteristics of the child–child interactions. These negotiations centred around decision-making as to who, when and how might be included in playing different games.

Quote 5.8   Summarising the findings on negotiation

Summing up our findings on negotiation, we found evidence that (a) negotiation is a broader based notion that goes beyond negotiation of meaning (b) negotiations in child–child interactions occur frequently and in multiple contexts within or between play sequences and (c) misunderstandings that prompt negotiation of meaning are not limited to NNSs in NS–NNS interactions.

(Bongartz and Schneider 2003: 24)

Perry tended to use imperatives whereas Martin was a more careful negotiator when playing with friends. Martin was often recorded negotiating carefully in order to maintain equity and integrity in play activities. In the following extract, Martin and his friend discuss how many toy ships they each have and this careful negotiation is continued until a status quo is achieved.

Sample data 5.7   Bongartz and Schneider (2003: 23)

Martin (M) and Peter (P) making boats out of cork bottle stoppers on the patio at home:

M: Ich will mein Schiff noch, und sehen, wieviel Schiffe ich habe. Ich hab' drei Schiffe, zwei Guten, wieviel Schiffe has du? ['I want my ship still and see how many ships I have. I have three ships, two good ones. How many ships do you have?']
P: (pointing) Diese here ['These here'].
M: Du hast drei auch. ['You have three too'].
P: Und die davon noch ein ['And one more over there'].
M: Oh, du hast vier. Ich habe gedacht, nix was runter. ['Oh, you have four. I thought nothing was underneath)']
P: Nein, du hast vier. ['No, you have four'].
M: Du darfst nich so viel machen. ['You can't make so many'].
P: Martin, jetzt habe ich auch vier. Jetzt hast du nur drei. ['Martin, now I also have four. Now you have only three.']
M: Das ist okey, ich mach' mehr: Ich habe noch viel Schiffe, viel, viel Schiffe noch. ['That's ok, I'll make more. I already have a lot of ships, many, many ships.']

In these lengthy negotiations Martin tried hard to get what he wanted, but when he did not, he compromised rather than disrupted smooth play. His younger brother was more directive and less ready to compromise.

Sample data 5.8   Bongartz and Schneider (2003: 23)

Perry (P) and Fatih (F) playing a table-top soccer game at kindergarten:

F: Perry, hey ['Perry, hey!']
P: Was gemacht? ['What did you do?']
F: Perry, Perry, Tor, Tor jetzt. ['Perry, Perry goal, goal, now']. I hab 'drei Tor jetzt. ['I have three goals now.']
P: Ja einfach. Einmal has du (blasting sounds) Boof! Boof! Boof! ['Yeah, simple. Once you (past)']
F: (F wants to be goalie) Ich bin xxx nicht und du hast xxx Perry. ['I'm xxx not, and you have xxxx Perry']
P: (Ignoring F, hitting the ball) Schaumal, boof! Und da ist ein Mann ['Look, Boof! And there is a man']

As this extract illustrates, Perry's skills or willingness to negotiate are not quite the same as his brother's. Here he simply ignores his friend's plea to be the goalie.

The linguistic approach

As part of the quantitative, linguistic analysis, Bongartz took an inventory of the boys' linguistic competence at five different times over the year to allow for comparisons of their development. The linguistic data were drawn from five transcripts of play interactions for each boy with comparable dates of recording. Bongartz focussed the analysis on aspects of German syntax that were different from English. The linguistic analysis revealed that Martin's syntax developed further than his brother's and there was a marked difference between the two boys' use of the German dependent clause.

Sample data 5.9   Bongartz and Schneider (2003: 30): dependent clauses

	Martin		Perry	
	N	%	N	%
Time 1	2	8.5	2	2.0
Time 2	1	2.2	–	–
Time 3	25	10.5	3	1.9
Time 4	26	17.3	9	5.5
Time 5	1	6.0	–	–
Total	55	11.7	14	2.4

N = number of tokens

Quote 5.9   Comparing the two boys' use of dependent clauses

The difference in the use of dependent clauses appears quite substantial: 55 of 471 sentence tokens (11.7%) from Martin's transcripts were dependent clauses whereas Perry used only 14 out of 584 sentences (2.4%), albeit with a marked increase at time 4. Because of the word order differences between main and dependent clauses in German...the acquisition of dependent clauses serves as a criterion to identify differences in proficiency.

(Bongartz and Schneider 2003: 30)

Martin's sentences generally contained more elements than Perry's and thus Martin emerges as a more advanced speaker of L2 German. In order to explain Perry's linguistic results, the authors use social information to shed light on his grammatical competence. Perry tended to use more imperatives to directly engage his playmates and to initiate and control the interaction. Alternatively, Perry may have chosen to avoid using dependent clauses.

Quote 5.10   The importance of personality in language learning

Considering imperative production in the context of Perry's outgoing personality and vivaciousness, his linguistic choices can be seen as motivated through his social self.

(Bongartz and Schneider 2003: 32)

The two boys' linguistic choices are inseparable from their interactive contexts and their different personalities. The findings suggest that linguistic competence may be interfaced with interactional competence and this is part of the learner's psychological disposition.

Implications of the study

Quote 5.11   On the implications of the study

Moving beyond the learning and the teaching of German, we see many implications for our research in L2 and foreign language assessment, language teaching pedagogy, and in linguistic research in SLA.

(Bongartz and Schneider 2003: 34)

The authors discuss several implications emerging from their study:

1. Implications for assessment: de-contextualised tests of linguistic knowledge fail to capture what learners know and are capable of doing in particular contexts.
2. Implications for language teaching pedagogy: the importance of peer-learning as a source of linguistic development is underlined and the authors suggest that opportunities for peer learning can be created in formal classrooms as well.
3. Implications for SLA research: combining the two analytical approaches is fruitful.

Overall, the authors conclude that the two boys' acquisition of German was more similar than different. They proceeded according to the social context and the opportunities for social and linguistic practices.

Discussion

Immediate implications for testing/assessment practices arise as the authors themselves point out. Testing procedures for young children need to be able to capture the richness of their language competence, such as language play. The importance of peer–peer interactions is underlined and the paper illustrates this unique learning potential. Even in contexts where all children share the same L1 but happen to be learning an L2 in a formal context, peer–peer interactions are important in providing qualitatively different learning opportunities, compared to school-based adult–child interactions. The data are noticeably characteristic of boys' discourse (Barbie bashing), so, an interesting question arises about how different the interactions would have been with girls. Would patterns of peer interactions between girls or mixed gender siblings be different from boys?

The two boys' acquisition of German as an L2 was largely unproblematic and successful. It may be the case that their temporary stay in Germany made this experience easier as they knew that they were going to return to the USA after a year. The other factor that could have contributed to their success is related to the status of US English and culture in Germany. The two boys' L1 and their American culture were probably very popular among their German-speaking peers and this would have contributed to the ease with which they made friends and had opportunities to participate in a variety of peer interactions.

This paper may inspire parents and teachers who may wish to track the development of just a small number of children. Regular recording sessions throughout the year will provide you with a large amount of data. Many different approaches to analysis are available to the researcher as a consequence of the large amount of data. In fact, the paper illustrates the importance of considering different methodological and epistemological options and their consequences when embarking on a research project. This study combines both ethnographic and linguistic analyses, but the ethnographic/social analysis is primary and the linguistic analysis is integrated into, and analysed against, the backdrop of the social data. In this way, the linguistic analysis further enriches the ethnographic findings. However, interesting questions arise about the data selection. One of the researchers, the mother of the children, read through the data and started to look for themes emerging from the recordings. Given that there was an enormous amount of data to choose from, it is not really clear what was left out and what was selected. Some explanation of the criteria here would have been useful. The selection procedures are important in discussing the boys' production of dependent clauses, too. Given that both home-based and school-based activities as well as interactions with both NS and NNS children were recorded, there is quite a variety of situations to choose from. For example, it would be interesting to know whether the data selection took into account the types of contexts involved. How much of the data was analysed with both boys present in the conversations, how much was recorded with other native speakers or non-native speakers (e.g. speakers such as Perry's Turkish friend)? In addition, how much of the data was taken from formal school activities where Martin would have naturally encountered more dependent clauses and how much data from preschool activities where the discourse may have been qualitatively different, perhaps much more based on simple sentences? Decisions about data selection in ethnographic studies always pose dilemmas, as we discussed in Chapter 4.

There are also interesting ethical issues raised by the authors regarding the dual role of the parent-researcher in particular, but also in terms of working with young children as respondents and addressing their particular sensitivities as compared to adult research subjects (see Chapter 6). Being aware of these issues and explicitly discussing their effects in your research is essential.

5.2.4   Case study 4 Swain and Lapkin (2003): focus on individual learners

Introduction

This study is a good example if you want to focus on just two learners. A particular advantage is that it can be conducted outside your regular lessons. This is also a brief but intensive study that can be completed within just weeks or days.

Background

Teachers and researchers working in the French immersion programmes in Canada came to realise that despite the excellent language learning conditions (i.e. plenty of comprehensible input, plenty of opportunities for interaction) students did not develop target-like grammatical competence in French. Swain (2000) proposed that students should be pushed beyond their comfortable levels of language competence via specific tasks that were designed to get them to produce L2 in speaking and writing and then teachers should get them to reflect on their own output. Collaborative writing tasks (such as a dictogloss task, or a jigsaw story-writing task) are especially effective activities because they push learners to focus on language forms (in addition to meaning). Collaborating with a friend during writing tasks leads to learners discussing, comparing, and evaluating their ideas about language use in an explicit manner.

Concept 5.7   Dictogloss

This is an activity where the teacher reads out a text at normal speed once, while the learners listen. Then the teacher reads the text out again and asks the learners to take some notes. Next, the learners are put in pairs to reconstruct the story in writing. It is important that their text resembles the original as much as possible. During this process the learners are encouraged to discuss specific aspects of language use (such as spelling, word order, syntax, and others) before they arrive at the best possible solution collaboratively. For further examples refer to Wajnryb (2003).

In these collaborative tasks learners rely on using language (L1 or L2) as a cognitive tool to mediate their learning (see Vygotsky in Chapter 1).

Aims and research questions

The focus is on how two grade 7 (12-year-old) learners evaluate the changes a native French speaker (reformulator) has made to their original story, which they wrote collaboratively. The aim of the project was to answer the following research questions:

1. What did students notice when they compared their own L2 writing with the NS reformulation?
2. What changes did they accept and reject and why?
3. What changes did they make to their stories at a later stage when they re-wrote it individually?
4. Were these based on the reformulations and/or the collaborative dialogue?

Participants

The two students, Dara and Nina, were selected by the teacher as average students. The two students were working with the researchers outside their French classes for a period of two school weeks.

The research procedures

These were somewhat complex, consisting of five stages.

Stage 1 (Collaborative writing): The research assistant played a five-minute video lesson which focussed on pronominal verbs in French. In the video, two students demonstrated a jigsaw task. Then Nina and Dara carried out the jigsaw task and they wrote a story together in French (the *Alarm clock* story) based on a series of eight pictures. One of them had pictures 1, 3, 5, and 7 and the other one had 2, 4, 6 and 8. Their joint story was then given to a NS French 'reformulator' who was asked to change non target-like language use while preserving the students' original meaning.

Stage 2 (Noticing): Nina and Dara were handed back their reformulated story to notice differences between their original story and the one re-written by the reformulator. The students used a highlighter to discuss their observations in the text and they commented on the differences. This discussion was video-recorded.

Stage 3 (Stimulated recall in L1 English): The researchers played the video of stage 2 for Nina and Dara to watch. They stopped the tape every time the girls were discussing a new difference. Nina and Dara were asked at these points what exactly they had been thinking at the time of comparing the two texts. This was done in order to probe more deeply into their thought processes.

Stage 4 (Post-test individual writing): The students were given a copy of their original story (from stage 1) and they were asked to re-write the story incorporating some changes they wanted to include. Here Nina and Dara worked on their individual stories independently.

Stage 5 (Individual interviews): The girls were interviewed independently to elicit their perceptions about the whole process of writing together, comparing texts and re-writing the original story.

All written products (the joint story, the reformulated story and the individual rewritten stories) were copied and analysed. In addition, all interactions between the two students and between the researchers and the students were recorded and transcribed. In the interactions between the two students the researchers were looking for evidence of language learning by isolating language-related episodes (LREs).

Concept 5.8   Language-related episode (LRE), defined by Swain and Lapkin (1995: 292)

'(LREs are defined as)...any part of the dialogue where learners talk about the language they are producing, question their language use or correct themselves or others.'

For stages 2 and 3, language where the learners were accepting or rejecting the reformulator's changes was also included in this definition. Three main categories of LREs emerged: lexical, form-focussed and discourse-related.

- Lexical – includes adverbs, nouns, adjectives and verbs.
- Form – includes article, gender, possessive pronoun/article, preposition, preposition+article, pronoun reference, sentence structure, spelling, pronominal verb, verb form.
- Discourse – includes discourse marker, logical sequencing, stylistics, tense sequencing, temporal sequencing, text structure.

Results

The main part of the article is devoted to the discussion of examples of LREs drawn out of the data at different stages of the project.

Sample data 5.10   Swain and Lapkin (2003: 295)

Original story (pre-test):	Elle sort du maison	
Reformulation:	de la maison	
Post-test Nina:	du maison	
Post-test Dara:	de la maison	

State 1 writing	Stage 2 noticing	Stage 3 stimulated recall
Form LRE (preposition+article)		*Nina rejects (and Dara accepts) reformulation*
464. N. OK, elle... vingt minutes plus tard elle sort du maison. Elle sort de la maison? Ou du maison?	107. N. Elle sort du maison	213. R. Ok so de la maison and du maison
465. D. De, non, du	108. D. en courant.	214. D. uh, it could have been any way.
466. N. Non, parce que de la c'est du	109. N. du mai?... de...Ils ont mis. Qu'est-ce qu' on a mis? On a mis du maison, ils ont fait de la maison.	215. N. it has to do with du, de la. I remember when we were first writing it.
467. D. Oui	110. D. Je t'ai dit! Ou tu as dit... [laughs]	216. D. Yeah.
468. N. sort du maison...sort...en courant		217. N. and we went like "is it either du or de la?" And we agreed that it was du but I don't know [laughs]
469. D. sort du maison...		218. D. I don't think I can remember it exactly, but
		219. N. Yeah, sometimes it's like de la? Isn't it de la equals du? I don't know.
		220. D. Nooo! Shoot, uh, ok
		221. R. So you know there's a rule in there, but
		222. D. um-hum, like I cannot remember things that I learned in grade five. They are a complete blur [laughter], so
		223. R. Many things are blurry to me.
		226. D. de la does make more sense. Well, I don't know. De la
		227. N. equals...
		228. D. Really?
		229. N. Yeah.

The researchers were able to document language learning through the analysis of the LREs. They argued that the research procedures involving the stages of writing, comparing texts and re-writing the story proved to be effective in stimulating noticing and reflection on language use. The reformulator's explicit corrections served as an additional stimulus for thinking and learning. The stimulated recall, despite its limitations, further helped these students to reflect on what they had been thinking when they had been looking at the differences. Interestingly, however, Nina and Dara did not correct all the mistakes identified by the reformulator in their writing, which suggests that learners' own convictions about what is correct and right are very hard to change.

Discussion

This study suggests that students do not just automatically accept reformulations and corrections from teachers. There are two main reasons why Nina and Dara rejected some of the reformulations. At times they felt that they knew a grammar rule and even though their 'rule' ended up being incorrect, their conviction was so strong that they insisted on hanging on to it even in the face of corrections from the NS. At other times they felt that the original story conveyed a different meaning compared to the reformulations offered by the NS and thus they rejected the correction on the basis that it altered their intended meaning.

Notwithstanding these rejections, it can be said that the repeated opportunities to talk through the same piece of writing led to learners reflecting on language points, learning new phrases, and coming to a deeper understanding of some grammatical points. The implications are clear to teachers in that peer–peer collaborative talk is an excellent context for learning to occur, and learners can, and will help and support one another. Teachers in L2 classrooms might like to consider using collaborative writing activities.

The generalisability of this study is very limited as it is based on just two learners, but research of this kind is more interested in exploring possibilities of learning and challenging existing assumptions about what is really going on. We do not know how typical or unusual these two girls' behaviour might have been. This is a common question with studies that focus on just one or two learners (see the discussion in Chapter 4). Conducting the same study with other students could have revealed some interesting similarities but also possibly important differences. The multi-stage methodology makes this a very complicated study and younger children would not be able to reflect on their reasons in a useful way. On the other hand, the methodology is quite flexible. It is not necessary to use all the steps. For example, after the jointly completed writing task the teacher may correct the texts and then hand them back to students to discuss any changes. Alternatively peer correction sessions may be organised for a second cycle of reformulations.

One issue that might arise is to do with the intensity of this research. Having the spotlight on just two students by recording all their conversations and copying all their work can have a negative effect on them as they may feel overwhelmed by the intensity of attention. A direct effect of being overwhelmed may be underperformance.

5.2.5 Case study 5 Lan and Oxford (2003): eliciting children's views

Introduction

This study was selected because it illustrates well both the advantages and the shortcomings of survey-based research with children. A large number of children were given questionnaires in Taiwanese schools and the paper offers statistical treatment of the elicited data. The focus of the study is on foreign language learning strategies.

Background

Researchers have only recently begun focussing their attention on implementing strategy instruction for elementary school learners and finding out more about what strategies children use and are conscious of (e.g. Chamot and El-Dinary 1999; Green and Oxford 1995). There is a shortage of studies in foreign language contexts.

Aims and research questions

This study was conducted in two stages. First, a questionnaire was administered to students and this is what the paper is reporting on. Later, some interviews were also used but these are not discussed here. The aim of this first research phase was to find out about the broad profile of strategy use among these learners. The researchers also wanted to see which strategies were most and least used by Taiwanese children. Finally, they were interested in the effect that gender, proficiency, and liking English may have had.

The research questions were:

1. For the entire group of students, what is the broad profile of strategy use overall and for each of the six categories?
2. How do these EFL results compare to those found in other studies involving elementary school children?
3. For the entire group of students, what are the most and least used strategies?
4. Are there significant differences by gender, proficiency level and/or liking English in terms of overall strategy use?
5. Are there significant differences by gender, proficiency level, and/or liking English in terms of use of any of the six strategy categories?
6. Are there significant differences by gender, proficiency level, and/or liking English in terms of any particular strategy items?

The participants

379 grade 6 students (202 boys and 177 girls) participated; they were 11 years old. They were students in a public elementary school which enjoyed an excellent reputation in Taiwan. The children's proficiency was tested using a criterion-referenced placement test designed by a local educational authority. According to this test the participants were divided into three proficiency groups: high proficiency (N = 179), medium (N = 65) and low (N = 35).

The questionnaire

The questionnaire was based on Oxford (1990) and Gunning (1997). The strategies to be investigated were categorised into six main groups.

Concept 5.9   Language learning strategies (summarised from Lan and Oxford 2003: 353–4)

(1) *memory strategies* (designed to help the learner to create mental frameworks which will allow new information to remain in long-term memory)
(2) *cognitive strategies* (these strategies help learners to process and use the language – ten techniques were incorporated into statements):

- repeat new expressions that I learn
- imitate native speakers
- practise the sounds of the English alphabet
- watch TV in English or listen to English tapes or CDs
- read books in English
- work with English computer programs
- try to find occasions outside of school to practise English
- practise with my parents what I am learning
- look for similarities in pronunciation between Chinese/Mandarin and English
- try to understand the main idea of what I read or hear without translating word for word and try to figure out rules of English grammar

(3) *compensation strategies* (these make up for missing knowledge):

- guess the meaning of a new word based on the rest of the sentence
- use gestures to express what I want to say
- ask for help
- find a different way to say what I want to say (e.g. synonyms, descriptions)

(4) *metacognitive strategies* (planning, monitoring and evaluating own progress, for example):

- organise my time so that I can study English often
- look for chances to practise English
- listen closely to someone who talks to me in English

- check my progress in English
- analyse my mistakes and try not to make them again

(5) *affective strategies* (these strategies are used to regulate emotional aspects of language learning):

- try to relax if I am anxious because of speaking English
- take risks such as guessing a word or phrase
- try to speak English even if I make mistakes, and reward myself for succeeding

(6) *social strategies*:

- ask the speaker to speak slowly, repeat or clarify what they said
- practise English with my classmates
- be interested and willing to learn information related to American culture.

Altogether 30 separate strategy items were created with 5-point Likert scale (Likert 1932) responses indicating the frequency from never $= 1$ to almost always $= 5$. At the end of the questionnaire the children were asked to indicate their gender and whether they liked English or not. The questionnaire was translated into Chinese with special attention to simplicity and comprehensibility.

The questionnaires were administered in the English classes by teachers who could provide help/clarification regarding the items. The teachers gave reassurance to the children that their responses did not count towards their assessment at school, and all responses were anonymous. To analyse the data, both descriptive and inferential statistics were used. Means and standard deviations were calculated for all items, the six categories and the strategy instrument as a whole. A three-way ANOVA (analysis of variance) with overall strategy use as the dependent variable, and the following three independent variables: (1) proficiency (2) gender and (3) students' liking of English were calculated. Then a three-way MANOVA was run to test whether significant differences arose in each of the six categories according to proficiency levels, gender and liking English. Finally, another three-way multiple analysis of variance (MANOVA) tested whether significant differences arose in strategy use in each of the 30 items. (For more practical information about these statistical measures, see Brown and Rodgers 2002).

Reported results

The results of the analysis of the questionnaire are reported according to the research questions (RQs) posed earlier:

RQ1. The data regarding the broad profile of the group point to a medium score for overall strategy use: the most frequent sets mentioned by the children were compensation and affective strategies.

RQ2. Compared to other studies (mainly in ESL contexts), these EFL learners used more rote memorisation strategies rather than strategies that provided opportunities to practise English.

RQ3. The five most often used strategy items included (1) ask for help when I do not know a word; (2) ask the speaker to slow down and repeat; (3) guess the meaning from the rest of the sentence; (4) try to relax when stressed about speaking; (5) find another way to say what I mean.

In summary, compensation, affective and social strategies were familiar to many of these learners. The five *least* often used strategies were: (1) mime words to remember them (2) work with classmates to practise English (3) make a drawing in my head or on paper to help me remember a word (4) be interested in and willing to learn information about American culture (5) look for occasions to speak English. This implies that less traditional memory strategies and occasions to practise English with peers and native speakers must be rare for these children.

Sample data 5.11   Lan and Oxford (2003: 358): the five most frequently used strategies in the whole Taiwanese EFL group

No. of children	Strategy	Mean	Category	Comment
18	When I don't know a word in English, I ask for help	3.5	Compensation	Lower end of high-use range
28	If I don't understand what is said to me in English, I ask the person to speak slowly, to repeat or clarify what has been said	3.5	Social	Lower end of high-use range
16	When I hear a new word in English, I try to guess the meaning by looking at the rest of the sentence	3.4	Compensation	Higher end of medium-use range
25	Whenever I am stressed by the idea of speaking English, I try to relax	3.3	Affective	Medium-use range

19	When I can't find an expression in English, I try to find another way to say what I mean	3.2	Compensation	Medium-range use

RQ4. Some significant differences emerged for each variable: (1) gender: girls use strategies more frequently than boys; (2) proficiency: high proficiency learners use more strategies; (3) those who liked English used significantly more strategies.

RQ5. Liking English had a significant effect on learners' employment of all six strategy types and thus this is the most influential of the three independent variables. Gender differences were evident in five categories, girls exceeding boys (except for the affective category). Proficiency affected four categories (not memory and social), with greater proficiency level correlating with more frequent strategy use.

Discussion

The authors conclude that young learners already use some L2 learning strategies, although the range of strategies is quite limited. They suggest that more cooperative learning should be used in English classes to encourage learners to practise some new strategies. Introducing different tasks in pairs or groups will certainly facilitate the use of language learning strategies and enhance the development of English skills. All children could benefit from explicit strategy instruction, and more of this should happen in English classes. Many students said they did not like English and it seems that liking English correlates highly with using strategies effectively. The implication is that it is important for teachers to tackle indifferent and negative attitudes to L2 at a young age, otherwise children might be put off language learning very early on.

This questionnaire is based on a standardised validated instrument and thus directly builds on previous research. It is also motivated by teachers' and the researchers' practical experience that EFL learners' strategies, and motivations to use them, might be very different from ESL learners. The statistics are powerful in terms of describing the trends but they do not tell us anything about important individual differences and reasons for using or not using certain strategies. Further interviews will complement this data. One issue that may have influenced the results is related to the number of questions in this instrument. When overloaded with questions, it is possible that some children ticked boxes without much reflection. In similar studies, therefore, reported strategy use may be usefully complemented with observations or think-aloud protocols focussed on certain classroom tasks.

5.2.6   Case study 6 Nagy (2009): eliciting children's views

Background

This study provides a contrast to the previous study in that it is much smaller in scope. It offers you a simple but innovative way of eliciting data. This is also a study that would be easy to replicate in a slightly altered form. In this study, the children were asked to reflect on their motivations and attitudes regarding learning English (e.g. Elliott and Hufton 2003; Nikolov 1999b).

Aims and research questions

The study aimed to investigate the views of Hungarian children aged 10–11 regarding their motivation to learn English and their attitudes to their English classes, using a 'participatory method' (see discussion in Chapter 6).
   Specifically there were three research questions:

1. What do pupils think helps or hinders them most while learning English?
2. What do pupils think the aims of learning and knowing English are at different stages of their lives?
3. Is there a difference between the perceptions of early beginners and late beginners?

Participants

49 fifth-grade pupils (aged 10–11) from four different primary schools in Budapest participated. They were divided into seven intact groups. All groups were taught by different teachers. Two of these schools started English in grade 1 (early starters, at age 6). These two schools enjoyed an excellent reputation and they had good resources. The other two schools started English in grade 4 (late starters, at age 9) in line with the recommendations of the National Curriculum Guidelines. Altogether there were 24 early beginners and 25 late beginners. The differences in perceptions between these two groups were also sought.

The data elicitation instrument

A special, participatory instrument was developed instead of conventional interviews. In each elicitation session six children were involved. Within a group of six, the children were further divided into self-selected pairs. The researcher felt that thinking about their views and opinions and articulating them would be easier in pairs than individually. After gaining permission, the children were taken out of class to work with the researcher in a quiet classroom. Within each group, all children worked with a partner. In the allocated room there were three 'stations' (tables) and the pairs moved around these 'stations'. Each station had a paper sheet which included open-ended questions written in L1, and invited the children to write their responses with different coloured pens. When one pair finished a question, they waited to get to the next station. This continued until all three pairs were finished with all three tasks. The questions on the three papers were designed to allow the children to write as much as they wished. It also enabled those in the same group to see what the others had written. They were allowed to read each others' sentences and ideas but they were told that if they felt their answer was already there, they still had to write it out again. The differently coloured pens allowed the researcher to identify different individuals.

Sample data 5.12   Nagy (2009: 234): The questions

Sheet 1 (station 1): In a big red heart, which was drawn on the paper, the children were asked to write *'Things that help me to learn English…'*
  At the bottom of the paper, outside the heart it was written: *Things that make it more difficult for me to learn English…'*

Sheet 2 (station 2): A time-line was drawn from left to right with words: *'Knowing English is good because now…, next year…, at the end of primary…. in secondary school…, at university…, when you are a grown-up……';* the children were invited to complete these sentences.

Sheet 3 (station 3): On the third piece of paper, in a speech bubble, they were asked to finish a sentence: *'When my teacher speaks only English it is good because…'* and outside the bubble another sentence: *It is also difficult because….'* (the answers to this last question are not presented in this paper)

In addition, children were asked to pick two or three 'smileys' from a large range of stickers and cut out and stick those that described best how they usually felt in their English classes.

The researcher was monitoring the children's work and was helping out when necessary but otherwise tried to stay in the background in order not to influence the children's responses.

The data analysis

The written responses were translated into English and grouped together according to emerging themes. The researcher acknowledges that this was a messy process and that it was not always straightforward to decide how to categorise the responses.

  The pupils' perceptions of beneficial factors included textbooks (22 mentions), the teacher (16 mentions), hearing the language (12 mentions), the dictionary (10 mentions), and studying a lot (6 mentions). Their perceived difficulties were different in the early and late starter groups. The early beginners thought that it was the teacher that made their learning difficult whereas the late beginners identified pronunciation as their biggest problem. In terms of their goal of study, both groups gave similar answers. The majority stated going to secondary school but many of them mentioned going abroad and working abroad when they grow up.

These children are learning English in a competitive test-oriented environment where their final assessment in English, which is based on frequent tests, can determine whether they will be admitted to a good secondary school or not. In this context teachers are torn between teaching for tests and teaching for communicative competence. A clearly instrumental motive seems to dominate even at a young age:

Quote 5.12   On a surprising finding

..., it is remarkable that none of the learners mentioned reasons related to any intrinsic motive: the pleasure of learning and knowing English. In fact, the opposite is true: many of the perceived problems relate to the language: vocabulary, pronunciation, grammar and the lack of paying attention. This is a vicious circle, as if they do not find the actual language learning activities intrinsically motivating, they cannot consciously focus on tasks.

(Nagy 2009: 241)

Another remarkable finding was about the role of the teacher. Frequent negative comments suggested that classroom practice must have been far from ideal, although there was no observation to gather alternative evidence.

Discussion

This study also emphasises that it is teachers, their enthusiasm, their commitment and personality that make the biggest difference in children's language classrooms. There is a danger here that these young learners will be put off learning because of the largely test-oriented learning environment where the enjoyment of the language does not get a single mention. Teachers may wish to ask themselves: How would my classes have answered these questions? What do children enjoy or find motivating to learn in my classes?

The study reported here is quite limited but this in a way justifies its place here. It is a good example of how to start with something small that can be built on, for example, by conducting observations of these classrooms, or by conducting interviews with the teachers.

Many interesting questions arise about the procedures and the researcher–child relationship. How well did the children know the researcher? What kind of relationship did they build up? The novelty effect of the task and the children's desire to please the researcher may have affected their answers. How would the children respond if this kind of task was repeated and their opinions were sought regularly about what was happening in their English classes? It is quite possible that on the one hand they would look upon the task as less exciting but on the other hand they might become more accustomed to formulating their opinions and views about their own learning processes. In this sense, one implication is to help children become more aware of their views and opinions by cultivating activities that regularly ask them to reflect and think about their own learning. Another issue concerns the quantity and the quality of the answers. Even though the children were told they could write as much as they wanted to, in reality most of them wrote only one or two sentences in response to each question. We might wonder whether the children could have provided the researcher with more interesting and more lively data in some other way, perhaps in a role play (see Gardner and Yaacob 2007). The researcher had to translate the children's written responses and then categorise them and this dual process may have distorted the original data.

5.2.7 Case study 7 Peng and Zhang (2009): focus on teachers

Introduction

This study focusses on primary English teachers' target language (TL) use in classrooms. In foreign language contexts, especially when resources are scarce, the teacher's input becomes the primary source of language learning. This study was selected because it illustrates the complexities of classrooms by juxtaposing different views and opinions from both teachers and their students in an attempt to uncover what is actually happening in lessons.

Background

In 2001, The Ministry of Education in China made English mandatory in primary schools from grade 3 and according to Ministry guidelines, teachers are encouraged to use the target language as much as possible in their teaching. Research into teachers' target language use indicates that it has positive effects on students' proficiency (e.g. Turnbull 2001). However, the authors warn that the majority of this research has focussed on college-level or secondary-level classrooms.

Quote 5.13   On research into teachers' target language use

Generally speaking, most of the existing studies focusing on teacher's TL use were conducted in the context of college foreign language (FL) classes (e.g. Duff and Polio, 1990, Polio and Duff 1994) or in secondary schools (e.g. Franklin,

> ## Quote 5.13   (Continued)
>
> 1990, Turnbull 1999). Very little research has been carried out in a context where teachers use the target language, the mother tongue (MT), or a mixture of both languages with young beginners whose TL proficiency is very low.
>
> (Peng and Zhang 2009: 213–40)

Aims and research questions

The following two research questions were proposed:

1. How much English do teachers use in their total teacher talk in elementary-school English classes?
2. How appropriate is their use of the TL?

The authors' larger research project indicated that there was a great deal of variety among English teachers in Chinese elementary classrooms with regard to how much target language they used. This paper focusses on just four classrooms.

Participants

The participants were four teachers and their 203 grade 5 learners (aged 10–11). Two of these teachers were in 'key' primary schools affiliated to universities and two teachers were in typical, ordinary elementary schools. Key schools generally require very high standards from their teachers.

Methods of data collection

The researchers carried out 'non-participant' observation using a checklist and they also audio-recorded the talk in the classrooms. Each teacher's lessons were recorded for seven weeks. During this time, the four teachers used the same thematic units, following procedures according to their normal daily teaching practices. Each teacher was observed and recorded four times and this produced 16 hours of classroom data. After the observations, semi-structured interviews were also conducted in order to gain deeper insights into their views about target language use. The following open-ended questions were used to allow freedom of expression:

1. What do you think about the feasibility of using only the TL for teaching?
2. Do you usually use the same words for classroom organisation?
3. How do you pay attention to the accuracy of your TL use in class?
4. What factors do you think may influence your effective use of English in class?

The children in the targeted classrooms all filled in questionnaires about their attitudes towards their teacher's use of English. The first seven questions concerned students' after-class English learning environment and the other eight questions concerned students' perceptions of their teachers' target language use. The questionnaire was piloted with 20 students before the study began.

Sample data 5.13   Peng and Zhang (2009: 227): the children's questionnaire (adapted)

1. *Do you like English classes?*
A. Yes, very much   B. Yes   C. Don't care   D. No   E. Not at all

2. *Do you spend a lot of time learning English?*
A. Yes, very much   B. Yes   C. Don't care   D. No   E. Not at all

3. *Have you got some tools for learning English such as computers or an MP3 player?*
A. Yes   B. No

4. *Have you got someone at home who can help you learning English?*
A. Yes   B. No

5. *How much do you understand your teacher when she is speaking English?*
A. Almost all of it   B. The majority of it   C. Half of it   D. A small part of it
E. Barely anything

6. *What do you think about the amount of English your teachers use in the class?*
A. Too little   B. A little   C. Just right   D. Quite a lot   E. Too much

7. *If the teacher uses a lot of verbal or non-verbal aids (such as repetition, miming, sketches) to help you understand English, how much can you understand?*
A. Almost all of it   B. The majority of it   C. Half of it   D. A small part of it
E. Barely anything

A questionnaire was also designed for 50 more teachers in the district. These responses were important in order to triangulate the results from the small-scale observation study. In this questionnaire the first 15 questions targeted the teachers' professional background and teaching contexts, and the second 15 questions targeted their English language use and attitudes to it.

Data analysis and findings

The following sample data box indicates the percentages for each teacher in terms of their target language use calculated from the audio-recording. A total time of 160 minutes was based on four recorded classes lasting 40 minutes for each teacher.

Sample data 5.14   Peng and Zhang (2009: 217): Total TL use
in minutes and percentages

These minutes and percentages are calculated taking the total talking time as 100
per cent. The low numbers indicate that there was a great deal of silent activity in
many of these classes.

Teachers	Class 1	Class 2	Class 3	Class 4	Mean
A	10 (90%)	8 (82%)	6 (82%)	7 (80%)	8 (83%)
B	11 (92%)	11 (94%)	10 (90%)	11 (93%)	11 (92%)
C	4 (62%)	4 (70%)	5 (68%)	5 (87%)	5 (71%)
D	5 (66%)	4 (63%)	5 (71%)	4 (59%)	5 (64%)

Teachers A and B used mainly English in their classes whereas teachers C and
D used less English. In the interviews, when asked about the feasibility of
using English only, all teachers expressed worries about students' frustration,
high anxiety levels and the difficulty of explaining grammar in L2. They also
mentioned that using the L2 may lead to losing control over the class and too
much time might be wasted when non-understanding occurs. From the 50
questionnaires 'only 20% of the respondents reported that more than 80%
of their talk was in English, and 42% admitted that they used English less
than 60% of their total teacher talk, while 12% of the respondents reported
their TL using was less than 20%' (Peng and Zhang 2009: 218).

Interestingly, the student questionnaires indicated that the students did
not think sufficient TL was used in any of these classes. More than 60 per
cent in each class reported that their teachers' use of TL was scarce. Even
in the case of the teacher who used mostly English (Teacher B), only 5 per
cent of the class believed that their teacher 'often' used English. No student
thought that the target language use by their teacher was too much.

Sample data 5.15   Peng and Zhang (2009: 218): students'
questionnaires, assessment of their teachers' TL use

Students	Too little	A little	Just right	Quite a lot	Too much
Teacher A's class	15%	52%	29%	2%	2%
Teacher B's class	27%	43%	25%	5%	0%
Teacher C's class	17%	53%	25%	2%	3%
Teacher D's class	15%	51%	23%	9%	2%

According to this table there is a sharp contrast between children's and teachers' views.

Quote 5.14   On the differences between learners' and teacher's opinions

...the four observed teachers believed that too much English tended to make their students more anxious and frustrated. Also, they thought it could be a waste of time if teachers could not make themselves understood. Thus their TL use was sometimes followed by Chinese explanations, or they chose to switch to Chinese and continue in the mother tongue. However, according to the students' feedback, the four teachers may have underestimated students' comprehension level as well as the ability to accept new things.

(Peng and Zhang 2009: 219)

The teachers' recordings were further analysed for language functions (differentiating between academic and social functions). Social discourse, i.e. real communication between students and teacher, was rare. A great deal of the talk was IRF-based.

Concept 5.10   IRF (initiation, response and feedback)

IRF is a specific discourse pattern observed in many language classrooms. The teacher is in complete control of the discourse and the questions are largely display type. Originally described by Sinclair and Coulthard (1975).

Initiation (T):   What's the capital of France?
Response (S):   Paris.
Feedback (T):   Yes, that's right.
Initiation (T):   What....?

Quote 5.15   On the results of the study

The results of the study revealed that there was considerable variation in the amount of teachers' TL use. For most of the teachers, the amount of TL use was not more than 60% of their talk. This may not be sufficient for students' foreign language learning. Furthermore, from the viewpoint of pragmatics, teachers' TL use was not varied enough and was often found inappropriate. The findings of the study indicate that the current use of TL in FL classes of elementary schools in the observed classes is far from satisfactory.

(Peng and Zhang 2009: 212)

Consider the restrictive nature of the following interaction between a teacher and a learner taken from one of these classes:

Sample data 5.16   Peng and Zhang (2009: 221)

Excerpt 4
Teacher D practising a structure

  T: Are you from England?
Ss: No!
  T: Are you from China?
Ss: Yes, I am (together with the teacher)
  T: Ok, follow me. Yes, I am.
Ss: Yes, I am.
  T: Yes, I am.
Ss: Yes, I am.
  T: Are you from China? (to one student)
  S: Yes, I am.
  T: Good.

Discussion

The results of this study are relevant for teacher development courses. Primary language teachers' awareness about effective TL use in the English classes must be raised. This study also illustrates that there may be differences between learners' and teachers' perceptions and that it is important for teachers to seek learners' views on all aspects of teaching and learning.

This study also illustrates the researcher's paradox very clearly. Researchers who observe teachers' classes may not actually be presented with reality, but instead they see an 'elevated' reality. It is argued that the researcher's presence leads to this distortion. The fact that the students' responses were so different from the teachers' responses indicates that such a researcher effect may have played a role here. In particular, if the teachers understood the research focus, they may have used more target language input during the observation period than they would usually have done.

Some questions arise about the data analysis. It is particularly striking that 10 minutes out of 40 minutes represents 90 per cent of the talk. Consequently, for the most part of the lesson the teacher is not actually talking at all. This either means that students are working silently and independently, or collaboratively in pairs or groups. It would be important too for the researchers to describe what was happening in these lessons when the teachers were not talking. It is also not quite clear how the target language utterances were coded. When code-mixing was used, for example, how was that calculated in terms of minutes and percentages of target language use?

Questions also arise about the teacher participants. For example, how were they selected? Were they volunteers, in which case they probably represent the most motivated and committed teachers among their colleagues. There is also an issue here with the researchers' status. Were they seen as colleagues or as authority figures? Potentially, this kind of research can expose teachers, by comparing them and pointing to the weak areas of their practice, and this can be problematic from an ethical point of view. A further question arises whether the four lessons were actually sufficient to come to these conclusions. Were these teachers following a/the book? To what extent was the resulting discourse a direct effect of the materials that the teachers were obliged to follow very closely? If they were all following the same book, the striking similarities in the discourse that emerge are not surprising.

5.2.8 Case study 8 Devlieger and Goossens (2007): focus on teachers

Introduction

This paper is part of a large-scale evaluation study exploring primary teachers' task-based language teaching practices in Brussels, Belgium. It focusses on the development of a particular assessment tool to help teachers implement language tasks effectively. It may be a suitable model for you, if you are interested in developing tools for teacher development purposes.

Background

Some schools in Brussels use French while others use Dutch as the medium of instruction. Most schools are multicultural and multilingual and Dutch is an L2 for many learners. The local Priority Policy Brussels organisation (PPB) supports local schools to adopt a task-based approach to Dutch language teaching across the curriculum to assist the learning of Dutch. The Centre for Language and Education (of the Catholic University of Leuven) was asked to conduct a longitudinal research study into the impact of this PPB support. This study is a snapshot of one particular aspect of the large-scale evaluation study.

Aims of the study

The study aimed to assess to what extent the teachers were translating the PPB input into observable classroom behaviour. Many teachers who were video-taped at the beginning of the PPB support were videoed again three years later. In order to evaluate the differences, the researchers were trying to construct an assessment tool that enabled them to objectively compare teacher behaviours.

Quote 5.16   On the need for the evaluation grid

The evaluation grid had to enable the researchers to compare actual classroom practice with 'ideal' teacher behaviour as spelled out from a task-based

---

Quote 5.16   (Continued)

perspective (i.e. the kind of task-based teacher behaviour the PPB counsellors were trying to promote). This called for the development of a standard of good task-based teacher practice, which meant translating the theoretical PPB framework of task-based language education into objectively observable parameters of teacher practice.

(Devlieger and Goossens 2007: 95)

Developing the grid

The first step was to make explicit the criteria underlying high-quality teacher behaviour. The researchers asked the PPB counsellors to write a report about optimal teacher behaviour during task-based teaching. This report was then combined with other sources from the literature recommended by the PPB. The end-product was a 'three circles' diagram. In this diagram, the outer circle represents a positive, safe environment. The middle circle represents using meaningful and relevant tasks. These tasks contain a bridgeable gap between students' current language levels and the task demands. The third, innermost, circle represents interactional support. During the task performances the teacher is available to provide interactional support but also makes it possible for learners to provide support for one another. In order to develop this basic grid further, the researchers had to translate these principles into observable teacher behaviours. Inspired by a similar framework developed for nursery classes by Verhelst and van den Branden (1999), a detailed framework was proposed:

Sample data 5.17   Devlieger and Goossens (2007: 99): the main indicators

1. **Establishing a safe class climate (outer circle)**
   1.1 classroom arrangement (children facing one another, eye contact)
   1.2 classroom management (children know what is expected of them)
   1.3 well-being (respectful, positive, calm)
   1.4 language climate (teacher does not oblige children to speak)

2. **Providing meaningful tasks (middle circle)**
   2.1 objectives
   2.2 motivation and commitment to the learning process
   2.3 language input and output
   2.4 organisational format

3. **Supporting pupils interactively (inner circle)**
   3.1 mediation
   3.2 construction and negotiation of meaning
   3.3 differentiation

Once these indicators were agreed, a rating scale had to be developed to use the above assessment grid with teachers in classrooms to measure behaviour. The researchers proposed five categories for rating each behaviour.

Sample data 5.18   Devlieger and Goossens (2007: 100): rating principles

(++) Good practice (positive teacher behaviour and actions occur systematically, no negative behaviours).

(+) On its way to good practice (positive teacher behaviour occurs regularly, negative behaviours are rare).

(+/−) A first step in the direction of good practice (mainly positive behaviours and negative behaviours occur only once or twice).

(−) Far from good practice (positive behaviours do not occur where they should but instead negative actions are frequent).

(?) Behaviour or actions are not observable during the observation or are seen far too rarely to be evaluated.

Extensive trials using videoed lessons followed and the raters worked towards a shared interpretation of the tool. During this process the tool was refined, items were rewritten and some items were excluded. The aim was to develop a tool that all users could interpret in a consistent manner.

Using the assessment tool in real classrooms

The paper discusses in detail how two real task-based classrooms were rated using just three criteria from the grid. The two classrooms that were contrasted were those of Mr Jones and Mrs White. The three indicators used were (1) well-being, (2) language input and output and (3) teacher mediation. Overall Mr Jones scored higher than Mrs White and he was thus labelled as the teacher who was putting task-based teaching into practice more consistently. For example, according to the seven indicators used for describing 'well-being' in class, Mr Jones scored much higher than Mrs White, gaining several ++ marks because he was supportive, patient and flexible with the children, while the second teacher was more rigid and directive.

With regard to the second criterion, language input and output, there are again five indicators to assess.

Sample data 5.19   Devlieger and Goossens (2007: 108): indicators of meaningful tasks

2.   Meaningful tasks
2.3.   Language input and output
2.3.1. T uses natural language; it relates to the experiences of the children

---

Sample data 5.19   (Continued)

2.3.2.   T provides varied language input without much simplification and using a variety of resources
2.3.3.   T promotes the children's academic language proficiency
2.3.4.   T uses interactive language, offers opportunities for output; she asks open-ended questions and extends children's output further
2.3.5.   T makes children use language in a meaningful way, as a means to an end; children formulate opinions, experiences and insights

---

The last indicator looked at the teacher's mediating behaviours according to the following five criteria:

1. T responds to children who have a problem.
2. T attempts to identify children's problems proactively.
3. T gives children opportunities to actively search for solutions and think for themselves.
4. T provides feedback to the children about their learning processes.
5. T provides feedback on the way the children work together.

The following extract illustrates how Mr Jones is getting the children to work out an answer by helping them to narrow down the focus:

Sample data 5.20   Devlieger and Goossens (2007: 111)

T: What do you have, you think?
       (The pupil does not respond)
T: When did we use that map?
P: To read the compass.
T: Yes, but mainly for something else....
       (The pupil does not respond)
T: I am going to show you.
       The teacher takes the map and unfolds it.
T: When did we use this map in particular? For our walk to..
P: .. the tunnel.

Overall, Mr Jones was scoring higher on all these indicators, which meant the instrument was able to describe better teacher behaviour in an objective criterion-referenced manner.

Reflecting on the design of the instrument

Altogether, the instrument contained 51 items and it took the researchers two full months to design it based on the analysis of approximately 80 hours of lessons from 36 different teachers. Some indicators were more difficult to rate than others. It was noticed that question marks were used by raters in an ambiguous way. Sometimes they indicated a lack of behaviour and sometimes a problem with the instrument.

Quote 5.17   On difficulties in analysis

Obviously, the boundaries between different items and indicators are highly artificial. Actions that the teacher takes at one level of the three circles are intrinsically entwined with the other two levels.

(Devlieger and Goossens 2007: 115)

A number of items always received question marks because to a certain extent this depended on the kind of lessons that the teachers were delivering.

The outcome

Although not without faults, the instrument was effective to the extent that it helped the researchers to compare teacher behaviours, enabled the researchers to draw differentiated conclusions concerning the impact of the PPB coaching and it also allowed them to make further recommendations for the next phase of the PPB support programme. Some items showed wide discrepancies among teachers. For example, many teachers did not implement small group work and the assessment also revealed poor transfer from PPB.

Quote 5.18   On the usefulness of the instrument

Evidently, individual teachers cannot live up to every single item in the instrument, nor can PPB coaches be expected to fill out the whole of the instrument during a single classroom observation. Nevertheless, the instrument helps coaches to detect which aspects of individual teacher's practices come close to their ideal of task-based language teaching and which aspects can still be improved. The formulation of the indicators and items suggest concrete ways in which this can be achieved.

(Devlieger and Goossens 2007: 119)

Discussion

The pedagogical implications of this study are broadly applicable to all task-based classrooms. The researchers handed over the instrument to headmasters and teachers but also returned them back to PPB coaches so that they could re-use them as observational tools. Having a concrete instrument, it is easier to grasp what task-based learning may mean in practice.

196 *Children Learning Second Languages*

This paper illustrates the multiple ways in which research, theory and practice interact and promote our understanding of task-based language learning. Note that task-based language learning was introduced in this context because of the convincing theoretical and research findings suggesting that it helps learners to develop language more effectively than do traditional methods. However, there was a clear need to translate these rather fuzzy theoretical ideas into tangible criteria that were observable and learnable by teachers in classrooms. So, one way to look at the assessment instrument is that it mediates between research, theory and practice and helps to achieve an understanding between researchers and their interpretations of task-based teaching and teacher's actions. At the same time, using the two classrooms as examples (Mr Jones's and Mrs White's), the researchers illustrate that the instruments can also be used to gather research data for further analysis and interpretation and/or to evaluate teachers' performance.

Since we, the readers, do not have access to the observational data or the original videotapes, we have to take the analysis of the two lessons on trust. One issue is that there are perhaps rather too many criteria, too many indicators (this is mentioned by the authors, too) and some of them do overlap. In fact the list is so long that it is difficult to see to what extent this only applies to task-based learning and teaching and to what extent it goes beyond tasks and describes classrooms in more general terms. Were the teachers aware of the range of indicators and if yes, were they perhaps a bit put off by them? Knowing that one has to fulfil so many criteria for so many descriptors may make the actual process of teaching impossibly difficult. The list of descriptors is also largely prescriptive in nature and this suggests that there is one specific way to do task-based teaching well. The grading principles are hard to use and they seem very 'black and white' in the way they claim everything in the classroom represents either positive or negative behaviour.

Notwithstanding these critical remarks, it is a good example of a project where the researcher is interested in developing, piloting and evaluating tools and learning materials.

5.3 Conclusion

These eight studies all represent types of research that you might like to replicate or use as an initial idea before developing your own unique interest. All these studies have clear implications for classroom practice in terms of what teachers in other contexts can learn from them. Some implications refer to what teachers might want to try and do (e.g. elicit/teach a range of different language functions to young L2 learners) or what approaches they may implement (e.g. a task-based approach based on a list of observable criteria), or what they may learn about their students' preferences and opinions. In fact, all studies here were selected because their basic motivation was to provide useful information for language classrooms of children.

All eight studies also function as individual building blocks in contributing to creating new knowledge. Whatever was discovered (e.g. that Taiwanese learners do not seem to use certain learning strategies or learners do not correct mistakes that are pointed out to them) will add to our accumulating knowledge about learning and teaching languages in primary classrooms. These findings will be vitally important to researchers who want to pursue their study in these content areas.

Several cycles of research and practice can be evident in a single study. For example, in case study 8, the motivation to construct an assessment tool is underlined a by a practical need. The actual items in the assessment tool are constructed based on features drawn from research but also from practice, i.e. the designers' extensive experience. The lengthy process of standardising this instrument involves negotiations among the members of the team but also practical trials with real classroom data. The tool that finally emerges is used to evaluate teacher behaviour, but in the future it may become a research tool, leading to further empirical data and knowledge building.

It seems that many questions arise about all the studies that were discussed here. In fact, no matter what type of research project or area of research we select, whether it is experimental or ethnographic, whether we work with large numbers of participants or small groups, or individuals, perfection will always elude us. Every research project will have some inherent shortcomings and it is always possible to ask critical questions. So, what is the value of research then? Why is it important? Research engages us in thinking about issues underlying our practice. Before we embark on our study we have to study other people's work and this creates useful links between our practice and research and other people's practice and research. Research also helps us to focus our mind on one specific question at a time without distractions while it encourages us to consider different alternative solutions. Research also drives our understanding about language learning forward in a cumulative way. Being familiar with a wide variety of research can sharpen our views and teaches us to take a questioning stance. Yet, through coming to appreciate the complexities of learning in language classrooms, we can become more measured and more careful about our judgment, decisions and opinions, both as teachers and researchers.

The next two chapters will consider possible future projects which can build on the types of approaches presented here. Chapter 6 considers issues related to methodology and ethics and Chapter 7 presents 15 feasible projects as a starting point for practitioners.

Part III

Issues in Future Research and Practice

6
Exploring Ethical and Methodological Issues in Research with Children

This chapter will

- discuss how children are different from adults as research subjects and participants
- discuss combined issues and dilemmas of methodology and research ethics in child-focussed research
- outline some ethical/methodological challenges in planned research projects

6.1 Introduction

Chapters 4 and 5 have already illustrated a range of methodological difficulties in studies with children of different ages. In particular, the use of different de-contextualised tests and tasks was highlighted as a potential risk in research. Methodological challenges are closely linked to ethical issues in child research and this chapter will aim to highlight some common difficulties and possible solutions.

When you decide to embark on a research project involving children, you may be reminded of the commonly held view that child subjects are less reliable, more problematic and less willing to participate than adult volunteer participants. Consider, for example, the following quote from Lewis (1992) summarising methodological difficulties with regard to interviewing children:

Quote 6.1 On the problems of interviewing children

...impediments to reliability include children's distractability, memory limitations, over-attention to certain perceptual features in the situation (Donaldson 1978), desire to give some sort of response however nonsensical (Hughes and Grieve 1980), susceptibility to leading questions from an adult because of the

---

Quote 6.1   (Continued)

adult's social status (Spencer and Flin 1990), willingness to be dishonest in some conditions (Ceci 1991), and receptive and expressive language limitations.

(Lewis 1992: 417)

If children are such difficult research subjects, what steps can we take to ensure that we gain useful data from them and how do we make them feel comfortable, able and willing to contribute? How can we ensure that our research data is 'authentic', and reflects the children's best ability? How do we have to alter our research tools to make them suitable for children of different age groups?

6.2   The researcher's own conception of childhood

Underlying all research are the researcher's own beliefs and assumptions about children and childhood. You, as a researcher engaged in projects with children, will have to think about how your own understanding and conception of 'childhood' and 'children' will influence the way you approach children, the way you talk to them and the kinds of roles and responsibilities you may assign to them.

Quote 6.2   On the researcher's underlying beliefs

... the research process is inevitably a product of the relationship forged between the researcher and the research participants and will therefore ultimately reflect the decisions made and approaches taken by the researcher as well as the particular responses adopted by the participants to these.

(Connolly 2008: 174)

Alderson (2005: 30) suggests that the particular model of childhood held by the researcher will influence all aspects of research from planning to analysing and interpreting the research data. Some popular and widely held models include: 'the innocent child' who needs protection, the 'ignorant child' who needs education, the 'badly behaved' child who needs adult control and the 'strong, resourceful child' who can work with adults towards solving problems and generating new ideas. Many other models can be constructed and it is also possible to combine features of different models. One important factor in the construction of these models is the degree of agency given to children. The first three models imply that researchers should not give too much space, control and responsibility to children because they are unable to handle it. It is only the last model that suggests that children are able to take control and responsibility, and while their thoughts and ideas may be different from adults', they are nonetheless important contributors to research with their own judgments.

This last model, embracing children's active participation in research has gained a great deal of ground recently and it proposes that we can learn an enormous amount from children when we listen to their voices and perspectives about second language learning processes and practices. Children might have a different emphasis or a different view compared to adults, such as their teachers or their parents, but the model suggests that their point of view is worth taking into account even if it seems puzzling or unusual at first sight.

Quote 6.3   On children's views being different from adults' views

... researchers need to set aside natural adult tendencies such as to take children for granted and to accord them a provisional status. The belief that children are inherently 'wrong' when they disagree with adults is an obstacle to be overcome.

(Fine and Sandstrom 1988: 75–6)

Whatever model of childhood is held by the particular researcher, it is important to keep in mind that all adults inevitably represent power and authority in children's eyes. This power gap is unavoidable even if children are invited to be active participants in research projects. Mayall describes the 'power gap' as the central characteristic of the relationship between adults and children:

Quote 6.4   On the power gap between adults and children

In order to get good data, children are to be taught by the researcher that power issues between children and adult can be diluted or defused to the point where children accept the adult as one of themselves, but according to my information from children, they think otherwise: a central characteristic of adults is that they have power over children.

(Mayall 2008: 110)

One of the most important tasks of the researcher at the planning stage is to think about the implications of this power distance, and if necessary, to take steps to reduce the gap by spending time with the children, getting to know them, by reassuring them about the focus of the research and by respecting their voices.

Related to the researcher's conception of childhood, according to Alderson (2005: 29–30) there are essentially three different ways in which children can become research subjects:

Children as unknowing objects
In this case children involved in the research project may be generally unaware of the research focus and may not have even been asked for their consent. This approach is described as completely adult-dominated research for adult interests. In the past this was very much the only way research with children was conducted.

Children as adult-controlled subjects
In this case children are subjects who have been asked for their consent and they would have been briefed about the research but they essentially agree to participate in a rigid adult-focussed study. This category comprises the majority of the studies in child SLA research.

Children as active participants
In this case children are involved as active participants who take part willingly in the research project, which uses some flexible methods of data collection. This is often referred to as 'participatory' research. The assumption is that this kind of research is more fun and relevant to children than surveys and traditional research approaches. According to O'Kane (2008), participatory methods may include the use of drawings, maps, flow diagrams, play, drama, stories or songs. Participatory research gives children agency and some control over the research agenda, and it emphasises the importance of understanding issues from the children's point of view.

Quote 6.5   On children's agency

I argue that the best people to provide information on the child's perspective, actions and attitudes are the children themselves. Children provide reliable responses if questioned about events that are meaningful to their lives.

(J. Scott 2008: 88)

While participatory research with children has been very popular, it is important to acknowledge that this approach is not without disadvantages either. While children can be experts on their own lives, they are not the only experts. Parents', siblings' and teachers' views are often equally important in order to understand children. Some critics of participatory research also argue that this type of research, although presented as child-focussed, is in fact ultimately adult-directed.

Quote 6.6   On the adult influence in participatory research

The very notion of empowerment implies that, without aid and encouragement from adult-designed 'participatory methods', children cannot fully exercise their 'agency' in research encounters. In this way, advocates of 'participatory methods' risk perpetuating the very model that they purport to oppose.

(Gallacher and Gallagher 2008: 503)

Some researchers suggest that research that concerns children should be conducted by children themselves (e.g. Kellett 2005). To this end, children are taught about how to conduct research and then they are free to choose topics to investigate to satisfy their own interests. This is an exciting idea but perhaps not feasible to be widely adopted in most contexts and with all age groups. However, in contexts where children are explicitly taught to develop responsibility for their own language learning, i.e. in autonomous classrooms (e.g. Thomsen 2003), such a research focus might be viable. Thomsen, whose learners are 13-year-olds in Denmark, comments on the importance of learners taking charge of their own learning:

Quote 6.7   On the importance of children taking charge of their own learning

...as in other types of work undertaken, learners themselves chose how to go about learning, with help and suggestions from other learners and the teacher. Learners in this particular class aim in general to become 'good language users and learners', so it is a natural thing for them to feel that they are in charge of their own learning.

(Thomsen 2003: 43)

In Thomsen's classroom, children are active participants, and they are already making decisions about their own learning. As a next step, they would also be able to discuss and decide on a suitable research project that they may want to engage in with their teacher. In a classroom where the learners are 12 to 13 years old and already work within an autonomous framework, handing over some control with regard to planning and implementing a language learning-related project might be possible. This approach however will require high levels of expertise on the teacher's part to facilitate the process, offer help whenever it is needed, and monitor any problems or sensitive issues that may arise.

Considering these different approaches to models of childhood, how do your underlying beliefs and models of childhood influence your project planning? There is not always a simple and straightforward relationship. For example, you may believe that ideally all children should be given responsibility in research and should be empowered, but this is not always possible and not always necessary either. If you are engaging in an experimental type of research project which requires the administration of a particular language test to a large group of children, inevitably, your research is going to fall into the more 'adult-controlled' category. This may be perfectly acceptable because the power relationships and the researcher's beliefs about childhood do not apply here in the same way as they might when you interview children about their thoughts and opinions. The focus of the research is on the actual test scores and the linguistic outcomes rather than on the children's thoughts and ideas. In addition, in some projects there may not be time to devote to developing a special rapport, and you simply cannot bridge the status gap between the researcher and the children. The children will see you as an adult figure of authority. While this is not an ideal situation, it may be acceptable, as long as the researcher acknowledges his/her relationship with the children and carefully considers the effects of this on the results and outcomes. In other situations, however, lack of adequate access to build rapport and develop a relationship will mean that the research project is seriously compromised or may not even be viable.

6.3   Ethics in child-focussed research

All research projects require clearance from an ethics committee and this is true for research with adult subjects as well. In this way, ethics is an integral part of planning any research project. Traditionally, research ethics cover issues such as the participants' rights, in particular, the right to refuse participation or to withdraw from the research without any negative consequences. Ethics also cover basic safeguards to ensure that the participants do not suffer any harm as a result of the research.

Ethical issues in child-related research have become increasingly important over the last decades, and this initiative can be directly traced back to the 'Declaration of Children's Rights' by the *United Nations Convention on the Rights of the Child* (United Nations 1989). This change of focus has brought a much wider recognition of the meaning of 'child protection', going well beyond children's physical protection. It has led to a commitment to displaying greater respect for children as 'equal' members of society and as research participants with their own perspectives.

In different countries there is specific legislation in place to cover the exact procedures that need to be followed when researchers work with children. For example, in the UK, every researcher who wishes to work in a school will need to be issued with a clearance certificate by the Criminal Record Bureau (CRB). The details of ethical guidelines change all the time to reflect the ongoing debate and discussions about 'best practice' in research with child subjects. Rather than a set of rigid rules, research ethics are therefore seen as a set of context-specific guidelines that help the researcher to think about all the challenges a project may present.

Quote 6.8   On research ethics

Ethics is about helping researchers to become aware of hidden problems and questions in research, and ways of dealing with these, though it does not provide simple answers...Ethical standards change and researchers need to be conversant with them. The safeguards of research ethics, such as applying to an REC (Research Ethics Council) for approval, take time but can protect the children who take part in research, and protect researchers from unnecessary criticism or litigation.

(Alderson 2008: 29)

One example of a set of guidelines regarding research with children in the area of second language learning comes from the British Association of Applied Linguistics (BAAL):

Example 6.1   Guidelines regarding issues of research ethics as they apply to children (BAAL)

Research with children
It is possible for even young children to be involved effectively in the planning, conduct and dissemination of research. Care is needed in providing explanations and consulting at all stages of research, including consultation about the outcomes of research.

Informed consent may be obtained even from young children, but researchers need to spend time ensuring children understand, to a degree commensurate with their capacities and interests, what they are agreeing to when they give consent.

For children under 16, consent also needs to be obtained from parents or other adults acting *in loco parentis*.

Children may be in a relatively powerless position vis à vis researchers and other adults: it is important that care is taken to ensure they do not feel under undue pressure to participate in or continue with research; it is also important not to exploit children's enthusiasm, and to ensure they do not undertake activities that may be against their own interests.

Researchers planning to work with children may be required by their institution, or other participating institutions, to obtain Criminal Records Bureau (CRB) clearance – see http://www.crb.gov.uk/. For an example of published guidelines see National Children's Bureau (undated). Other resources include Alderson and Morrow (2004) and Hill (2005).

Notice that the guidelines above emphasise children's active participation in the research process, which is broadly in line with the participatory approaches discussed earlier. It is also stated that children must give consent, must understand the research aims and must not be exploited to satisfy adult interests. The guidelines also send the reader to a government website and suggest reading some relevant literature about current debates and dilemmas in child-focussed research.

Morrow (2005: 151) argues that in the case of children ethical dilemmas are more complex than in adult research because children are both 'vulnerable and incompetent'. Vulnerability implies that children need protection from adults or other children because they are weak, passive and possibly open to physical or psychological abuse. Indeed, if at any point during your research project it comes to your attention that a child is vulnerable, or has been or is being mistreated, or is facing the risk of abuse of any kind, it is your obligation as a researcher to seek help, usually by consulting other responsible adults. This is a particularly important guideline in sensitive topic areas but the need might arise for this kind of protective action in any project. Incompetence implies that children are still only 'becomings' who are not fully developed, knowledgeable or skilful yet, so adults need to take control. Both these concepts, but in particular the idea of vulnerability, are associated with a concern for the safety of children and lead to strict risk management procedures. Risk management and protection however are in direct conflict with the idea of liberating children as research subjects and involving them as active participants in research. This tension will inevitably lead to some difficult dilemmas and decisions in research projects.

Quote 6.9   On tensions in ethics

Just as children's opportunities for participation in research may be declining due to risk management of their lives, so too is there a push towards transformative opportunities that seek to increase their engagement in research.

(Farrell 2005: 166)

Another dilemma concerns consent. If children's own views and opinions are respected, it is not sufficient to ask their parents' and teachers' permission when it comes to participation in any kind of research project. So, how do we approach the issue of consent with children? While this seems straightforward at first sight, many complex questions are unresolved, for example, what to do when children refuse consent but parents agree or when parents refuse and the children agree? Another question concerns the age at which children may be ready/sufficiently competent to consent at all.

Quote 6.10   On child consent

When are children competent enough to consent? This depends on each child's relevant experience, confidence, the type of research, and the researcher's skill. Standardized tests of competence tend to set unduly high thresholds that many children and some adults fail to reach. Instead, competence to consent to research can be assessed by asking children what they understand about the project and about their rights.

(Alderson 2005: 34)

McNaughton and Smith (2005: 114) further suggest that researchers need to check whether children are willingly participating in the research project and they need to present some sort of evidence for this. For example, it may be possible to ask children to talk about their understanding of what the project is about, using their own words. It is a good idea to create private and individual spaces for children to discuss questions and agree to participate in your project so that other children don't influence their responses.

In order to cover the most important aspects of ethical research and to highlight any dilemmas and how they will be dealt with, researchers working with children will have to fill in an ethical clearance form before they can embark on their project. This example is taken from the website of the Institute of Education in the University of Warwick in the UK.

Example 6.2   Ethical clearance form for postgraduate students engaging in research

Methodology
Please outline the methodology e.g. observation, individual interviews, focus groups, group testing etc.

Participants
Please specify all participants in the research including ages of children and young people where appropriate. Also specify if any participants are vulnerable e.g. children, as a result of learning disability.

Respect for participants' rights and dignity
How will the fundamental rights and dignity of participants be respected, e.g. confidentiality, respect for cultural and religious values?

Privacy and confidentiality
How will confidentiality be assured? Please address all aspects of research including protection of data records, thesis, reports/papers that might arise from the study.

Example 6.2 (Continued)

Consent

- will prior informed consent be obtained?
- from participants? Yes/No   from others? Yes/No
- explain how this will be obtained. If prior informed consent is not to be obtained, give reason:
- will participants be explicitly informed of the student's status?

Competence

How will you ensure that all methods used are undertaken with the necessary competence?

Protection of participants

How will participants' safety and well-being be safeguarded?

Child protection

Will a CRB check be needed?   Yes/No   (If yes, please attach a copy.)

Addressing dilemmas

Even well planned research can produce ethical dilemmas. How will you address any ethical dilemmas that may arise in your research?

Misuse of research

How will you seek to ensure that the research and the evidence resulting from it are not misused?

Support for research participants

What action is proposed if sensitive issues are raised or a participant becomes upset?

Integrity

How will you ensure that your research and its reporting are honest, fair and respectful to others?
What agreement has been made for the attribution of authorship by yourself and your supervisor(s) of any reports or publications?

Other issues?

Please specify other issues not discussed above, if any, and how you will address them.

Notice that although the same form is used for all research projects (adult or child), specific questions are included about children. Researchers are encouraged to think about the vulnerability of their subjects: they are reminded that they need to safeguard their research subjects and support them to avoid negative outcomes. They are also reminded to obtain the government mandated CRB certificate and to disclose any anticipated ethical dilemmas. The very first question is about the methodology, which signals that initial decisions about methodology are closely related to issues in research ethics and it is best to think about these two issues at the same time.

Gaining access to the children could be a lengthy process, especially if many gatekeepers are involved such as university ethics councils, parents, child protection organisations and local education authorities. Researchers need to be aware that gaining access may take time and also be prepared to accept that aspects of the research may need to be changed following advice from research ethics councils. It is always advisable to have an alternative plan.

6.4 Methodological concerns: gaining data from children

6.4.1 Research contexts

The context in which the research tasks are administered, or where research conversations between the researcher and the children take place, is crucially important. It is quite different for a child to interact with a researcher in the playground (which is considered more the children's home territory) as opposed to a formal classroom or the headteacher's office. Where exactly the data collection is carried out will influence the way children respond. For example, in the case of interviews, some researchers have used home interviews as opposed to school-based interviews on the grounds that at school children are likely to be influenced by the proximity of their classmates. As Scott suggests, 'even if answers are supposedly confidential, children are likely to quiz one another on their responses and may be tempted to give answers that win favour with the peer group' (J. Scott 2008: 93). On the other hand, interviewing at home is more costly and time-consuming and because of the rest of the family present, it is often impractical.

Although most research involving children normally takes place on school premises, some researchers raise questions about school-based research:

Quote 6.11   On the problems of school-based research

In schools the balance of power is heavily skewed towards adults, and children are least able to exercise participation rights. Adults control children's use of time, occupation of space, choice of clothing, times of eating – even their mode of social interaction. So how does this impact on the nature and outcomes of school-based research?

(Robinson and Kellett 2004: 91)

When a research project is conducted at school, children may think that the research task is a test, and as such it may count towards their formal assessment. This may make them reluctant to speak up or be critical in any way. Class routines, such as teachers nominating those who are allowed to speak, may also interfere with the researchers' intentions when inviting children to contribute ideas freely to a discussion. Children know that most tasks and questions at school have a right or wrong answer and they have this same expectation when they participate in research. Careful briefing about what is expected of them is necessary. If this applies to your research, you may want to prepare a list of guidelines and expectations to discuss with the children. Once these guidelines are developed, you can display them on a poster so that everyone can be reminded of these during the research process.

Example 6.3   Poster showing 'Agreed rules for group interviews in our class'

- *We will listen to everybody and take note of all the views*
- *We will not use names to identify different children when we speak about events*
- *We will never mock each other or laugh at each other's views*
- *We can stay silent if we have no opinion or cannot think of anything to say*
- *We can contribute more than one idea at a time*
- *Other?*

6.4.2   Working with groups or individuals

One-to-one conversations with a researcher are often difficult for children. Recall that in Lamb's (2003) research, discussed in Chapter 4, many of the participants felt uncomfortable when being interviewed by the researcher even though they were 12–13 years old. Talking to children in groups is one way of alleviating unnecessary stress, anxiety or feelings of embarrassment. Children are more relaxed when interviewed in groups (Lewis 1992; Eder 1995; Fingerson 1999) because there is safety in being with familiar peers and outnumbering the adults. Being together gives children confidence and they are less intimidated in a group. In some sense group discussions will reveal a great deal more than individual interviews as children build on each other's talk and discuss a wider range of experiences. Tagging on to each other's ideas may indicate the importance of those ideas. A further advantage is that those who are not speaking are having time to think and thus they become more reflective. Being part of a bigger group may make it easier for children to question the interviewer, seek clarification, or express uncertainty. If the group interview is conducted in friendship groups, the children's talk is likely to be more indicative of naturally occurring discourse (Albrecht, Johnson and Walther 1993). This implies that rather than just responding with short sentences to the researchers' questions, in friendship groups children will begin to produce longer utterances, tell stories and anecdotes and use language naturally, as they would with friends, focussing on issues that seem important and meaningful to them.

It is important to think about the composition of these groups. Spencer and Flin (1990) suggest that children tend to give much fuller responses to questions in situations where they are allowed to sit next to someone they like. Friendship groups where individuals feel free to express their differences of opinion but trust one another work best. The size of the group is important, too. Smaller groups are more likely to encourage participation of all children, especially if the physical arrangements are appropriate. Hartup (1978: 418) also reminds us that gender, personality, age, ability as perceived by oneself, others and the teachers, attainments, attractiveness, popularity, friendship patterns and sibling relationships all have a bearing on the types of responses generated in group interviews. It is important to think carefully about how the children will be grouped for possible interviews or discussions. If the research project involves children from different year groups, it is important to make sure that older children do not dominate. In some contexts boys and girls may be interviewed separately as they have such different communication styles (J. Scott 2008: 100).

In one of the case studies in the previous chapter (case study 6), Nagy (2009) pointed out that the children she worked with were more confident and able to respond because they were in a group. Being in a group also helped the children to construct meaningful responses to the questions posed by the researcher. The researcher argues that had the children been left to answer on an individual basis, they might have panicked and might have stayed silent. Pair interviews also work well. Two children can also support one another, in a way similar to the group interviews.

Quote 6.12   On pair interviews with children

I asked a child to choose a friend. This social context did seem to be supportive and enabling. At ease with each other, and thereby perhaps more confident with the third, adult participant, children could follow on each other's leads, pick up points and confirm, comment or move on.

(Mayall 2008: 112)

6.4.3 'Child-friendly' research instruments

Researchers will have to think carefully about the linguistic demands their research instruments impose on children. Language considerations apply to all research tools, including testing instruments, tasks, and interviews, discussions and questionnaires of all kinds.

Quote 6.13   On the lack of understanding between researcher and child

The researcher has to communicate the nature of the problem to the child. If, however, the child does not share the experimenter's understanding of the words being used, then a failure to complete the task might well be due to a breakdown in communication rather than the child's inability to reason appropriately.

(Kellett and Ding 2004: 163)

In addition to the common emphasis on adults producing questions and instructions that children do not understand, Punch (2002) reminds us that the language challenge can be mutual.

Quote 6.14   On mutual language difficulties between adults and children

In any research with adults or children, when forming research tools and questions, clarity of language is vital. However, adult researchers tend to be more conscious of their use of language in research with children. This stems from adult perceptions of children as non-competent (Mahon *et al.* 1996), or as having 'limitations of language and lack of articulateness' (Ireland and Holloway 1996: 156). Younger children may have a more limited vocabulary, but equally they may use different language which adults do not understand. Thus the language dilemma is mutual.

(Punch 2002: 328)

The language the children need to understand and respond to (either in their L1 or L2) will have to be planned as much as possible. Ideally, children's stronger language (L1) should be used in research instruments when researchers construct instructions and explanations. Sometimes bilingual instructions may be given and children can select whichever language they want to use (L1 or L2), for example in an interview. This may be necessary when the researcher is working with bilingual children and cannot be sure which language individual children might select. Sometimes, the researcher may not have a choice and has to rely on the child's L2 when conducting a research study. This may be a serious limitation in some cases where the child's L2 competence is limited.

When eliciting young children's views, questionnaires may be altogether unsuitable. When children are presented with a set of instructions to compose responses to open questions and/or tick responses that best describe their own opinions and feelings, they may be unable to work out the intentions behind questions and to judge the amount of information required. Younger children also find it difficult to distinguish between what is said and what is meant and thus almost any hypothetical question is problematic (Robinson 1986). However, questionnaires can be made more child-friendly by including visual elements. These will clarify/simplify meaning and at the same time reduce the pressure of reading and writing. Consider the simplicity of the questionnaire adapted from Ionnou-Georgiou and Pavlou (2003):

Example 6.4   Sample questionnaire adapted from Ionnou-Georgiou and Pavlou (2003: 117)

Name:......... Unit............. Date:.........

How well did I do in this unit?

	Very well	OK	Not so well
I can say what things I have got			
I can say things I have not got			
I can ask my friend 'Have you got a ?'			
I know when to say 'yes I have' or 'No, I have not'.			
I can count from 1 to 20 in English			
I played the game on page 38.			
I liked the song			
I liked the game.			

For slightly older children a simple modification of adult-like question formats may be sufficient. For example, the standard Likert scale can be turned into a choice between (1) 'do you agree' or (2) 'disagree' and then a separate question can be used to probe for the intensity of the feeling. Writing at length in response to open questions will be both difficult and boring and thus open questions should be avoided. To help children further, questionnaires may be administered personally, which means that the researcher/teacher is present while the children are tackling the questions. This gives the adult the opportunity to monitor the children, spot any confusion, and clarify any misunderstandings or problems.

For younger children, especially, in order to put them at ease, it may be possible to place the research task within a larger, familiar activity (Tammivaara and Enright 1986). You may want to think about embedding interviews into everyday activities such as 'show and tell', 'circle time', or other regular activities that the children are used to. Interviews can also be embedded in games such as 'Telling stories', 'Let's pretend' or 'Act out'. In these contexts children feel free to speak their minds, assume roles, and imitate both real and imaginary characters. Role plays, for example, can be particularly enlightening, as we saw in Gardner and Yaacob's study (2007) in Chapter 4.

In interviews, the researcher needs to be careful to ground the questions in the discourse of the children. There may be words and phrases that the children are not familiar with or certain ways of probing and questioning may be too threatening and linguistically unusual to the children. Some researchers believe that less structured methods of interviewing are more appropriate (e.g. Mayall 2008) because this gives children a chance to relax and contribute points that they see as relevant. There is less chance for language problems to occur.

Quote 6.15   On the use of less structured interviewing

...though these discussions (with the children) were initiated by me, they were not very different in character (perhaps a little more focussed) from conversations I heard around the classroom and the corridors. The children were working through points, elaborating, confirming, opposing and diverging.... Talking with friends is an important way of acquiring knowledge, so for the researcher listening to conversations can be one means of learning about this process.

(Mayall 2008: 114)

Just as in the case of questionnaires, in interview situations it may be possible to support children with visual clues. Visual stimuli make questions and issues more concrete than verbal representations alone. For example, in a study by Pinter (2007), Hungarian children were interviewed about their L2 task performances in pairs. Before the interview began, all the pictures and prompts were placed in front of the children to help them recall their experiences with the tasks.

Quote 6.16   On the use of visual prompts during interviewing children

During the interview, to focus the discussion, they (the children) all watched some of the videotape of their first and last performances in English on both tasks. They also had the original pictures in front of them to help them recall their task performances and the experiences they had. . . . the aim was not to recall the children's moment-by-moment cognitive processes but rather help them contextualise the interview questions and to bring their views and opinions to the surface. The intention was that these concrete reminders would trigger children's thoughts and feelings to start the discussions.

(Pinter 2007: 138–9)

Another technique that works well is the so-called 'bounded recall'. This means that the researcher uses events like Christmas, school terms and birthdays to establish a period of time. For example, rather than asking 'Have you watched any English films in the last three months?' this question might work better: 'Have you watched any English films since Christmas?'

Sentence completion is also an effective technique because it invites structured yet open-ended responses. For example, before interviewing bilingual children about language practices at home and at school, you might ask them to complete the following sentences:

Example 6.5   Worksheet

Complete these sentences. Write Spanish (L1) or English (L2) in the spaces.

- *With my parents at home I use . . .*
- *With my brothers and sisters I speak . . . . . .*
- *With my best friend I speak . . . .*
- *At school I speak more . . . . than . . . . . .*
- *At the weekend I speak more . . . than . . . . .*

Children whose second language proficiency is quite low for various reasons, may find that they cannot overcome the linguistic obstacles presented in certain research instruments. If the researcher does not speak their L1, one interesting solution is to use visually based research tools such as photographs, drawings, pictures and videos rather than rely on spoken or written output, i.e. 'visual methods' (Thomson 2008). Cook and Hess (2007) suggest that taking photos is a quick and relatively easy way of obtaining data. Children are likely to enjoy it and it is open to all children including those who are young or who have learning difficulties. The choice of the photos is more likely to represent what the child is interested in rather than the adult researcher. Photos are also excellent prompts for further discussions with children.

Similarly, Johnson (2008) describes a project in an Australian school where she used visual research methods with children aged 10–11. The children were co-researchers in a project which aimed to make sense of their own experiences at school. The artwork produced by the children was the basis for developing new understandings of school life and school places. The children selected the content and the composition of their photos. The research project helped to uncover child interpretations of school life that were new and unexpected to adults. In fact, the children's representations were powerful and transformative in their potential to challenge adult views. Johnson specifically stresses the appropriateness of visual research methods with children who do not speak English fluently.

Quote 6.17   On the appropriateness of using visual methods with L2 children

... the use of visual images in this research was inclusive of the abilities of all children. It enabled all children who wished to participate to have a 'say' to reflect on their daily lives, to identify issues of concern, and to make informed judgments. The use of artwork and photography enabled children to develop expertise in having their 'voices heard'. Because words were not a privileged source of data, children who were deaf and communicated with AUSLAN (sign language), those with identified language disorders and who did not speak fluent English were all able to participate.

(Johnson 2008: 81)

While the above visual approaches are inherently attractive, they also have challenges. For example Punch (2002) explains that while using drawings with a group of children helped to elicit children's views about the research focus, it was fun to do and it gave children control over their form of expression, several disadvantages remained, such as being inhibited by lack of artistic competence or copying from one another. Similarly, when the children were invited to take photos, they may have taken those that make a good picture or may have copied adult examples of typical photos, rather than thought about their own perspectives.

6.5   Using multi-methods

Given that all research tools, even the child-friendly ones, or those inviting children to be active participants and co-researchers have their inherent disadvantages, it is important to use a variety of different tools aiming to collect different sets of data from the same group of children. Sometimes even carefully prepared and piloted instruments do not work for some reason. The best way to proceed is for the researcher to use multiple methods and collect evidence from different perspectives, rather than rely on one specific tool.

For example, start with a brief period of observation before implementing a particular instrument or prior to interviews. Observations will help you to identify routines and communicative norms; they may also assist you in developing good rapport with the children and to fine-tune your tasks and other instruments.

Gallacher and Gallagher (2008) usefully point out that in some research situations children may actually actively resist the planned research instruments and do not involve themselves at all.

Quote 6.18   On children resisting research tools

In our research projects, by contrast, some of the most fascinating insights have emerged from children acting in unexpected ways: appropriating, resisting or manipulating our research techniques for their own purposes. Taking an ethnographic approach, our respective projects were able to view such forms of action as potential data, rather than viewing them negatively as instances of non-compliance.

(Gallacher and Gallagher 2008: 508)

These researchers suggest that if such resistance happens, it may be useful to consider why this is the case and consider the children's natural actions and reactions as spontaneously emerging data. This is more likely to happen with younger children than older children, who are used to specific instructions and tasks. When children resist one particular task, the researcher may then decide to collect alternative data using different tools and approaches.

Punch (2002) argues that a combination of different methods is most valuable with children for a number of reasons.

Quote 6.19   On using a variety of methods in child research

Using a range of methods, both traditional and innovative, can help strike a balance and address some of the ethical and methodological issues of research with children. Like other researchers, I found that using a variety of techniques was valuable: to prevent boredom and sustain interest (Hill 1997); to prevent biases arising from overreliance on one method (Ennew and Morrow 1994: 70; Morrow and Richards 1996: 101); to triangulate and cross-check data (INTRAC 1997; Lucchini 1996; Morrow 1999) and to strike a balance between traditional and innovative methods.

(Punch 2002: 336–7)

6.6   Conclusion

The following questions can be used as an initial guide or thinking tool before you embark on conducting a research project involving children.

- *What are my underlying beliefs about children and childhood? How do my beliefs influence the type of project I am planning?*

It is useful for every researcher to reflect on this issue but this does not mean that you can take on projects only if they fall in line with your beliefs. Your area of interest may be one where children's agency and active participation is less important.

- *What are my research questions?*

Each researcher intending to work with children needs to take the age of the children into account. When you are working with very young children, certain research questions cannot be answered because the types of tools required to probe into the questions may be completely unsuitable for the given age group. For example, a researcher may be interested in what young children say about their language learning strategies but would have to accept that it would be difficult to formally interview children aged 4 or 5 with such an objective. Children that young will be reluctant to talk to researchers/outsiders and any formal questioning and probing will lead to awkward silences and possibly a total withdrawal on the children's part. In addition, children at that age are unable to verbalise their strategies and in fact the whole concept of a 'strategy' will be too abstract and meaningless. So, in this case, the researcher is advised to change the research focus or questions and/or pursue the research questions with a more suitable group, i.e. with older children. As a general rule, it is safer to use observation with younger learners or to devise short, focussed activities with visual and/or hands-on elements. When in doubt about the suitability of a particular tool, it is best to observe the children first and get some advice from colleagues. Older learners may be more reliable in terms of their expected behaviours and responses but even with them we need to expect surprises, be prepared to encounter problems and keep an eye on signs of lack of willingness or hesitation to participate.

- *What are the implications of my status as a researcher in the given context? What is the level of the researcher's knowledge and experience in child research? What is the time frame for the project?*

If the researcher is the regular class teacher, the children know the researcher well and thus their responses and behaviour can be expected to be natural and reflect their 'best' ability. It is still important to explore the researcher's role in relation to the children and make this an explicit part of the project. For example, young children often idolise their teachers and want to please them by giving responses that are over-optimistic or over-enthusiastic. If the researcher is the parent of the child, the parents' extensive access to the child may be a problem in that parents find it hard to separate research from private life. In fact, both teachers and parents need to juggle two personalities, i.e. the teacher versus the researcher and the parent versus the researcher.

Outsider researchers do not have such a burden of trying to be two people at the same time but they need to invest time and effort into being accepted by the children they wish to work with. Depending on the type of project, this may take any time between a few days to several weeks.

If the class teacher is the researcher then it is likely that he or she will share the children's first language, whereas this might not be the case for outsider researchers. When the L1 is shared, teachers and researchers will be able to conduct interviews or observe children playing and talking in natural contexts. If the researcher does not have access to the children's L1 (in some contexts children's L1 will be varied within a whole class) then this will again limit the opportunities available to the researcher. Bilingual assistants who speak the children's L1 could offer help by mediating between two languages and between the researcher and the children. In some cases, it might be possible to conduct the research entirely in L2, without any need to rely on the children's L1. Depending on the situation, you may want to consider all the available language options and select the most appropriate one.

If you are the class teacher, you are likely to know what the children are learning in other subjects and this knowledge can be usefully built on. Depending on the research focus, the outsider researcher will need to get to know the school and the curriculum. Certain types of projects are more suitable for certain contexts. For example, in a school where the children only have two short formal lessons per week in L2, the researcher is more limited when planning a focussed intervention. In schools where the children are exposed to the L2 every day, e.g. in immersion programmes, a greater range of project types and generally greater intensity are feasible.

It is also important for the researcher to know what working methods the children are used to and what resources are available in the school. For example, an outside researcher might be interested in a computer-assisted learning project but this is only possible if the children have stable access to computers and the software that the study requires. No matter how interesting, relevant and exciting this computer-mediated project might be to the researcher, if the resources in the school are not adequate, a different type of question or focus is needed.

If you are an experienced researcher, you may embark on a more challenging project, whereas if this is your first project, you may want to plan a project that is brief and less complicated by methodological and ethical dilemmas.

In many cases research studies need to be completed by a given dead-line, e.g. many Masters programmes set a hand-in date for research-based dissertations, and they generally allow only four months for the whole project. If the research project requires the researcher to travel to different schools and pilot different instruments, realistic time frames for these activities need to be planned carefully. When the researcher is not working to specific deadlines and there is no time pressure, this allows for more reflection, more interaction with colleagues, and more time to shape the project in view of the researcher's changing and developing interests. If the researcher has more time, it may be possible to try out experimental materials and approaches and/or to plan a study that lasts for a longer period of time. A great deal of research in the real world is conducted by researchers working on their own but some researchers work as part of a team and this is an exciting option which again will have an effect on the kind of project one may initiate. For example, teachers in your school may decide to initiate a research project together. This is likely to be more motivating than working on your own.

- *What research ethics guidelines apply in my context/ country/ institution?*
  - *What steps do I need to take to negotiate access to the child participants? Who are the gatekeepers?*
  - *How will I safeguard and protect the children who consent to participate? How will I safeguard their well-being?*
  - *How will I make sure that the children understand the focus of the research and their own role?*

Every researcher needs to consult the ethics guidelines in their institution. If you are conducting a research study which is part of the course in a higher education institution, that institution will have its own guidelines. If the data collection takes place in another context, i.e., in another country, you need to consider another set of rules/guidelines applicable in that context. For example, if you are conducting an MA dissertation in the UK and want to gather data from Japanese children, you need to consider ethical guidance for both the UK and Japan.

If the research project is in any way sensitive – for example, if the children disclose information about their classroom teacher that is problematic, or the tasks and activities in the research project upset the children, it is important to reassure them and elicit help from another colleague.

Think of various ways in which you can explain, demonstrate and discuss with children the focus of the research. Think of ways in which the children can convince you that they understand the focus of your research and think about what level of understanding is necessary, for example, when you are introducing a new activity.

- *What methodological decisions can I take?*

  o *How will the children participate in this study? Why? Would there be other ways?*

  o *Where is the research project going to take place? At school or in some other context?*

  o *What linguistic, cognitive or other difficulties may be hidden in my selected research tools?*

  o *How can I adapt or supplement my research tools to make them more accessible to the needs of the children?*

Think of different ways in which you may elicit data from the children. Consider the advantages of pairing them up, putting them in groups or eliciting their views individually. There may be different options available to you regarding the venue for data collection and it is good to consider possible advantages and disadvantages of all options. If you have a draft tool, such as a list of interview questions, you might like to think about possible ways of wording the questions, supplementing them with visuals, or turning some questions into simple role play exercises.

Having drawn up some preliminary plans based on the questions above, it is a good idea to discuss your plans with other colleagues and researchers. The next chapter will offer further ideas in the shape of 15 feasible studies. The aim is to help you polish your ideas so far and give you workable solutions that can be adapted to suit both the local context and your specific needs and interests.

7
Some Feasible Studies for Future Research

This chapter will

- provide some ideas for feasible research studies to carry out in different contexts of teaching languages to children
- illustrate research steps in more traditional and innovative projects
- illustrate ways in which studies can fill some of the gaps identified in Chapter 4

7.1 Introduction

You may already have some ideas about what you might like to do. In this case, the studies described below will help you focus your study or offer some workable alternatives. They may also alert you to possible pitfalls or ethical considerations. If you do not yet have a project in mind, it is hoped that you will find a topic or a type of data collection method that is feasible in your context and attractive, to motivate you to take the first steps.

7.2 Selecting project ideas

Overall, the range of studies suggested in this chapter corresponds to the methodological organisation of Chapter 4. Accordingly, some studies will fall into the experimental/ comparative category (e.g. Studies 1 and 2), while others will focus on possible studies with individual learners or small groups of learners (e.g. siblings in Study 5). There will be ideas for studies focussing on eliciting data from children about their opinions and perceptions (e.g. Studies 9 or 10) and then, finally, studies that incorporate a focus on primary teachers (e.g. Studies 14 or 15). All these projects are broadly applicable to a variety of contexts and they all contain optional elements, to enable researchers to tailor the study to suit their interests but also to suggest ways in which they can be extended into bigger, more ambitious projects.

Some of these ideas are included because they represent popular approaches in currently published literature, while others are included because they attempt to contribute to filling a gap identified earlier in Chapter 4. For example, the study that encourages teachers to explore ways of promoting autonomous learning in their classrooms (Study 14) is included because teacher-initiated studies are rare as compared with the vast majority of studies published by outsider researchers, often academics. A further reason for including this study is because it incorporates a focus on learner-initiated ideas in research. Rather than the teachers deciding what aspects of autonomous learning they want to implement and focus on, the students' ideas are invited and the final decisions are negotiated between teachers and learners.

Chapter 4 also identified a general lack of longitudinal studies in the literature even though the complex processes of second language learning are best captured by longitudinal studies. Chapter 4 indicated that many more longitudinal studies will be necessary in the future. Project ideas such as the one that encourages you to explore children's writing over a period of a whole academic year (Study 3) would yield extremely valuable data about the complexities of individual learners' trajectories. Another gap exists in that formal and informal learning opportunities are rarely connected, and here the study that focusses on children's home learning incorporates information about both home and school learning (Study 5). Finally, there are more studies needed in foreign language learning contexts and for this reason several of these studies are located in foreign language environments (e.g. Studies 1, 4 and 6).

In terms of the different approaches to research, both quantitative and qualitative approaches were included, although a combination of these, referred to as 'mixed method' research, is almost always preferable (Dörnyei 2007). This is the reason why in the experimental studies that are largely quantitative, it is advisable to incorporate data collection that takes account of the *processes* in addition to the quantifiable *products*. For example, when children's task performances are analysed, coded, and linguistic features are quantified (e.g. in Study 2), it is useful to explore how the children engaged with the tasks, and why and exactly how they interpreted the tasks. These processes may throw fresh light on the product and may explain some of the potentially puzzling statistics that the data may show up.

Regarding the models of childhood discussed in Chapter 6, it is fair to say that most of the recommended studies here are teacher/researcher-directed. Yet, elements of participatory methods and some control on the part of the children have been incorporated into several projects. For example, when exploring children's views in relation to assessment (Study 8), the researcher is encouraged to use role plays rather than ordinary interviews alone. In your particular context, if the circumstances allow you, you may wish to incorporate other flexible methods, including visual methods (e.g. Study 11).

Particularly careful ethical procedures have been suggested in the projects so that children can be fully protected, fully informed, and fully aware of their rights to withdraw from research without negative consequences. Some of the project ideas are more suited to outsider researchers and others to teachers or parents. All these types of research are equally valuable, but whoever is the researcher, issues to do with relationships, building rapport, and conflicting roles will have to be considered carefully. Additional ethical concerns may arise in your context that cannot be anticipated here.

Additional steps are included with every study because depending on the scope of the study, the developing interest of the researcher, and the time available to continue working with a project, the direction of the research may change. At the same time, there may be an unexpected opportunity that arises to complement the views, perceptions or the products of selected participants, using an alternative set of data. Alternative angles are important because in research projects, when something does not go according to plan, e.g. some participants drop out, the school restricts originally agreed access, or the researcher comes across something unexpected and surprising, the focus of the study may have to be extended or altered. This is more likely to happen in the case of longer, more complex projects rather than shorter experiments but researchers are always advised to have an alternative plan.

7.3   Classroom experiments

These studies are relatively short in duration and they seek to establish cause and effect relationships between approaches, materials, techniques and language learning (see Chapter 4). It is very difficult to create genuinely experimental conditions and this is why researchers often choose to complement their statistical results with additional evidence relating to processes.

A great deal of the literature in child SLA is experimental in design and therefore researchers and teachers need to be familiar with this approach. Experiments are also 'convenient' in certain circumstances – for example, for researchers who cannot stay in the field for a long time.

Study 1

Research question: *Will a 'discovery method' to teaching vocabulary lead to better word learning?*

Age: 8-9 years of age (not suitable for age groups with limited literacy skills)

Context: foreign language context

Problem: Teachers/researchers need some empirical evidence that a new/ alternative method is working. An experimental approach allows researchers to compare the relative merits of two methods.

Some similar studies: Llinares Garcia (2007), Harley (1998), Peñate Cabrera and Bazo Martínez (2001)

Researcher(s): class teacher

Language of elicitation: mixture of L1 and L2

Procedures:

i. Select two learner groups. In practical terms, it is often not possible to assign the members of the control group and the experimental group randomly, so you may decide to use two comparable classes. One class will be the experimental group (Group A) and the other class will be the control group (Group B).

ii. Aim to show that the two classes are similar in their level of L2 language proficiency, motivation and the content they have covered so that the most important variables are controlled.

iii. Design a pre-test which contains elements that measure proficiency and learning motivation and include a standard test for vocabulary recognition (e.g. Meara 1996). The vocabulary section should be adapted to suit the children's level and should contain both some of the new words that you intend to teach to the groups and some other random words.

iv. Compare results of the pre-test using means and standard deviation calculations for the proficiency scores and the vocabulary scores.

v. If the two groups are comparable, i.e. the pre-test does not show significant differences between them, you can procede with the treatment in Group A (experimental group).

vi. Establish your hypothesis, i.e., learners following the discovery approach will learn/remember their vocabulary better.

vii. Design the experimental materials according to the principles inherent in the discovery method. Use activities such as word detective tasks, guessing tasks, dictionary tasks, and other suitable discovery games.

viii. Pilot some experimental materials with a class of the same age to ensure that the tasks and activities are appropriate for the age group, the level of L2, and that they are fun and motivating to do.

ix. Decide on the duration of the intervention. It is better to opt for a relatively longer period of time because the effects of the treatment might not be immediately observable/measurable. One academic term may be ideal.

x. Continue with the 'normal' teaching in Group B.

xi. Begin the intervention and record your observations in a research diary. You may also want to record some lessons in both classes to shed light on the learning processes during vocabulary activities.

xii. Administer a post-test after the treatment. This may comprise two sections. First, re-run the vocabulary part of the pre-test again in both groups. Then administer a specific vocabulary test just focussing on the words taught during the treatment to both groups. It is important that the test activities need to be familiar and meaningful to both groups of children, so use, for example, gap filling or multiple choice questions.

xiii. Using a t-test, compare pre- and post-test results in both groups. The t-test will show you whether the differences in the children's vocabulary scores between the two groups are significant or not.

xiv. If necessary, use the analysis of the recorded activities from the classroom and your journal to complement the numerical data.

xv. Discuss the results and draw up some implications for subsequent research and/or classroom practice regarding the usefulness of the discovery approach.

xvi. Discuss limitations, such as small sample size, difficulty in controlling all variables, and one teacher in both groups.

Additional steps:

(Option) Consider supplementing the data with views and opinions gained from the children as these might highlight further benefits or problems related to the treatment.

Ethical considerations/ possible dilemmas:
- Issues about the tension between teacher and researcher roles
- Issues about exposing children to an approach that may well be inferior to the new, progressive approach (in Group B)
- Issues about the tension of a school-based project and issues about consent
- Issues about how to gain evidence that children understand what the research entails

---

Study 2

Research question: *What are the differences between two groups of children regarding their L2 communication strategies when using two different communication tasks in L2?*

Age: 8-year-olds compared with 12-year-olds
(It would be difficult to work with children who are younger than 6 years of age, as they might not be readily able to work with an interactive task.)

Context: foreign or second language contexts

Problem: Teachers and material designers need to know how children work with different communicative language tasks so that they can design suitable materials for different age groups and also help children tackle these tasks more effectively. Data that show what strategies children are able to use can help teachers decide about where to focus teaching.

Some similar studies: Pinter (2007), Mackey, Oliver and Leeman (2003), Philp, Oliver and Mackey (2006), Shrubshall (1997)

Researcher: class teacher

Language of elicitation: mixture of L1 and L2

Procedures:

i. Design the two tasks you want to work with. For example, design a 'Spot the differences' task and a 'Follow the route on the map' task. They may be based on the content of a unit in the course-book. Make sure these are familiar task types in the given context, otherwise the children need some training.

ii. Identify the two groups of learners.

iii. Organise the recording facilities. In this case, because there is an interest in the children's observable strategies, video-recording is appropriate to capture body language.

iv. Make sure the children are comfortable with the process of video-recording.

v. Pilot the tasks with similar-aged children to identify any problems with the design of the tasks.

vi. Plan the implementation of the tasks during specific lessons or outside the class. In reality, it will be very difficult to record everyone working and speaking at the same time in the classroom because of the noise levels. It may be better to make arrangements to record the children outside class, one by one. Think about possible places for the recording and the implications for the children's performance.

vii. Record the tasks.

viii. Transcribe the recorded task performances.

ix. Analyse the transcripts according to your selected framework, in this case, according to a communication strategies framework (e.g. Bialystok 1990).

x. Quantify the different strategies in the performances and compare their occurrence in the data elicited from the two groups of learners.

xi. Treating task 1 and task 2 in both groups as variables, you can run an ANOVA test to analyse variance. This will show you significant differences between the two tasks and the two groups. For example, it may be the case that the older children used significantly more strategies during their performance in one task as compared to the younger children.

xii. Discuss the results and the implications for classrooms. You may be able to argue the case for teaching different strategies to the two age groups or teaching strategies in a particular order.

xiii. Discuss the limitations such as small group sizes and dilemmas related to coding.

Additional steps:

(Option) Invite the children to comment on the tasks either by talking to them or asking them to evaluate them in some way.

Ethical considerations and possible dilemmas:

- Issues about the tension of a school-based project and consent
- Issues about gaining evidence from the children that they understand what the project is about
- Issues about negotiating access to the recorded data and confidentiality
- Issues about dealing with anxiety, i.e. reassuring children that their performance is not formally assessed or evaluated

---

Both these projects are suitable for the class teacher to conduct, but it is also possible for an outside researcher to take over the class for a short time. The first project is planned for a whole academic term, while the second project is very short, lasting just a week or two. The focus is on the children's performances in both cases and the coding of these data will be geared to address the research questions. However, in both studies it is possible to incorporate other evidence from the learners that can help to cast further light on the numerical results. Both projects would ideally require that the researcher be bilingual, but in the second case it may be possible to administer the tasks in L2.

7.4   Documenting children's language learning and growing awareness over time

This second group of studies tend to be longitudinal in design and focus on a smaller number of learners rather than on whole classes or larger groups. It simply would not be manageable to track the development of every learner in an average-size class for several years. Since there is a general need for longitudinal studies, studies like these, focussing on the 'ups and downs' of the learning process as learning unfolds in time, are particularly necessary. Some studies in this group also aim to fill gaps in combining school and home learning (Study 5), in exploring processes in foreign language contexts (Studies 4 and 6), and in exploring trilingual children's competences (Study 7).

Study 3

Research question: *How do young L2 children, who have experienced schooling and been introduced to L1 literacy, develop their L2 spelling over the first year of learning English?*

Age: flexible, but the learner needs to be at the beginning stage of acquiring L2 literacy and with a background in L1 literacy; typically 5–7 years of age, depending on context

Context: L2 immersion context

Problem: Currently we do not know a great deal about how language development occurs over time and, in particular, writing is a neglected skill, especially for younger learners.

Some similar studies: Nassaji and Cumming (2000), Bae (2007)

Researcher: teacher or outsider

Language of elicitation: mixture of L1 and L2

Procedures:

   i. Select your participants. Focus on a maximum of four learners in the same group: two girls and two boys or four children with different L1 backgrounds. You can also focus on just one learner or two or three. Your subjects would typically have some background in L1 literacy (1–2 years) and they should be beginners immersed in an L2 environment.
   ii. Decide on what kind of writing you are going to focus on. This will depend on what the children are familiar with, what they enjoy and what you can have access to. For example, you may want to work on a joint journal-writing project.
   iii. Make a decision about how regularly the children will be asked to write, maybe once or twice a week, over a period of the whole academic year.
   iv. If you are their teacher, you need to monitor their other writing tasks and experiences. If you are not the teacher, you will need to obtain information about this.
   v. Introduce the idea of the journal writing. Make it sound exciting. You may want to give some instructions about what sort of things to write about and show examples of diaries written by other children.
   vi. Buy some note-books that the children can use as diaries and let them decorate these as they like.
   vii. When writing begins, don't overtly correct mistakes in children's messages but respond naturally to their entries using correct spelling when you write.
   viii. After continuing the writing for some time, transfer the texts into an electronic file and start marking/coding all the different examples of spelling mistakes in the texts. For example, you may find spelling mistakes that seem to be the direct products of L1 transfer, whereas others might be explained by the child's developing awareness between letter and sound correspondence patterns in English.
   ix. Keep adding further data to the file until the end of the project.

    x. Complete the analysis and describe the main patterns of development observable in the data produced by the four children.

   xi. Compare and contrast the individual patterns of development across the four cases.

  xii. Discuss implications for teaching spelling in L2 English. You may be able to suggest spelling rules that may be beneficial to teach early on.

 xiii. Discuss limitations such as the small number of children, the type of writing you explored and the limited context and issues/problems of coding.

Additional steps:

(Option) If this is possible, get the children to talk about their writing. This may help you to make sense of some of the possibly fragmented content and give you the perspective of the writer.

(Option) A particularly interesting opportunity arises in trying to explore whether the children themselves see any evidence of their own development from their own texts and how they evaluate their own writing.

Ethical considerations/possible dilemmas:

- Issues about the tension between school-based writing and willingness to participate; more specifically, how to handle children's refusal to carry on with the journal, if this happens
- Issues about gaining consent (from parents, teachers and children)
- Issues about handling sensitive topics in writing
- Issues about access to and ownership of diaries

Study 4

Research question: *What patterns of interactions are evident, and thus what language learning opportunities present themselves in small groups in L2 classes?*

Age: 10-year-olds (Children younger than 6–8 will not be able work effectively in groups.)

Context: foreign language context

Problem: Little research has explored to date what actually happens when children are talking together in groups in L2 foreign language classrooms. While group work would ideally offer opportunities for practice, children often do not have sufficient competence to use their L2 and do not know how to manage L2 conversations effectively.

Similar studies: Hawkins (2005), Nikolov (1999a)

Researcher: teacher or outsider researcher

Language of elicitation: mixture of L1 and L2

Procedures:

i. Identify the groups you want to focus on. Since it may be too difficult to focus on all the children in a class of 30 or more students, it may be best to identify two groups in your class, e.g. two groups of three or four children who regularly sit and work together. You may select members for the groups according to further criteria such as background, gender, level of proficiency or just leave them as intact friendship groups.

ii. Explain the research focus and make sure the children are comfortable with the idea of recording their talk.

iii. Record the talk that occurs in these groups whenever communicative tasks are set, such as an information gap task, a collaborative writing task, or a role play task. You can put the children in charge of the recording. Check the level of the background noise.

iv. Continue with the recording sessions over time, aiming to get data emerging from different communicative tasks.

v. Listen to the recorded interactions and identify different patterns. Define what you mean by successful or less successful interaction and analyse the interactions, for example, according to how much L1 the children needed to complete the task or how effectively they dealt with misunderstandings.

vi. Transcribe some sample interactions that illustrate your claims.

vii. Discuss implications for classrooms, e.g. identify phrases, strategies or language functions that would help the children work more effectively on similar communication tasks and suggest pre-teaching these before introducing group tasks.

viii. Discuss the limitations such as small number of participants, only one L1 background.

Additional steps:

(Option) Children may be asked to listen to their own interactions and notice aspects of the talk that can be improved.

(Option) You may also want to explore the children's abilities to evaluate their group work over time.

Ethical considerations /possible dilemmas:
- Issues about the tension of school-based research, consent and children's willingness to participate
- Issues about anxiety: reassuring children that the project is not part of their formal assessment
- Issues about access to the recorded materials and confidentiality

Study 5

Research question: *How do siblings who share the same L1 incorporate L2 into their spontaneous play at home?*

Age: flexible, but the data is likely to be more useful if the children are closer in age, e.g. 5 and 7, or 8 and 10.

Problem: In situations where siblings are immersed in a new L2 environment, a great deal of learning and language practice takes place outside children's formal education. In fact, the home provides a safe and secure context to practise language learnt at school. Even though the importance of outside-school learning has been recognised, very little is known about the language use of siblings who share their L1 but will use L2 some of the time at home as they play. The expectation is that they will spontaneously use more and more L2 in their play as a result of being exposed to it at school.

Similar studies to consult : Mitchell and Lee (2008), Bongartz and Schneider (2003)

Context: Immersion/second language contexts

Researcher: parent or a close friend who has regular access to the children at home

Language of elicitation: mixed L1 and L2

Procedures:

  i. Discuss with your children your intention to carry out some research.
 ii. Observe and record your children when they play together after school and decide which play activities you will focus on, e.g. joint reading in L2, playing school, playing computer games in L2, or others.
iii. Record these activities regularly. You may agree to record on certain days or when certain games are played. You may want to consider putting the children in charge of the recording.
 iv. In addition to the recording sessions, keep a diary about your observations regarding the children's L1 and L2 language use.
  v. When the data collection stage is over, e.g. after a few weeks or months, listen to the data and select relevant sections where changes occur in the use of particular linguistic features, functions or phrases, shifting from L1 to L2.
 vi. Transcribe relevant sections of the data.
vii. Examine the patterns of development over time for both children, focussing on similarities as well as differences.
viii. Discuss implications for other families and for teachers who do not have access to informal learning.
 ix. Discuss limitations such as single language background and single family.

Additional steps:

(Option) Follow your children's progress at school, ask to speak to the teacher regularly and look at their school work.

Ethical considerations/possible dilemmas:

- Issues about the tension inherent in the differing roles of parent/ researcher
- Issues about safeguarding tapes, ownership and access to tapes

Study 6

Research question: *Does getting children to record their spoken performances regularly have an impact on their ability to evaluate and improve their performance in L2?*

Age: children aged 9–10 (The element of reflection in this study makes this difficult to implement with children younger than this age.)

Problem: Spontaneous communication and oral competence seem to be difficult to achieve in foreign language contexts where children are not exposed to L2 for more than just one or two hours per week. Yet, it is motivating for children to be able to communicate meaningfully at the beginning stages of their learning an L2. Teachers will be interested to find out what approaches may help improve children's oral communication skills.

Similar studies: Pinter (2006), Simard (2004)

Researcher: class teacher

Language of elicitation: mixture of L1 and L2

Procedures:

i. Select a group of learners and explain the research focus.
ii. Select a suitable recording facility (e.g. mp3 players) and make sure all learners who are participating have got one.
iii. Focus on practising particular speaking tasks in class (such as short monologues, storytelling, or role plays).
iv. Get the learners to record their spoken performances. This may have to be done at home if the class is big and noisy.
v. Get them to listen to the tapes and notice any aspects of the performance that they think they can improve next time, e.g. choice of words or phrases, intonation, pronunciation or content. Ask children to jot down these ideas to remind themselves before the second recording.
vi. Get the children to re-record their performances and listen to the differences between the first and the second recording.

vii. Continue this for several weeks, using different speaking tasks.

viii. Organise lessons when you elicit children's experiences with the task of recording and evaluating/comparing performances. Audio-record these sessions.

ix. Encourage the children to select their best performances for a 'portfolio tape'.

x. Combine all data sources to identify important insights: i.e. children's first and second recordings, their observations about their first recordings and the recorded discussions in class.

xi. Look for important patterns in the data: What aspects of the performances did the children comment on in their writing and in the discussion sessions? Were there any differences between these? Did they pick up on their friends' suggestions?

xii. Discuss implications regarding the use of this approach in raising awareness about aspects of speaking with this age group; incorporate reflection of this kind with other activities in your classes.

xiii. Discuss limitations, such as small group size, one language background.

Additional steps:

(Option) Interview children about the perceived benefits of the process.

(Option) If they are comfortable with this, let them ask a friend to listen to both their recordings and get some peer-feedback.

Ethical considerations/possible dilemmas:

- Issues about the tension of a school-based project and willingness to participate
- Issues about safeguarding the recordings
- Issues about negotiating access to recordings
- Issues about completing the tasks at home: parent influence

---

Study 7

Research question: *How does a trilingual child's ability to tell stories in three languages change over time in a given context?*

Age: flexible, but it is important to take into account that young children's ability to tell stories can be very limited

Problems: Little is known about trilingual children's acquisition processes and data illustrating their abilities in three languages would give teachers and researchers invaluable insights. There may be particularly interesting times in the life of the learner when a project like this may be useful, e.g. when a bilingual child starts an L3.

Similar studies: Wang (2008)

Researcher: outsider researcher

Language of elicitation: mixture of L1, L2 and L3

Procedures:

i. Select appropriate picture stories with a clear outline, appropriate cultural and motivating content. Make sure the story is not previously known or otherwise familiar.

ii. Using a set of picture prompts, get the learner to tell the story in three languages, e.g. L1: German, L2 English and L3 Spanish.

iii. Repeat the task with new pictures and new stories once a month for a year.

iv. Record the child telling the story in L1, L2, and L3. This order means that in L1 the story line and all the important elements of the story will be established and the child will attempt to 'translate the story' into their L2 and L3. In order to counteract the effect of the language choice, the researcher should vary the order of the languages in which the story is told/recorded on different occasions.

v. Identify an aspect of storytelling that you wish to focus on, e.g. use of cohesive devices, developing a coherent story line, referencing, use of communication strategies or other aspects of interest.

vi. Examine patterns of development over time and across languages.

vii. Draw implications for researchers and teachers interested in the processes of trilingual development.

viii. Discuss limitations, such as the particular languages involved and a single learner.

Additional steps:

(Option) Consider obtaining interview data from the participant regarding his/her feelings about the storytelling task and perceived difficulties in each language.

(Option) Consider obtaining interview data regarding the functions of the three languages in the child's life and the frequency of use.

Ethical considerations/possible dilemmas:

- Issues related to undue pressures on the participant
- Issues related to keeping the participant interested and motivated
- Issues related to the ownership of and access to the recordings
- Issues related to researcher/child relationship and consent

The focus here is still on the learners' performances, as in the previous group of studies, but, in the optional steps, you are advised to consider getting data from the children about their feelings and opinions. In some of these studies the researcher can easily be an outsider (e.g. Study 7) and some of these studies can be completed partly outside school or entirely outside school (e.g. Studies 5, 6 and 7). Many of these studies are open-ended and exploratory. The data itself will offer different directions the researcher can take. Researchers may find interesting and even unexpected insights while exploring their data set. Even though all these studies are longitudinal in nature, some of them can produce useful data after just a few weeks (e.g. Study 6).

7.5   Eliciting children's voices about their language learning

In this group of studies the focus is on children's views related to second language learning. In Chapter 4 this was identified as a gap, especially in terms of using alternative ways of eliciting data from younger children who may struggle with traditional data collection methods.

Study 8

Research questions: *How do children view/understand the L2 assessment practices in their classrooms in different types of schools, in a particular country/ context?*

Age: 8-year-olds (Role plays with older children might not work because they may be shy about acting and performing.)

Problem: Assessment is a difficult area because it is unavoidable in most contexts to test children, yet teachers often feel that young L2 learners can be easily put off language learning if their performance in L2 is assessed in formal ways. In order to construct suitable assessment tools, it is important for teachers to know about children's perceptions about assessment practices.

Researcher: outsider researcher

Similar studies: Gardner and Yaacob (2007), Lamb (2003)

Context: foreign language or second language contexts

Language of elicitation: L1

Procedures:

i. Identify some school types (such as private and state schools, urban or rural schools, large, well-equipped or small, under-resourced schools) and decide which types of schools you are going to work with.

  ii. Depending on the local possibilities, decide how many schools you will work with (e.g. 4–5).

 iii. Familiarise yourself with the officially described assessment practices in the country, and specifically, in these schools. If possible, interview teachers about their assessment practices in L2 with 8-year-olds.

 iv. Observe the children for 1–2 weeks in each school to familiarise yourself with their particular context, their level of development, their concerns, interests. Use this time to brief the children about the project and develop rapport.

  v. In preparation for the interviews, ask the children to draw some pictures depicting how assessment is done in their English classes. These can be used in the interview sessions as prompts.

 vi. Set up friendship groups for interviews with groups of 4–5 children.

 vii. Draft the interview questions. In addition, or instead of, ordinary questions, include a 'role play task'. Get the children to act out what happens when they have a test in their L2 class. Bring along props such as test booklets, score sheets, textbooks and invite them to make use of these, if they wish.

viii. Write specific instructions for the role play and establish an audience, e.g. imagining younger children who come as visitors to see what an English test is like.

 ix. Record the interviews, including the role plays.

  x. Analyse the data, focussing on the children's interpretations of assessment.

 xi. Discuss implications for classrooms, teachers and materials/test designers.

 xii. Discuss limitations such as a single context, children's eagerness to please the researcher or overacting in the role-play.

Additional steps:

(Option) Consider interviewing test designers, head-teachers, parents with regard to their views on L2 assessment.

Ethical considerations/possible dilemmas:

- Issues about organising/negotiating access to these schools
- Issues about the tension between a school-based project and consent
- Issues about the power gap between the researcher and the children
- Issues about protecting the identities of children, teachers and specific schools

Study 9

Research questions: *How do children evaluate their textbook, in particular, the illustrations in their textbook?*

Age: 10-year-olds (Children much younger may find reflecting on their opinions difficult.)

Problems: There is very little known about how children evaluate materials they work with. What features of the textbook do they find attractive and why? This information would be valuable to teachers and material designers.

Similar studies: Hewings (1991), Nagy (2009)

Researcher: outsider researcher or class teachers

Language of elicitation: L1

Procedures:

   i. Select a textbook or a range of textbooks. These can be textbooks familiar to you but possibly not so familiar to the children or textbooks that the children are currently using.
  ii. Design a simple questionnaire to find out what aspects of the book the children like and why, and what features they do not like and why. You can use a simple 'finish these statements' exercise (see Chapter 6). Illustrations may be mentioned here as either positive or negative features.
 iii. Organise group interviews focussing on the illustrations and their interpretations, e.g. cultural content, or the way children are portrayed in the book.
  iv. Explore in the interview what style of illustrations they like and why, what they think the function of the illustrations may be, and, if this is a book they are already using, when and how these illustrations are used in class, looking at a unit they have already covered.
   v. Get the children to design some illustrations to go with their favourite unit in the book. Children may be keen to design these on the computer.
  vi. Discuss implications for textbook and materials design of children's insights regarding textbook illustrations.
 vii. Discuss limitations, such as small group size and one L1 background.

Additional steps:

(Option) Interview the teacher about their opinion regarding the illustrations in the textbook.

Ethical considerations/possible dilemmas:

- Issues around the tension regarding a school-based project, consent and willingness to participate
- Issues around the power-gap between the researcher and the children

Study 10

Research questions: *What activities do children enjoy most in my English classes? Comparisons between different age groups and classes.*

Age: flexible, but children need to be able to reflect on their learning processes. This ability improves dramatically from age 8–9 onwards.

Problems: There is a dearth of this kind of practitioner research when teachers embark on projects to explore their own classrooms. Discovering what your learners enjoy and why will be invaluable in terms of planning future teaching. There is often a gap between what teachers think learners like and enjoy and what learners actually say they like.

Similar studies: Nagy (2009)

Researcher: class teacher is researcher

Language of elicitation: L1

Procedures:

   i. Design a simple questionnaire to use in class regularly. It may be possible to use it after every unit, or once a week, or once a fortnight.
  ii. Get the children to rate the activities in your classes.
 iii. Monitor their choice of activity over time (say for several months) and compare different classes, e.g. a class of children aged 6–8, and a class of 10-year-olds.
  iv. Organise some group interviews to explore their questionnaire responses. This is an opportunity to explore the reasons behind their statements or choice of responses.
   v. Use the questionnaire responses as prompts to help them remember activities they enjoyed.
  vi. Compare the reasons provided by the two groups and highlight any differences.
 vii. Organise class discussions regularly to monitor children's changing opinions.
viii. Continue your explorations based on your own and the children's growing insights about the learning processes in your classes (no set time scale).
  ix. Discuss implications, such as mutual benefits, i.e. learners become more aware of what they do and like and why, and teachers get valuable insights about what children enjoy and why.
   x. Discuss limitations, such as only two classes involved.

Additional steps:

(Option) Get the children to create enjoyable activities for each other. Spend some time in class to do these and let the children get peer-feedback on their activities.

(Option) Encourage children to have a learning diary where they record what they learnt and what they enjoyed most in their language classes.

Ethical considerations/possible dilemmas:
- Issues related to wanting to please the teacher and not being truthful about their opinions
- Issues related to rating new things high because of the novelty effect
- Issues related to the tension of being both the teacher and the researcher;
- This project resembles the features of exploratory practice (e.g. Allwright and Hanks 2009) and it has the potential of benefiting both learners and the teacher and improving classroom life. This is considered an important advantage from an ethical point of view.

Study 11

Research question: *How do child sojourners (temporary visitors) in a new target country make sense of their experiences?*

Age: flexible, but more suited to children who are 6 or older.

Problems: Many postgraduate student/parents who spend a year completing a Masters degree at an overseas university (e.g. UK or USA) relocate their families for a year and send their children to local schools. Parents consider this as a great opportunity for their children to learn a new language (often English) and experience a different culture. However parents often find this a difficult time as they have to juggle study and family life and have very mixed experiences. Very little is known about the children's lives in a new country and their interpretations of their new experiences.

Similar studies: Johnson (2008) and Cook and Hess (2007)

Researcher: outsider researcher

Language of elicitation: partly non-linguistic, partly L2

Procedures:

  i. Introduce the project idea to the parents and their children. The project would be worthwhile even if you had only one family to work with but it would be possible to work with several families from different backgrounds.
  ii. Give some notebooks to the children to use as their diaries to be completed in L2, or a mixture of L1 and L2. Explain that they can personalise it by drawing in it and sticking favourite pictures and photos in it. Explain that they can write once a week in the diary rather than every day.
  iii. Towards the end of their stay, give the children a disposable camera and ask them to take pictures for a photo album that they might like

to take back to their country to show their friends. This photo album would represent their most important/interesting experiences. Give a time limit to think about the pictures and let them use the camera to capture aspects of their lives they want to include. Try to ensure that parents do not influence their children in what to photograph. Alternatively, it would be possible to get the children to create video projects. Many children are experienced video editors and enjoy making films.

iv. When the pictures are developed, ask the children to write short descriptions to accompany the photos and to create an album using those pictures that they are happy with, or to add commentary to their video projects.

v. Organise group or individual interviews to discuss the photos or videos in L2.

vi. Discuss findings about children's interpretations of their experiences.

vii. Discuss implications for other similar families and local schools.

viii. Discuss limitations such as small number of families and children involved in the study.

Additional steps:

- (Option) Consider obtaining interview data from parents who often have slightly different interpretations of their children's experiences (3–5 times during the year).
- (Option) Consider organising observations in school and/or talking to the teacher (3–5 times a year). You may have access to their school work and assignments.

Ethical considerations/possible dilemmas:

- Issues related to the power and language gaps between the researcher and the children
- Issues related to possible conflict between parents' and children's consent
- Issues related to exposing potentially negative/painful experiences
- Issues related to the ownership of and access to diaries, photo albums and video projects

This group of studies comprises some ideas that are suitable both for the classroom teacher and an outsider researcher. They all focus on the children's views and a consequence of this is that the language of elicitation is almost always the children's L1. Outsider researchers who are unable to communicate with children in their L1, may be able use visual materials (e.g. in Study 11) although such material without the opportunities to discuss intentions and meanings can be somewhat limiting. Some of these projects resemble features of exploratory practice (e.g. Study 10), and therefore they do not have set time limits at all. Others are longitudinal (e.g. Study 11) and yet others are shorter and more manageable for someone with time constraints (e.g. Studies 8 and 9). Many of these projects can be conducted as part of your normal classroom practice (e.g. Study 9 or Study 10) while others are conducted outside the classroom (e.g. Study 11). The main focus and the starting point is always the children's views and opinions, but all studies attempt to bring in additional evidence from other people, such as parents or teachers, in the optional steps.

7.6   Focus on teachers

Following the structure in Chapter 4, this last section is devoted to a group of studies focussing on teachers. In order to understand learning in children's language classrooms, it is important to study teaching and teachers. There are four project ideas listed here. The first two projects (Study 12 and Study 13) are about exploring other teachers' (e.g. your colleagues') views, opinions and understandings about issues related to their classrooms. The next study (Study 14) focusses on exploring your own practice, in this case your own language use, in your own classroom. This falls into the category of practitioner research (similar to Study 10); and the very last study focusses on collaborative action research involving several teachers and their students.

Study 12

Research questions: *What are primary language teachers' perceptions about 'good young language learners' in a particular context? How is this reflected in what they do in their classes? How is this related to the amount of experience they have?*

Age: N/A

Problem: All over the world, L2 programmes for young children have become widespread but little is known about the actual processes of learning and teaching on a day-to-day basis. Teachers' beliefs about learners and learning are crucial to understand, since they shape classroom practices. Research attempting to understand what teachers believe about good learners and how they relate to them during their lessons is important.

Similar studies: Butler (2004), Carless (2006), Peng and Zhang (2009)

Context: foreign language context

Researcher: outsider researcher

Language of elicitation: L1

Procedures:

   i. Consider what number of teachers you may be able to access and how many teachers you wish to involve.

ii. Discuss your research project with the selected teacher participants from different schools. This may be possible by organising face-to-face meetings or it is possible to do it in writing.

iii. Design a questionnaire related to teachers' views, beliefs and practices regarding good language learners in primary classrooms. The questionnaire should contain a section about the teacher's language teaching experience and background. The questionnaire is best to administer in the individual teacher's L1.

iv. Pilot the questionnaire with a comparable but smaller group of teachers and adjust the design, e.g. the wording of difficult questions, following the feedback from the pilot participants.

v. Decide how you will administer and collect the completed questionnaires. You may want to opt for a variety of different options including using postal delivery and return, delivering and collecting it personally, or simply uploading it to the web for teachers to open and fill in electronically. This flexibility may increase the return rate.

vi. Collect the questionnaires and use descriptive statistics to analyse the results. Draw some conclusions, and take note of any questions or responses that emerged. Add these to the interview questions.

vii. Interview some teachers in order to gain further insights into their views and the reasons behind their beliefs. You may want to select participants from different types of schools and with varying levels of experience, e.g. 5–8 participants according to the selection criteria.

viii. Arrange observations to find out whether their reported practices and their real practices match up.

ix. Analyse the combined data set of interviews and observations, and draw implications for classroom practice and teacher development.

x. Discuss limitations, such as a single context.

Additional steps:

(Option): Organise interviews with children to find out about their views regarding who is a good language learner. Elicitation techniques such as role playing good learners in class may be an effective way of getting child data. Drawings or pieces of writing about good learners may be revealing too.

Ethical considerations/possible dilemmas:

- Issues about accessing schools and teachers, consent
- Issues about the tension between the head of school's expectation that teachers will participate and teachers' genuine willingness and interest
- Issues about protecting teachers' identities
- Issues about the relationship and the status gap between the researcher and teachers

Study 13

Research questions: *What are primary language teachers' understanding of task-based teaching and learning in primary schools in a certain country?*

Age: N/A

Problem: Task-based teaching and learning is a widely accepted approach but teachers' understanding of this approach differs from context to context. It is important to explore teachers' understanding of concepts and approaches because this will have a direct effect on their practice.

Similar studies: Carless (2004)

Context: foreign language context

Language of elicitation: L1

Researcher: outsider researcher

Procedures:

- Explain the project idea to the recruited teachers. This can be done in face-to-face meetings or in writing.
- Organise some focus group interviews with the participants to explore issues of concern to teachers in the given context (e.g. 2–3 groups of 4 teachers). The aim of this step is to gain some deeper understanding of teachers' practices, ideas and concerns before the questionnaire is designed.
- Based on your reading and the insights from the focus group interview, design a questionnaire to explore aspects of practice related to task-based teaching.
- Administer the questionnaire using a variety of methods, e.g. face-to-face, postal, on-line, with a cover letter and clear instructions.
- Analyse questionnaire data and describe the results using descriptive statistics.
- Discuss most prevalent practices and problems related to task-based learning based on the results.
- Discuss implications such as content for in-service teacher development sessions.

Additional steps:

(Option) Consider exploring learners' views in order to complement the teacher data.

(Option) Consider conducting observations of some teachers' classrooms.

(Option) Consider examining the textbooks and other official guidelines and documents in the given context about the benefits of task-based learning.

Ethical considerations/possible dilemmas:

- Issues about accessing schools and teachers
- Issues about the tension between the head of school's expectation of teachers to participate and teachers' genuine willingness and interest
- Issues about protecting teachers' identities
- Issues about the relationship and the status gap between researcher and teachers

Study 14

Research question: *How can we encourage children to take more responsibility for their own language learning?*

Age: 12–13 years of age

Problems: Teachers working together in an action research project can benefit professionally a great deal but there is very little documented evidence in the literature about the process of such small group collaboration. There is also a gap in the area of handing over some responsibilities to learners in the process of directing the focus of research. This study idea combines both these perspectives.

Similar studies: Thomsen (2003), Dam (1995), Denos *et al.* (2009)

Researcher: class teachers

Procedures:

i. Organise a small group of teachers to share/discuss ideas about encouraging the development of more language learner autonomy in their classrooms.

ii. Get together informally to discuss your ideas about what autonomy is and why it is important to develop it. You may agree to read studies in the area of promoting learner autonomy.

iii. As part of the discussion, you can agree to devote a number of lessons to brainstorming with the children what aspects of their language learning they would like to take control of.

iv. After this brainstorming session, meet up with your colleagues again to share your own and the children's ideas, and plan to implement some of the ideas that the children suggested, for example, designing activities for one another, selecting homework tasks for themselves, selecting a topic to explore according to their interests rather than simply follow the outline of the next unit in the textbook.

v. Your group will agree on the period of time to spend implementing the selected ideas. This may take two or three weeks, or longer.

  vi. During the implementation, keep diaries about aspects of the classes that worked well and those that did not.

 vii. Obtain feedback from the children regularly.

viii. At the end of the agreed period of time, meet together again and discuss/share experiences.

  ix. Implications can be drawn for future projects based on what worked and why and what did not work.

  x. Your group may decide to continue exploring this topic with a new/altered focus.

Ethical considerations:

- Issues related to the conflict between being the researcher and the teacher at the same time
- Issues about trust, commitment and conflict management within the teachers' group
- Issues of about the researcher's role in the group; whether you are all colleagues with the same professional status or whether one of you might be a group leader with additional status and power

---

Study 15

Research question: *How can I improve my interaction with the children in my class?*

Age: flexible

Problems: Teachers can benefit a great deal from audio-recording their classes because a close examination of their language use can prompt them to make conscious changes that will benefit their learners. This project is also a type of practitioner research as the idea for the research is initiated by the teacher rather than an outsider.

Similar studies: Tang and Nesi (2003), Peng and Zhang (2009)

Researcher: class teacher

Procedures:

  i. Identify the class or classes where the recordings can be made. It is especially useful to do this with a class where the learners are too young to give other type of feedback by reflecting on the activities or talking about their likes and dislikes (for example, a class of children aged 3–4).

 ii. Record several lessons and after listening to the tapes, identify an aspect of your language use to work on, e.g. your questioning techniques, your pronunciation, the way you give feedback, your instructions, or other features.

iii. Alternatively, identify your focus before the recordings begin.

iv. Transcribe the lessons and quantify/analyse the features of interest.

v. Discuss implications of your findings, as they may be useful to other teachers as well.

vi. Draw practical conclusions for yourself and implement some changes to your language use. Record yourself again.

vii. Note any changes in the children's reactions and responses to the changes.

viii. With young children, especially at beginning stages, you may be using a great deal of body language and therefore it may be appropriate to consider video-recording rather than audio-recording.

Additional steps:

(Option) You may consider encouraging a colleague to do the same and discuss your insights.

(Option) You may want to consider other types of projects using the 'self' as a source for development (further ideas in Bailey, Curtis and Nunan 2001).

Ethical considerations:

- As an example of practitioner research, this project is likely benefit both learners and the teachers and the quality of life in the classroom and may thus be especially sound practice form an ethical point of view.
- Safeguarding tapes

The above project ideas allow both classroom teachers to explore their own practice and outsider researchers to explore other colleagues' classrooms and practices. All these studies would fill important gaps that Chapter 4 identified. Reports on collaborative action research related to issues in primary language classes are scarcely reported and disseminated and studies like this would be invaluable.

7.7 Concluding thoughts

The ideas above are intended to serve as initial plans only, to stimulate motivation to undertake research, and it is not expected that any researcher/teacher will be able to follow these outlines fully. What changes might you consider as you work with a study? First of all, in terms of the focus of the study and the content area, it is easy to think of alternative ideas. For example, in Study 12, where primary teachers' perceptions about good language learners are sought, it is possible to use the same procedures to explore other aspects of teacher knowledge, such as teachers' conceptions of language tests, grammar teaching, project work, or vocabulary teaching. Once the focus and the content of the project are settled, it is important for researchers to engage with the relevant literature and to simultaneously explore the restrictions and opportunities in the given context. Understanding the context is particularly important for outsiders, as original plans often need to be adjusted to meet local restrictions. The numbers of participants suggested in each study can also be altered, depending on the circumstances, the researcher's purpose and the size and scope of the project. At the data collection stage, again, it is quite natural to develop insights and questions that may take you away from the suggested procedures into new, alternative territories. This may lead to trying alternative ways of approaching the data, using new frameworks of analysis.

It is my hope that the list of ideas above will inspire much-needed creative projects with children and their language teachers in the broad area of second language learning and pedagogy.

Part IV
Resources

8
Resources in Child SLA and Pedagogy

This chapter offers a range of useful resources to teacher practitioners and researchers, as well as to families and parents. Since the content of this book is quite broad – it gives an overview of processes of language learning in very different contexts, both in families and in different types of school – it would not be possible to cover all of these areas in a comprehensive manner. The selected sources offer a starting point and they represent my personal choice and preference. The lists below include practical teaching materials, teachers' handbooks, theoretical books, research journals, websites, tests and relevant organisations where a wealth of additional information is available. *Full publishing details for all books and articles are given in the Bibliography.*

8.1 Hands-on teaching materials

Many of these books contain adaptable ideas that can be used with different age groups and in different languages. The commentary to go with the ready-to-use activities is minimal and very easy to follow. Many of these books offer worksheets to copy and take in class with you.

R. C. Clark and P. R. Moran (2002) *Index Card Games for ESL.*
C. Cant and W. Superfine (1997) *Developing Resources for Primary.*
S. Cave, L. Murray and J. Thatcher (2006) *100+ Fun Ideas for Practising Modern Foreign Languages in the Primary Classroom: Activities for Developing Oracy and Literacy Skills.*
C. Chaves, A. Graham and W. Superfine (1999) *Fun and Games in English: Photocopiable Language Activities for Young Learners.*
E. Claire (1998) *ESL Teachers' Activities Kit.*
O. Dunn, (1984) *Developing English with Young Learners.*
K. Einhorn (2001) *Easy and Engaging ESL Activities and Mini-books for Every Classroom.*
I. Forte and M. A. Pangle (2001) *ESL Active Learning Lessons: 15 Complete Content-based Units to Reinforce Language Skills and Concepts.*
G. Gerngross and H. Puchta (1996) *Do and Understand.*
C. Graham (1978) *Jazz Chants for Children.*
L. Henny and S. Rixon (1990) *Look Alive!*

C. A. Josel (2002) *Ready-to-use ESL Activities for Every Month of the School Year.*
P. McKay and J. Guse (2007) *Five-minute Activities for Young Learners.*
S. Rixon (1981) *How to Use Games in Language Teaching.*

One particularly useful website for browsing hands-on language teaching-related books for primary level is the CILT (Centre for Information on Language Teaching and Research) site **http://www.cilt.org.uk**. Here, a range of resources are available to teachers working with children, teaching modern foreign languages. Many of these resources and ideas can be used with any second or foreign language in any context. The site offers advice regarding language learning and teaching at primary, secondary and tertiary levels, and there is information about teacher training and development opportunities. Readers can access web-based discussion forums and blogs. The following is a taster from the large selection of books relevant for primary level:

R. Bailey and C. Dugard, C. (2007) *Lights, Camera, Action. New Pathfinder 6.*
A. Barnes and M. Hunt (2003) *Effective Assessment of Modern Foreign Languages.*
B. Clinton and M. Vincent (2009) *Leading the Way. Young Pathfinder 16.*
M. Datta and C. Pomphrey (2004) *A World of Languages: Developing Children's Love of Languages. Young Pathfinder 2.*
P. Satchwell and J. de Silva (2009) *Speak Up! Young Pathfinder 15.*

All major ELT/ESL publishers produce series of children's textbooks, children's dictionaries, simplified readers, audio/video materials, computer-based and interactive whiteboard materials. For teachers, publishers produce resource books with hands-on ideas and advice. One example is the 'Primary Resource Books for Teachers' series at Oxford University Press (series editor: Alan Maley) **http://www.oup.com/elt/catalogue/**. Some titles in this series are listed here but consult the website for an up-to-date full list of current publications and also consult other major ELT/ ESL publishers (e.g Pearson, Macmillan, Cambridge and many others).

S. Ioannou-Georgiou and P. Pavlou (2003) *Assessing Young Learners.*
G. Lewis (2004) *The Internet and Young Learners.*
S. Phillips (1999) *Drama with Children.*
J. Reilley and V. Reilley (2005) *Writing with Children.*
A. Wright (1997) *Creating Stories with Children.*

Hands-on teaching and learning materials are also available freely from a large number of websites. Many of these sites offer worksheets, games, songs, stories, and general advice to teachers working with younger learners. The following are some of my favourites:

http://www.ihes.com/bcn/tt/yl-sites.html#
This is the 'International House' site which offers a range of excellent links for older children as well as younger ones. Some of the sites are aimed at

teenage learners and some sites were produced by teenagers themselves. This site also offers great resources for teacher training.

http://www.britishcouncil.org/kidsenglish
This is a British Council website aimed at children learning English. There are creative activities, opportunities to listen to stories, songs, short podcasts related to different topics and children can play interactive language games. Children are encouraged to write feedback about their experiences. This is also an excellent resource for teachers searching for fresh ideas and specific advice is also given to parents.

http://www.eslcafe.com/search/Kids/index.html
This is Dave's Café, the internet meeting place for all EFL and ESL learners and teachers. Overall, the site offers a great deal of useful advice, hands-on teaching materials and over 3,000 links to relevant sites including many for language teachers of younger learners.

http://www.esl-galaxy.com/index.htm
This is an EFL/ESL lesson plan and teaching resource portal with over 2,000 free printable worksheets and downloadable games and e-books.

http://www.eslkidsworld.com/
'Eslkidsworld.com' offer free ESL printable worksheets, flashcards, songs, phonics exercises, games, and PowerPoint materials for lesson planning.

http://www.onestopenglish.com
With over 7,000 resources, including lesson plans, worksheets, audio, video and flashcards, 'onestopenglish' [Macmillan English] is a very useful resource site for English language teachers.

www.songsforteaching.com
This site offers thousands of songs, lyrics, sound clips and teaching suggestions. There are songs available in a wide range of topic areas and in different languages.

You are encouraged to search for your own sources, as there are many excellent sites created by teachers, schools and organisations in different parts of the world.

8.2 Resources integrating research with practice

The next category of resources contains examples that still maintain a practical focus and refer to teaching activities and tasks frequently, but at the same time they also attempt to incorporate underlying theoretical principles. Here are some examples:

J. Brewster and G. Ellis (1991) *The Storytelling Handbook for Primary Teachers.*
J. Brewster, G. Ellis and D. Girard (1992) *The Primary English Teacher's Guide.*

C. Brumfit, J. Moon and R. Tongue (1991) *Teaching English to Children.*
L. Cameron (2001) *Teaching Languages to Young Learners.*
H. Curtain and C. A. Dalhberg (2010) *Language and Children: Making the Match: New Languages for Young Learner Grades K-8.*
P. Driscoll and D. Frost (1999) *The Teaching of Modern Foreign Languages in the Primary School.*
G. Ellis and J. Brewster (2002) *Tell it Again: The New Storytelling Handbook for Primary Teachers.*
P. Edelenbos, R. Johnstone and A. Kubanek (2006) *The Main Pedagogical Principles Underlying the Teaching of Languages to Very Young Learners.*
D. Freeman and Y. Freeman (2007) *English Language Learners. The Essential Guide: Theory and Practice.*
E. Garvie (1990) *Story as a Vehicle.*
P. Gibbons (2002) *Scaffolding Language, Scaffolding Learning: Teaching Second Language Learners in the Mainstream Classroom.*
T. Gordon (2006) *Teaching Young Children a Second Language.*
S. Halliwell (1992) *Teaching English in the Primary Classroom.*
J. Haynes (2007) *Getting Started with English Language Learners: How Educators can Meet the Challenge.*
J. D. Hill and K. M. Flynn (2006) *Classroom Instruction that Works with English Language Learners.*
M. Jimenez Raya, B. Faber, W. Gewehr and A. J. Peck (eds.) (2001) *Foreign Language Teaching in Europe: Effective Foreign Language Teaching at the Primary Level.*
C. Kennedy and J. Jarvis (eds.) (1991) *Ideas and Issues in Primary ELT.*
B. Law and M. L. Eckes (2000) *The More-Than-Just-Surviving Handbook: ESL for Every Classroom Teacher.*
M. K. Legutke, A. Müller-Hartmann, and M. Schocker-von-Ditfurth (2009) *Teaching English in the Primary School.*
P. McKay (2006) *Assessing Young Language Learners.*
J. Moon (2000) *Children Learning English.*
A. Pinter (2006) *Teaching Young Language Learners.*
C. Scott (2008) *Teaching Children English as an Additional Language: A Programme for 7–12 year olds.*
W. A. Scott and L. H. Ytreberg (1990) *Teaching English to Children.*
M. Slattery and J. Willis (2001) *English for Primary Teachers: A Handbook of Activities and Classroom Language.*
D. Vale and A. Feunten (1995) *Teaching Children English.*

8.3   Research-focussed books related to child SLA, the 'age factor' and language policy in different contexts

These are just some examples:

J. Enever, J. Moon and U. Raman (eds.) (2009) *Young Learner English Language Policy and Implementation: International Perspectives.*
E. E. Garcia, E. A. Frede and D. Perkins (eds.) (2010) *Young English Language Learners: Current Research and Emerging Directions for Practice and Policy.*
B. Harley (1986) *Age in Second Language Acquisition.*
R. Johnstone (2002) *Addressing the Age Factor: Some Implications for Language Policy.*

A. Moyer (2004) *Age, Accent and Experience in Second Language Acquisition.*
C. Muñoz (ed.) (2006) *Age and the Rate of Foreign Language Learning.*
M. Nikolov (ed.) (2009) *Early Learning of Modern Foreign Languages: Processes and Outcomes.*
M. Nikolov (ed.) (2009) *The 'Age Factor' and Early Language Learning: Studies on Language Acquisition.*
M. Nikolov, J. Mihaljević Djigunović, M. Mattheoudakis, G. Lundberg and T. Flanagan, (eds.) (2007) *Teaching Modern Languages to Young Learners: Teachers, Curricula and Materials.*
J. Philp, R. Oliver and A. Mackey (eds.) (2008) *Second Language Acquisition and the Young Learner: Child's Play?*
S. Rixon (ed.) (1999) *Young Learners of English: Some Research Perspectives.*
D. Singleton and L. Ryan (2004) *Language Acquisition: The Age Factor.*
M. Shatz and L. C. Wilkinson (eds.) (2010) *The Education of English Language Learners: Research to Practice: Challenges in Language and Literacy.*

8.4   Child development and L1 acquisition

Many teachers and researchers working with children are interested to know more about developmental psychology and cognitive, social and emotional development in childhood, as well as first language acquisition. This information may serve as useful background knowledge when teaching and researching second languages with children. Here is a selection of useful books:

N. Applebee (1978) *The Child's Concept of Story.*
L. Berk (2000) *Child Development.*
R. Brown (1973) *The First Language.*
R. Cattell (2000) *Children's Language: Consensus and Controversy.*
M. Donaldson (1978) *Children's Minds.*
S. Foster-Cohen (1999) *An Introduction to Child Language Development.*
S. Foster-Cohen (ed.) (2009) *Language Acquisition.*
L. Galda and A. D. Pellegrini (eds.) (1985) *Play Language and Stories: the Development of Children's Literate Behaviour.*
R. Grieve and M. Hughes (eds.) (1997) *Understanding Children.*
M. T. Guasti (2002) *Language Acquisition: the Growth of Grammar.*
M. A. K. Halliday (1975) *Learning How to Mean: Explorations in the Development of Language.*
S. McNaughton (1995) *Patterns of Emergent Literacy: Processes of Development and Transition.*
S. Meadows (1993) *The Child as Thinker.*
N. Mercer and K. Littleton (2007) *Dialogue and the Development of Children's Thinking.*
K. Nelson (1996) *Language in Cognitive Development.*
J. Piaget (1926/1955) *The Language and Thought of the Child.*
K. Richardson and S. Sheldon (eds.) (1988) *Cognitive Development to Adolescence.*
B. Rogoff (1990) *Apprenticeship in Thinking: Cognitive Development in Social Context.*
P. K. Smith, H. Cowie and M. Blades (1998) *Understanding Children's Development.*
S. Thornton (2008) *Understanding Human Development.*

M. Tomasello (2003) *Constructing a Language: a Usage-based Theory of Language Acquisition.*

K. Trott, S. Dobbinson and P. Griffiths (2004) *The Child Language Reader.*

G. Wells (1981) *Learning through Interaction: The Study of Language Development.*

D. Wood (1998) *How Children Think and Learn.*

8.5   Bilingual/multilingual upbringing and development

Much language learning in childhood happens in families with parents speaking different languages to their children and many families intending to raise their children to become bilingual or even trilingual. These families can access advice about strategies that work best according to research and other people's experiences. Some of these sources give hands-on advice whereas others are more theoretical in their focus.

Examples of websites giving practical advice:

Multilingual Family
http://www.multilingualfamily.co.uk/
This website offers practical advice to multilingual families and additional sources relevant to specific languages. There is a message board where you can send in specific questions.

Bilingual Family Newsletter
http://www.bilingualfamilynewsletter.com/index.php
At this site you can download regular newsletters relating to advice and resources for bilingual and multilingual families. There is also a good range of books recommended for these families.

Bilingual/Bicultural Family Network
http://www.biculturalfamily.org/index.html
This site was started by a bilingual family and it offers advice, tips, on-line resources, a calendar of events, and a magazine for families that wish to join.

Bilingual Families in Perth
http://www.bilingualfamilies.net/pages/en/home.php
This is also a website offering advice. Although it is aimed at families in the Perth area, in Australia, some advice is generic and there are excellent resources included, in particular, some advice on running kids' language clubs.

Examples of books offering advice to bilingual families:

A. Arnberg (1987). *Raising Children Bilingually: The Pre-school Years.*

B. Baker (2000) *A Parents' and Teachers' Guide to Bilingualism.*

S. Barron-Hauwaert (2004) *Language Strategies for Bilingual Families: the One Parent – One Language Approach.*

U. Cunningham-Andersson and S. Andersson (1999) *Growing up with Two Languages: A Practical Guide.*
E. De Jong (1986) *The Bilingual Experience: a Book for Parents.*
E. Harding-Esch and P. Riley (2003) *The Bilingual Family: A Handbook for Parents.*
K. King and A. Mackey (2007) *The Bilingual Edge: Why, When and How to Teach Your Child a Second Language.*
G. Saunders (1982) *Bilingual Children: From Birth to Teens.*

Examples of websites that promote multicultural understanding for children:

The 'International Children's Digital Library'
http://en.childrenslibrary.org/about/mission.shtml
It contains over 4,400 books in 54 languages that readers can search, buy or read on-line. The mission of the organisation is to promote intercultural understanding among young people. There is a community forum that you can join and you can volunteer to translate books or help the organisation in other ways.

The 'Global Gateway'
http://www.globalgateway.org.uk/default.aspx?page=2396
This organisation wants to bring an international dimension to education. Schools are encouraged to find international partners. More than 20,000 schools are registered and there is support and advice for both UK and non-UK schools to register and implement successful international partnerships.

'Skipping Stones'
http://www.skippingstones.org/canvas-vol154-page2.htm
A US-based international multicultural magazine that promotes intercultural understanding. The magazine contains poetry pages, teen talk and book sections. Outstanding books and teaching resources are regularly featured.

The 'Language Lizard'
http://www.languagelizard.com/v/vspfiles/families.htm
You can search for award-winning books, CDs and posters in 40 languages. There are different combinations of dual language books available. The aim of this organisation is to inspire children through languages. There are unique and entertaining supplementary materials for teachers and information for librarians.

Examples of theoretical books about child bilingualism:

C. Baker and S. Prys Jones (1998) *Encyclopedia of Bilingualism and Bilingual Education.*
T. K. Bhatia and W. C. Ritchie (eds.) (2006) *The Handbook of Bilingualism.*
N. B. Chin and G. Wigglesworth (2007) *Bilingualism: An Advanced Resource Book.*
S. J. Caldas (2006) *Raising Bilingual-Biliterate Children in Monolingual Cultures.*
O. Garcia (2008) *Bilingual Education in the 21st Century: A Global Perspective.*
F. Genesee (ed.) (1994) *Educating Second Language Children.*

F. Grosjean (1982) *Life with Two Languages: An Introduction to Bilingualism.*
K. Hakuta (1986) *Mirror of Language: The Debate on Bilingualism.*
K. Potowski (2007) *Language and Identity in a Dual Immersion School.*
J. Simpson and G. Wigglesworth (eds.) (2008) *Children's Language and Multilingualism.*
X. Wang (2008) *Growing Up with Three Languages: Birth to Eleven.*
T. Williams Fortune and D. J. Tedich (eds.) (2008) *Pathways to Multilingualism: Evolving Prespectives on Immersion Education.*

8.6   Child-friendly research methods

This is a collection of books offering advice on using different research methods with child subjects, often through presenting and critiquing empirical studies conducted with different age groups. Both traditional and more innovative approaches to research, as well as appropriate aspects of ethics, are addressed.

P. Christensen and A. James (eds.) (2008) *Research with Children: Perspectives and Practices.*
R. Davie and D. Galloway (eds.) (1996) *Listening to Children in Education.*
R. Davie, G. Upton and V. Varma (eds.) (1996) *The Voice of the Child: A Handbook for Professionals.*
D. Eder and L. Fingerson (2001) 'Interviewing children and adolescents'. In J. B. Gubrium and J. A. Holstein (eds.) *Handbook of Interview Research.*
A. Farrell (ed.) (2005) *Ethical Research with Children.*
G. A. Fine and K. L. Sandstrom (1988) *Knowing Children: Participant Observations with Minors.*
S. Fraser, V. Lewis, S. Ding, M. Kellett and C. Robinson (eds.) (2004) *Doing Research with Children and Young People.*
M. Hill (2005) *Ethical Considerations in Researching Children's Experiences.*
R. M. Holmes (1998) *Fieldwork with Children.*
A. James and A. Prout (1997) *Constructing and Reconstructing Childhood.*
M. Kellett (2005) *How to Develop Children as Researchers: A Step-by-Step Guide to Teaching the Research Process.*
M. Kellett (2010) *Rethinking Children and Research: Attitudes in Contemporary Society.*
G. McNaughton, S. A. Rolfe and I. Siraj-Blatchford (eds.) (2001) *Doing Early Childhood Research: International Perspectives on Theory and Practice.*
A. Pollard (1996) *The Social World of Children's Learning.*
P. Thomson (ed.) (2008) *Doing Visual Research with Children and Young People.*
J. Tinson (2009) *Conducting Research with Children and Adolescents: Design, Methods and Empirical Cases.*
K. Tisdall, J. B. Davies and M. Gallagher (2009) *Researching with Children and Young People: Research Design, Methods and Analysis.*

8.7   Journals

Research articles related to children's language learning in different contexts can be located in a wide variety of journals. These are some examples:

- *ELT Journal* http://eltj.oxfordjournals.org/
- *Applied Linguistics* http://applij.oxfordjournals.org/
- *Child Development* http://www.wiley.com/bw/journal.asp?ref=0009-3920& site=1
- *Elementary School Journal* http://www.journals.uchicago.edu/toc/esj/ current
- *Oxford Review of Education* http://www.tandf.co.uk/journals/titles/ 03054985.asp
- *Child Development* http://www.tandf.co.uk/journals/titles/03054985. asp
- *Childhood* http://chd.sagepub.com/
- *Children and Schools* http://www.naswpress.org/publications/journals/cs. html
- *Comparative Education* http://www.tandf.co.uk/journals/titles/03050068. asp
- *Developmental Psychology* http://psycnet.apa.org/index.cfm?fa=browsePA. volumes&jcode=dev
- *International Journal of Bilingual Education and Bilingualism* http://www. tandf.co.uk/journals/1367-0050
- *International Journal of Multilingualism* http://www.tandf.co.uk/journals/ 1479-0718
- *International Journal of Bilingualism* http://ijb.sagepub.com/
- *Cognitive Development* http://www.sciencedirect.com/science/journal/ 08852014
- *Journal of Child Language* http://journals.cambridge.org/action/display Journal?jid=jcl
- *Journal of Multilingual and Multicultural Development* http://www.tandf.co. uk/journals/0143-4632
- *Language and Education* http://www.tandf.co.uk/journals/0950-0782
- *Language Awareness* http://www.tandf.co.uk/journals/
- *Language Culture and Curriculum* http://www.tandf.co.uk/journals/ 07908318
- *Language Learning* http://www.wilcy.com/bw/journal.asp?ref= 00238333
- *Language in Society* http://journals.cambridge.org/action/displayJournal? jid=lsy
- *Literacy* http://www.wiley.com/bw/journal.asp?ref=1741-4350
- *Studies in SLA (SSLA)* http://journals.cambridge.org/action/displayJournal? jid=SLA
- *System* http://www.elsevier.com/wps/find/journaldescription.cws_home/ 335/description#description
- *The Modern Language Journal* http://mlj.miis.edu/
- *TESOL Quarterly* http://www.ingentaconnect.com/content/tesol/tq

8.8   Tests and examinations for children

Content and language

In countries like the USA, Canada, Australia or the UK, ESL learners are tested in the subject areas targeted at the general learner population, and in addition, they take ESL-specific tests. For example, in the USA:

ACCESS (Assessing Comprehension and Communication in English for English Language Learners) is a large-scale test that addresses English language development standards. *ACCESS for ELLs* (English Language Learners) assesses language proficiency and does not assess content area knowledge, unlike the *WKCE* (Wisconsin Knowledge Concepts Examination) which assesses a student's comprehension in the content area as well. **http://dpi. state.wi.us/oea/access.html**

As an example, this website from the Connecticut State Department of Education, illustrates the benchmarks and standards for English language learners (ELLs) together with standards necessary to exit English Language Learning Programmes. **http://www.csde.state.ct.us/public/cedar/ assessment/ell/index.htm**

English as a second language

One of the most well-known English language tests that have been specifically designed for young learners is the *Cambridge Young Learners English Tests* developed and administered by *the University of Cambridge ESOL Examinations*. Large numbers of young learners take this examination every year from countries such as China, Argentina, Spain and Italy. The *YL* test is specifically designed to take into account research and latest developments in methodology, curriculum design and textbook content for EFL children.

The *Cambridge Young Learners* tests are organised according to the following levels:

- Starters Exam (for age 7, or Year 1 to 2 elementary students)
- Movers Exam (for age 8 to 11, or Year 3 to 4 elementary students)
- Flyers Exam (for age 9 to 12, or Year 5 to 6 elementary students)

In the examination, candidates are being tested under three aspects:

- Reading and Writing
- Listening
- Speaking

Teachers and parents can purchase practice books and test papers for all the levels. **http://www.cambridgeesol.org/exams/young-learners/yle.html**

Other English as a Second Language tests for children include:

Common European Framework of Reference for Languages (CEFR)
http://www.coe.int/t/dg4/linguistic/DNR_EN.asp
This website is a rich source of documents describing the background to the European standardised framework of language learning and assessment using detailed descriptors. Originally, the *CEFR* was aimed at adult learners but gradually it is being extended to all school-level learning and teaching in Europe and outside. The framework can help learners and teachers to measure proficiency and progress in different languages. Examples of language portfolios and language passports for different levels in different languages are available on the website. One example of a *CEFR*-based English language test for young learners is Hasselgren (2005), which was developed for Norwegian schools.

Many of the following internationally marketed *YL* tests are also linked to the *CEFR*:

Pearson PTE Young Learners, formerly known as *London Tests of English for Children* **http://www.pearsonpte.com/PTEYOUNGLEARNERS/Pages/home.aspx**

Anglia's General English tests, levels suitable for children and teenagers, i.e. First Step, Junior, Primary, Preliminary, Elementary and Pre Intermediate **http://eu.anglia.nl/index.php?option=com_content&task=view&id=4&Itemid=6**

Trinity's GESE grades suitable for children, i.e. grades 1–4
http://www.trinitycollege.co.uk/site/?id=1803

LCCI Junior English Tests (JET)
http://www.britishcouncil.org/burma-exams-english-exams-lcci-esol.htm

TOEFL
TOEFL is a test for adults but many middle school and high school level students in the USA and worldwide take it in preparation for further studies. Pre-TOEFL preparation courses are often offered to grades 3–5, and grades 6–7. Official TOEFL preparation may start in grades 8–12.

The last category of tests comprises some commonly used cognitive and L1 related tests often cited in research publications. Some examples:

Stanford-Binet Intelligence Scale
This is used for ages between 2 and adulthood and is designed to measure abilities in verbal reasoning, visual reasoning, quantitative abilities and short-term memory capacity. Results are age-appropriate scores.

Wechsler Intelligence Scale for Children
This is used for ages 6–16 years. It measures verbal abilities and visual reasoning.

Differential Ability Scales (DAS)
This measures cognitive abilities and achievement between the ages of 2 and 17.
www.PsychCorp.com

Raven's Progressive Matrices
Non-verbal assessment of perception and thinking skills between the ages of 5 and 11.
www.opp.co.uk.

The Peabody Picture Vocabulary test
This is used for ages between 2 and adulthood. It assesses single word receptive language. It gives an age-equivalent score.

8.9   Organisations and projects

The CHILDES Project
http://childes.psy.cmu.edu/intro/
This is a rich source of recorded and transcribed child talk for researchers.
See B. McWhinney (1991) *The CHILDES Project: Tools for Analysing Talk.*

IATEFL Young Learners Special Interest Group (YL SIG)
This organisation is focussed on recent developments in English language education for children and teenagers aged 3–17. Members receive a biannual publication (*Children and Teenagers*) with articles and book reviews in addition to the *IATEFL Voices Newsletter*. The YL SIG has a comprehensive website with web sources and downloadable articles. Members can also join an active discussion group. **http://groups.yahoo.com/group/younglearners**
    You can find local *IATEFL* branches in most countries worldwide. You will find information about conferences on the website.
http://www.countryschool.com/ylsig2/

TESOL K-12 (Teaching English to Speakers of Other Languages) K 12 (from kindergarten to age 12)
This US-based organisation caters for second language children's needs in the mainstream school system. If you are a member of *TESOL*, you can have access to a large database of primary and secondary level teaching materials as well as teacher development opportunities.
http://www.tesol.org

Council of Europe Languages
This is a rich resource that contains a wealth of information about language policies across Europe, including primary and pre-primary levels. You can find a calendar of activities and schemes, publications, research reports and assessment instruments for different language learning levels.

http://www.coe.int/t/dg4/linguistic/
One example project that is relevant for primary language teachers is ELLiE (*Early Language Learning in Europe*) with partners from England, Italy, the Netherlands, Poland, Spain, Sweden and Croatia. Here is the project website where you can read about the project aims and objectives, the events, the outcomes and publications, and can view further links and contacts: http://www.ellieresearch.eu/calendar.html

Child Research NET: an Internet-based Research Institute
http://www.childresearch.net/ABOUTUS/index.html#mess
This is a research institute which publishes international research articles and resources in the area of child research, education and development, including language education. There is a special section devoted to research and resources in Japan and Asia. There is an extensive list of international researchers associated with its board and the site provides links to over 180 relevant institutions worldwide.

National Capital Language Resource Center
http://www.nclrc.org/html
This is a US-based resource centre offering language teaching resources in multiple languages, research publications, project reports, podcasts and training materials. There is also up-to-date information about relevant conferences and workshops.

Center for Advanced Research in Language Acquisition (CARLA) in the University of Minnesota
http://www.carla.umn.edu/research.html
This is another national language resource centre in the USA. It has an excellent resource bank of information related to immersion education and research, content-based learning, culture and assessment. You can subscribe to receive their regular newsletter.

Center for Applied Linguistics (USA, Washington)
http://www.cal.org/index.html
Their site offers extensive information about research, resources, projects and services related to language teaching and learning both in childhood and adulthood. You can also buy *CAL* publications and join the *CAL* list and receive regular *CAL* news.

Australian Council of TESOL Associations
http://www.tesol.org.au/Teacher-Education/Links/ESL-Teacher-Resources
Their site offers publications, ideas for teacher education, conferences and events and it has got links to hundreds of relevant sites for language teachers.

VicTESOL (Australia)
http://www.vatme.vic.edu.au/about/
With resources and links to professional organisations, a special section is devoted to children and schools. Their site offers links to articles, reports, conference news and resources for teachers.

TESL Canada
http://www.tesl.ca/Home.htm
This is a rich site with local branches according to geographical locations in Canada. There are extensive, free resources for language teachers, including teachers of children.

References

Albrecht, T. L., Johnson, G. M. and Walther, J. B. (1993) Understanding communication processes in focus groups. In D. L. Morgan (ed.), *Successful Focus Groups: Advancing the State of the Art*. Newbury Park, CA: Sage, pp. 51–64.

Alderson, P. (2005) Designing ethical research with children. In A. Farrell (ed.), *Ethical Research with Children*. Maidenhead: Open University Press, pp. 27–36.

Alderson, P. (2008) Children as researchers: Participation rights and research methods. In P. Christensen and A. James (eds.), *Research with Children*. London: Routledge, pp. 276–90.

Alderson, P. and Morrow, G. (2004) *Ethics, Social Research and Consulting with Children and Young People*. Barkingside: Barnardo's.

Alexiou, T. (2009) Young learners' cognitive skills and their role in foreign language vocabulary learning. In M. Nikolov (ed.), *Early Learning of Modern Foreign Languages: Processes and Outcomes*. Second Language Acquisition Series. Bristol: Multilingual Matters, pp. 46–61.

Allen, S., Genesee, F., Fish, S. and Cargo, M. (2002) Grammatical constraints on early bilingual code-mixing: Evidence from children learning Inuktitut and English. Paper presented at the Boston University Conference of Language Development.

Allwright, D. and Hanks J. (2009) *The Developing Language Learner: An Introduction to Exploratory Practice*. Basingstoke and New York: Palgrave Macmillan.

Alptekin, C., Ercetin, G. and Bayyurt, Y. (2007) The effectiveness of a theme-based syllabus for young L2 learners. *Journal of Multilingual and Multicultural Development*, 28 (1): 1–17.

Anderson, J. (1985) *Cognitive Psychology and its Implications*. New York: Freeman.

Anglin, J. M. (1993) *Vocabulary Development: A Morphological Analysis*. Monographs for the Society for Research in Child Development, 58 (10, Serial number 238).

Aoyama, K., Guion, S. G., Flege, J. E., Yamada, T. and Akahane-Yamada, R. (2008) The first years in an L2-speaking environment: A comparison of Japanese children and adults learning American English. *International Review of Applied Linguistics (IRAL)*, 46: 61–90

Applebee, N. (1978) *The Child's Concept of Story*. Chicago: University of Chicago Press.

Arnberg, A. (1987) *Raising Children Bilingually: The Pre-school Years*. Clevedon: Multilingual Matters.

Atkinson, R. C. and Shiffrin, R. M. (1968) Human memory: A proposed system and its control processes. In K. W. Spence and J. T. Spence (eds.), *Advances in the Psychology of Learning and Motivation 2*. New York: Academic Press, pp. 90–195.

Azmitia, M. and Montgomery, R. (1993) Friendships, transactive dialogues, and the development of scientific reasoning. *Social Development*, 2: 202–21.

Baddeley, A. D. (1992) Working memory. *Science*, 255: 556–9.

Baddeley, A. D. (1994) The magic number seven: Still magic after all these years? *Psychological Review*, 101: 353–6.

Bae, J. (2007) Development of English skills need not suffer as a result of immersion: Grades 1 and 2 writing assessment in a Korean/English two-way immersion programme. *Language Learning*, 57 (2): 299–332.

Bailey, K. M, Curtis A. and Nunan, D. (2001) *Pursuing Professional Development: The Self as a Source*. Boston: Heinle and Heinle.

Bailey, N., Madden, C. and Krashen, S. (1978) Is there a natural sequence in adult second language learning? *Language Learning*, 24: 235–43. Reprinted in E. Hatch (ed.) (1978) *Second Language Acquisition: A Book of Readings*. Rowley, MA: Newbury House.

Bailey, R. and Dugard, C. (2007) *Lights, Camera, Action: New Pathfinder 6*. London: CILT.

Baker, C. (2000) *A Parents' and Teachers' Guide to Bilingualism*. Clevedon: Multilingual Matters.

Baker, C. (2006) *Foundations of Bilingual Education and Bilingualism*. Clevedon: Multilingual Matters.

Baker, C. and Prys Jones, S. (1998) *Encyclopedia of Bilingualism and Bilingual Education*. Clevedon: Multilingual Matters.

Baker-Ward, L., Ornstein, P. A. and Holden, D. J. (1984) The expression of memorisation in early childhood. *Journal of Experimental Child Psychology*, 37: 555–75.

Barnes, A. and Hunt, M. (2003) *Effective Assessment of Modern Foreign Languages*. London: CILT.

Barron-Hauwaert, S. (2004) *Language Strategies for Bilingual Families: The One Parent – One Language Approach*. Clevedon: Multilingual Matters.

Berk, L. (2000) *Child Development*. Needham Heights, MA: Pearson Education Company.

Berman, R. A. (2007) Developing linguistic knowledge and language use across adolescence. In E. Hoff and M. Shatz (eds.), *Blackwell Handbook of Language Development*. Oxford: Blackwell Publishing, pp. 347–67.

Berndt, T. J. (1982) The features of effects of friendship in early adolescence. *Child Development*, 53 (6): 1447–60.

Berndt, T. J. and Keefe, K. (1995) Friends' influence on adolescents' adjustment to school. *Child Development*, 66 (5): 1312–29.

Best, D. L. and Ornstein, P. A. (1986) Children's generation and communication of mnemonic organisational strategies. *Developmental Psychology*, 22: 845–53.

Bhatia, T. K. and Ritchie, W. C. (eds.) (2006) *The Handbook of Bilingualism*. Malden, MA: Blackwell.

Bialystok, E. (1990) *Communication Strategies*. Oxford: Blackwell.

Bialystok, E. and Hakuta, K. (1999) Confounded age: Linguistic and cognitive factors in age differences for second language acquisition. In D. Birdsong (ed.), *Second Language Acquisition and the Critical Period Hypothesis*. Mahwah, NJ: Erlbaum, pp. 161–82.

Bigelow, B. J. and La Gaipa, J. J. (1980) The development of friendship values and choice. In H. C. Foot, A. J. Chapman and R. J. Smith (eds.), *Friendship and Social Relations in Children*. Chichester: Wiley, pp. 15–44.

Binet, A. and Simon, T. (1916) *The Development of Intelligence in Children*. Vineland, NJ: Publications of the Training School at Vineland (reprinted 1980 by Williams Publishing Co, Nashville, TN).

Birdsong, D. (1992) Ultimate attainment in second language acquisition. *Language*, 68: 706–55.

Birdsong, D. (1999) Introduction: Whys and why nots of the critical period hypothesis for second language acquisition. In D. Birdsong (ed.), *Second Language Acquisition and the Critical Period Hypothesis*. Mahwah, NJ: Erlbaum.

Birdsong, D. and Molis, M. (2001) On evidence for maturational constraints in second language acquisition. *Journal of Memory and Language*, 44: 235–49.

Bjorklund, D. F. (1980) Children's identification of category relations in lists presented for recall. *Journal of Genetic Psychology*, 136 (1): 45–54.

Bjorklund, D. F. (2003) Evolutionary psychology from a developmental systems perspective: Comment on Lickliter and Honeycutt, *Psychological Bulletin*, 129 (6): 836–41.

Bjorklund, D. F. and Douglas, R. N. (1997) The development of memory strategies. In N. Cowen (ed.), *The Development of Memory in Childhood*. Hove: Psychology Press, pp. 83–111.

Bjorklund, D. F. and Hock, H. S. (1981) Age differences in the temporal locus of memory organization in children's recall. *Journal of Experimental Child Psychology*, 33(2): 347–62.

Bjorklund, D. F. and Jacobs, J. W. (1985) Associative and categorical processes in children's memory: The role of automaticity in the development of organisation in free recall. *Journal of Experimental Child Psychology*, 39: 599–617.

Bjorklund, D. F., Miller, P. H., Coyle, T. R. and Slawinski, J. L. (1997) Instructing children to use memory strategies: Evidence of utilisation strategies in memory training studies. *Developmental Review*, 17: 411–41.

Bjorklund, D. F. and Zeman, B. (1982) Children's organisational and metamemory awareness in their recall of familiar information. *Child Development*, 53: 799–810.

Björklund, S. (1997) Immersion in Finland in the 1990s: A state of development and expansion. In R. K. Johnson and M. Swain (eds.), *Immersion Education: International Perspectives*. Cambridge: Cambridge University Press, pp. 85–101.

Bley-Vroman, R. W. (1989) What is the logical problem of foreign language learning? In S. M. Gass and J. Schachter (ed), *Linguistic Perspectives on Second Language Acquisition*. Cambridge: Cambridge University Press, pp. 41–68.

Bongaerts, T. (1999) Ultimate attainment in L2 pronunciation: The case of very advanced late L2 learners. In D. Birdsong (ed.), *Second Language Acquisition and the Critical Period Hypothesis*. Mahwah, NJ: Erlbaum, pp. 133–60.

Bongartz, C. and Schneider, M. L. (2003) Linguistic development in social contexts: A study of two brothers learning German. *The Modern Language Journal*, 87: 13–37.

Bosch, L. and Sebastián-Gallés, N. (1997) Native-language recognition abilities in 4-month-old infants from monolingual and bilingual environments. *Cognition*, 65: 33–69.

Bouffard, L. A. and Sarkar, M. (2008) Training 8-year-old French immersion students in meta-linguistic analysis: An innovation in form focused pedagogy. *Language Awareness*, 17 (1): 3–24.

Brainerd, C. J. and Gordon, L. L. (1994) Development of verbatim and gist memory for numbers. *Developmental Psychology*, 30: 163–77.

Brainerd, C. J. and Reyna, V. F. (1990) Gist is the grist: Fuzzy trace theory and the new intuitionism. *Developmental Review*, 10: 3–47.

Brewster, J, and Ellis, G. (1991) *The Storytelling Handbook for Primary Teachers*. Harmondsworth: Penguin Books.

Brewster, J., Ellis, G. and Girard. D. (1992) *The Primary English Teacher's Guide*. Harmondsworth: Penguin Books.

Broom, Y. (2004) Reading English in multilingual South African primary schools. *International Journal of Bilingual Education and Bilingualism*, 7 (6): 506–28.

Brown, A. L., Smiley, S. S. and Lawton, S. Q. C. (1978) The effects of experience on the selection of suitable retrieval cues for studying texts. *Child Development*, 49: 829–35.

Brown, J. D. and Rodgers, T. S. (2002) *Doing Second Language Research*. Oxford: Oxford University Press.

Brown, R. (1973) *The First Language: The Early Stages*. Cambridge, MA: Harvard University Press.

Brumfit, C., Moon, J. and Tongue, R. (1991) *Teaching English to Children*. London: Collins ELT.

Brunswick, E., Goldscheider, L. and Pilek, E. (1932) Unterssuchungen zur Entwiklung des Gedachtnisses (Studies on the development of memory). In W. Stern and O. Lippmann (eds.), *Beihefte zur Zeitscrift fur Angewadte Psychologie 64*. Leipzig: Ambrosius Barth.

Brunzel, P. (2002) *Kulturbezogenes Lernen und Interkuturalität. Zur Entwicklung kultureller Konnotationen im Französischunterricht der Sekundarstufe I*. (*The Topic of Culture and Interculturality: Study on the Development of Cultural Connotations in the Teaching of French at the Lower Secondary Level*). Tübingen: Narr.

Burstall, C., Jamieson, M., Cohen, S. and Hargreaves, M. (1974) *Primary French in the Balance*. Windsor, UK: NFER Publishing Company.

Butler, Y. (2004) What levels of English proficiency do elementary school teachers need to attain to teach EFL? Case studies from Korea, Taiwan, and Japan. *TESOL Quarterly*, 38 (2): 245–78.

Butler, Y. and Lee, J. (2006) On-task versus off-task self-assessment among Korean elementary school students studying English. *The Modern Language Journal*, 90 (4): 505–18.

Caldas, S. J. (2006) *Raising Bilingual-Biliterate Children in Monolingual Cultures*. Clevedon: Multilingual Matters.

Cameron, L. (2001) *Teaching Languages to Young Learners*. Cambridge: Cambridge University Press.

Cameron, L. (2003) Challenges for ELT from the expansion in teaching children. *ELT Journal*, 57: 105–12.

Cancino, H., Rosansky, E. and Schumann, J. (1978) The acquisition of English negatives and interrogatives by native Spanish speakers. In E. Hatch (ed.), *Second Language Acquisition: A Book of Readings*. Rowley, MA: Newbury House, pp. 207–30.

Candlin, C. and Derrick, J. (1973) *Language*. London: CRE.

Cant, A. and Superfine, W. (1997) *Developing Resources for Primary*. Richmond Publishing.

Carless, D. (2004) Issues in teachers' reinterpretation of a task-based innovation in primary schools. *TESOL Quarterly*, 38 (4): 639–62.

Carless, D. (2006) Collaborative EFL teaching in primary schools. *ELT Journal*, 60 (4): 328–35.

Case, R. (1972) Validation of a neo-Piagetian mental capacity construct. *Journal of Experimental Child Psychology*, 14: 287–302.

Case, R. (1985) *Intellectual Development: Birth to Adulthood*. Orlando, FL: Academic Press.

Case, R. (1991) *The Mind's Staircase: Exploring the Conceptual Underpinnings of Children's Thought and Conceptual Knowledge*. Hillsdale, NJ: Lawrence Erlbaum.

Cattell, R. (2000) *Children's Language: Consensus and Controversy*. London: Cassell.

Cave, S., Murray, L. and Thatcher, J. (2006) *100+ Fun Ideas for Practising Modern Foreign Languages in the Primary Classroom: Activities for Developing Oracy and Literacy Skills*. Dunstable, UK: Brilliant Publications.

Ceci, S. J. (1991) How much does schooling influence general intelligence and its cognitive components? A reassessment of the evidence. *Developmental Psychology*, 27 (5): 703–22.

Ceci, S. J. and Roazzi, A. (1994) The effects of context on cognition: Postcards from Brazil. In R. J. Sternberg (ed.), *Mind in Context*. New York: Cambridge University Press, pp. 74–101.

Cekaite, A. (2007) A child's development of interactional competence in a Swedish classroom. *The Modern Language Journal*, 91: 45–62.

Cenoz, J. (2000) Research on multilingual acquisition. In J. Cenoz and U. Jessner (eds.), *English in Europe: The Acquisition of a Third Language*. Clevedon: Multilingual Matters, pp. 39–54.

Cenoz, J. and Genesee, F. (1998) Psycholinguistic perspectives on multilingualism and multilingual education. In J. Cenoz and F. Genesee (eds.), *Beyond Bilingualism, Multilingualism and Multilingual Education*. Clevedon: Multilingual Matters, pp. 16–32.

Chamot, A. U. and El-Dinary, P. B. (1999) Language learning strategies in language immersion classrooms. *The Modern Language Journal*, 83 (3): 319–38.

Chapman, M. and Lindenberger, U. (1988) Functions, operations and decalage in the development of transitivity. *Developmental Psychology*, 24: 542–51.

Chaves, C., Graham, A. and Superfine, W. (1999) *Fun and Games in English: Photocopiable Language Activities for Young Learners*. Surrey, UK: Delta Publishing.

Chi, M. T. H. (1978) Knowledge structures and memory development. In R. S. Siegler (ed.), *Children's Thinking: What Develops?* Hillsdale, NJ: Lawrence Erlbaum, pp. 73–96.

Chin, N. B. and Wigglesworth, G. (2007) *Bilingualism: An Advanced Resource Book*. London: Routledge.

Chomsky, C. (1969) *The Acquisition of Syntax in Children from 5 to 10*. Cambridge, MA: MIT Press.

Chomsky, N. (1987) Transformational grammar: Past, present and future. *Studies in English Language and Literature*. Kyoto: Kyoto University, pp. 33–80.

Christensen, P. and James, A. (eds.) (2008) *Research with Children: Perspectives and Practices*. London: Routledge.

Claire, E. (1998) *ESL Teacher's Activities Kit*. Upper Saddle River, NJ: Prentice Hall.

Clark, E. V. (1990) On the pragmatics of contrast. *Journal of Child Language*, 17: 417–31.

Clark, R. C., and Moran, P. R. (2002) *Index Card Games for ESL*. Brattleboro, VT: Pro Lingua Associates.

Clahsen, H. (1984) The acquisition of German word order: A test case for cognitive approaches to L2 development. In R. Andersen (ed.), *Second Language: A Cross-linguistic Perspective*. Rowley, MA: Newbury House, pp. 219–42.

Clinton, B. and Vincent, M. (2009) *Leading the Way. Young Pathfinder 16*. London: CILT.

Cohen, S. P., Tucker, R. and Lambert, W. E. (1967) The comparative skills of monolinguals and bilinguals in perceiving phoneme sequences. *Language and Speech*, 10: 159–68.

COLT (Comunicative Orientation of Language Teaching Scheme) http://openlibrary.org/books/OL12064664M/Colt_Observation_Scheme_(Research)

Comeau, L., Genesee, F. and Lapaquette, L. (2003) The modeling hypothesis and child bilingual code-mixing. *International Journal of Bilingualism*, 7: 113–26.

Connolly, P. (2008) Race, gender and critical reflexivity in research with young children. In P. Christensen and A. James (eds.), *Research with Children: Perspectives and Practices*. London: Routledge, pp. 173–88.

Cook, G. (2000) *Language Play, Language Learning*. Oxford: Oxford University Press.

Cook, T. and Hess E. (2007) What the camera sees and from whose perspective: Fun methodologies for engaging children in enlightening adults. *Childhood*, 14 (1): 29–45.

Creese, A. and Martin, P. (2003) Multilingual classroom ecologies: Interrelationhips, interactions and ideologies. *International Journal of Bilingual Education and Bilingualism*, 6 (3–4): 161–7.

Cummins, J. (1981) The role of primary language development in promoting educational success for language minority children. In California State Department of Education (eds.), *Schooling and Language Minority Students: A Theoretical Framework*. Los Angeles: Evaluation, Dissemination and Assessment Centre, pp. 3–49.

Cummins, J. (1983) Language proficiency and academic achievement. In J. Oller (ed.), *Issues in Language Testing Research*. Rowley, MA: Newbury House, pp. 108–29.

Cummins, J. (1984) *Bilingualism and Special Education: Issues in Assessment and Pedagogy*. Clevedon: Multilingual Matters.

Cummins, J. (2000) Putting language proficiency in its place. In J. Cenoz and U. Jessner (eds.), *English in Europe; The Acquisition of a Third Language*. Clevedon: Mutilingual Matters, pp. 54–83.

Cummins, J. (2003) Bilingual education. Basic principles. In J.-M. Dewaele, A. Housen and Li Wei (eds.), *Bilingualism: Beyond Basic Principles*. Multilingual Matters, pp. 56–66.

Cummins, J. and Corson, D. (eds.) (1997) *The Encyclopedia of Language and Education 5: Bilingual Education*. Dordrecht: Kluwer.

Cunningham-Andersson, U. and Andersson, S. (1999) *Growing Up with Two Languages: A Practical Guide*. London: Routledge.

Curtain, H. (2000) Early language learning in the USA. In M. Nikolov and H. Curtain (eds.), *An Early Start: Young Learners and Modern Languages in Europe and Beyond*. Graz, Austria: European Centre for Modern Languages,Council of Europe, pp. 191–208.

Curtain, H. and Dalhberg, C. A. (2010) *Language and Children: Making the Match: New Languages for Young Learner Grades K-8*. Boston: Allyn and Bacon Publishers.

Curtiss, S. (1977) *Genie: A Psycholinguistic Study of a Modern-day 'Wild Child'*. New York: Academic Press.

Dagenais, D., Day, E. and Toohey, K. (2006) A multilingual child's literacy practices and contrasting identities in the figured world of French immersion classrooms. *International Journal of Bilingual Education and Bilingualism*, 9 (5): 205–18.

Dam, L. (1995) *Learner Autonomy 3: From Theory to Classroom Practice*. Dublin: Authentik.

Datta, M. and Pomphrey, C. (2004) A *World of Languages: Developing Children's Love of Languages: Young Pathfinder 2*. London: CILT.

Davie, R. and Galloway, D. (eds.) (1996) *Listening to Children in Education*. London: David Fulton.

Davie, R., Upton, G. and Varma, V. (eds.) (1996) *The Voice of the Child: A Handbook for Professionals*. London: Falmer Press.

Davine, M., Tucker, R. and Lambert, W. E. (1971) The perception of phoneme sequences by monolingual and bilingual elementary school children. *Canadian Journal of Behavioural Science*, 3: 72–6.

Day, E. and Shapson, S. (1996) *Studies in Immersion Education*. Clevedon: Multilingual Matters.

De Courcy, M. (2007) Disrupting preconceptions: challenges to pre-service teachers' beliefs about ESL children. *Journal of Multilingual and Multicultural Development*, 28 (3): 188–203.

De Houwer, A. (1995) Bilingual language acquisition. In P. Fletcher and B. MacWhinney (eds.), *The Handbook of Child Language*. Oxford: Blackwell, pp. 219–50.

De Jong, E. (1986) *The Bilingual Experience: A Book for Parents*. Cambridge: Cambridge University Press.

de Mejía, A.-M. (2005) Bilingual education in Colombia: Towards in integrated perspective. In de Mejía (ed.), *Bilingual Education in South America*. Clevedon: Multilingual Matters, pp. 48–64.

de Mejía, A.-M. and Tejada, H. (2002) Empowerment y cambio en la construcción de currículos bilingües (inglés – español) en colegios monolingües. In A.-M. de Mejía and R. Nieves Oviedo (eds.), *Nuevos Caminos en Educación Bilingüe en Colombia*. Cali: Universidad del Valle.

DeKeyser, R. (2000) The robustness of critical period effects in second language acquisition. *Studies in Second Language Acquisition*, 22: 499–533.

Denos, C., Toohey, K., Nielson, K. and Waterstone, B. (2009) *Collaborative Research in Multilingual Classrooms*. Clevedon: Multilingual Matters.

Derrick, J. (1977) *Language Needs of Minority Group Children*. Windsor, UK: NFER.

Deutsch, W. and Pechmann, T. (1982) Social interaction and the development of definite descriptions. *Cognition*, 11: 159–84.

Devlieger, M. and Goossens, G. (2007) An assessment tool for the evaluation of teacher practice in powerful task-based language learning environments. In K. Van den Branden, K. Van Gorp and M. Verhelst (eds.), *Tasks in Action: Task-based Language Education from a Classroom-based Perspective*. Newcastle upon Tyne: Cambridge Scholars Publishing, pp. 92–130.

Dimroth, C. (2008a) Perspectives on second language acquisition at different ages. In J. Philp, R. Oliver and A. Mackey (eds.), *Second Language Acquistion and the Younger Learner: Child's Play?* Amsterdam: John Benjamins Publishing Company, pp. 53–82.

Dimroth, C. (2008b) Age effect on the process of L2 acquisition? Evidence from the acquisition of negation and finiteness in the L2 German. *Language Learning*, 58 (1): 117–50.

Donaldson, M. (1978) *Children's Minds*. London: Fontana Press.

Donaldson, M. (1992) *Human Minds: An Exploration*. London: Penguin.

Döpke, S. (2000) *Cross-linguistic Structures in Simultaneous Bilingualism*. Amsterdam: John Benjamins.

Dörnyei, Z. (2007) *Research Methods in Applied Linguistics*. Oxford: Oxford University Press.

Dörnyei, Z. (2009) *The Psychology of Second Language Acquisition*. Oxford: Oxford University Press.

Doyé, P. (1995) Exemplarischer Fremdsprachenunterricht. In P. Doyé (ed.), *Kernfragen des Fremdsprachenunterrichts an der grundschule*. Braunschweig: Westermann, pp. 30–9.

Doyé, P. and Hurrell, A. (eds.) (1997) *Foreign Language Learning In Primary Schools (age 5/6 to 10/11)*. Strasbourg: Education Committee, Council for Cultural Co-operation, Council of Europe Publications.

Drew, I. (2009) Using the early years literacy programme in primary EFL Norwegian classrooms. In M. Nikolov (ed.), *Early Learning of Modern Foreign Languages: Processes and Outcomes*. Second Language Acquisition Series. Bristol: Multilingual Matters, pp. 108–20.

Driscoll, P. and Frost, D. (1999) *The Teaching of Modern Foreign Languages in the Primary School*. London: Routledge.

Duff, P. A. (2002) The discursive co-construction of knowledge, identity and difference: An ethnography of communication in the high school mainstream. *Applied Linguistics*, 23 (3): 289–322.

Duff, P. A. and Polio, C. G. (1990) How much foreign language is there in the foreign language classroom? *Modern Language Journal*, 74: 54–166.

Dulay, H. and Burt, M. (1974) Natural sequences of child second language acquisition. *Language Learning*, 24: 37–53. Reprinted in E. Hatch (ed.), *Second Language Acquisition: A Book of Readings*. Rowley, MA: Newbury House.

Dunn, O. (1984) *Developing English with Young Learners*. London: Macmillan.

Durgunoğlu, A. Y. and Öney, B. (1999) A cross-linguistic comparison of phonological awareness and word recognition. *Reading and Writing*, 11 (4): 281–99.

Edelenbos, P., Johnstone, R. and Kubanek, A. (2006) *The Main Pedagogical Principles Underlying the Teaching of Languages to Very Young Learners*. Brussels: European Commission.

Eder, D. (1995) *School Talk: Gender and Adolescent Culture*. New Brunswick, NJ: Rutgers University Press.

Eder, D. and Fingerson L. (2001) Interviewing children and adolescents. In J. B. Gubrium, and J. A. Holstein (eds.), *Handbook of Interview Research*. Thousand Oaks and London: Sage Publications, pp. 181–202.

Edwards, H. P., Doutriaux, C. W., McCarrey, H. and Fu, L. (1977) *Evaluation of the Federally and Provincially Funded Extensions of the Second Language Programmes in the Schools of the Ottawa Roman Catholic Separate School Board, Ottawa*. Ottawa: Roman Catholic Separate School Board.

Eilers, R. E., Pearson, B. Z. and Cobo-Lewis, A. B. (2006) Social factors in bilingual development: The Miami experience. In P. McCardle and E. Hoff (eds.), *Childhood Bilingualism: Research on Infancy through School Age*. Clevedon: Multilingual Matters, pp. 68–90.

Einhorn, K. (2001) *Easy and Engaging ESL Activities and Mini-books for Every Classroom*. London: Scholastic Teaching Resources.

Elliott, J. and Hufton, N. (2003) *Achievement Motivation in Real Contexts*. BJEP Monographs Series II, 155–72.

Ellis, G. and Brewster, J. (2002) *Tell it Again: The New Storytelling Handbook for Primary Teachers*. London: Longman.

Enever, J., Moon, J. and Raman, U. (eds.) (2009) *Young Learner English Language Policy and Implementation: International Perspectives*. Reading,UK: Garnet Education.

Ennew, J. and Morrow, V. (1994) Out of the mouths of babes. In E. Verhellen and F. Spiesschaert (eds.), *Children's Rights: Monitoring Issues*. Gent: Mys and Breesch, pp. 61–84.

Enomoto, K. (1994) L2 perceptual acquisition: The effect of multilingual linguistic experience on the perception of less novel contrast. *Edinburgh Working Papers in Applied Linguistics*, 5: 15–29.

Epstein, H. T. (1980) EEG developmental stages. *Developmental Psychobiology*, 13: 629–31.

Farrell A. (ed.) (2005) *Ethical Research with Children*. Maidenhead: Open University Press.

Felix, S. (1985) More evidence on competing cognitive systems. *Second Language Research*, 1: 47–72.

Fernald, A. and Morikawa, H. (1993) Common themes and cultural variations in Japanese and American mothers' speech to infants. *Child Development*, 64: 637–56.

Field, T. (1984) Separation stress of young children transferring to new school. *Developmental Psychology*, 20: 786–92.

Fine, G. A. and Sandstrom, K. L. (1988) *Knowing Children: Participant Observations with Minors*. Newbury Park, CA: Sage.

Fingerson, L. (1999) Active viewing: Girls' interpretations of family television programmes. *Journal of Contemporary Ethnography*, 28: 389–418.

Fischer, K. W. and Rose, S. P. (1995) Concurrent cycles in the dynamic development of brain and behaviour. *SRCD Newsletter* 3–4: 15–16.

Flavell, J. H. (1992) Cognitive development: past, present and future. *Developmental Psychology*, 28: 998–1005.

Flavell, J. H. (2000) Development of children's knowledge about the mental world. *International Journal of Behavioural Development*, 24: 15–23.

Flege, J., Monro, M. and McKay, I. (1995) Factors affecting degree of perceived foreign accent in a second language. *Journal of the Acoustical Society of America*, 97: 3125–34.

Flege, J., Yeni-Komshian, G. and Liu, S. (1999) Age constraints on second language acquisition. *Journal of Memory and Language*, 41: 78–104.

Forte, I. and Pangle, M. A. (2001) *ESL Active Learning Lessons: 15 Complete Content-based Units to Reinforce Language Skills and Concepts*. Nashville, TN: Incentive Publishers.

Foster, P. and Skehan, P. (1996) The influence of planning and task type on second language performance. *Studies in Second Language Acquisition*, 18: 299–323.

Foster-Cohen, S. H. (1999) *An Introduction to Child Language Development*. London: Longman.

Foster-Cohen, S. H. (ed.) (2009) *Language Acquisition*. Basingstoke and New York: Palgrave Macmillan.

Franklin, C. E. M. (1990) Teaching in the TL: Problems and prospects. *Language Learning Journal*, 2: 20–4.

Fraser, S. Lewis, V., Ding, S., Kellett, K. and Robinson, C. (eds.) (2004) *Doing Research with Children and Young People*. London: Sage.

Freeman, D. and Freeman, Y. (2007) *English Language Learners: The Essential Guide (Theory and Practice)*. London: Scholastic Teaching Resources.

Galda, L. and Pellegrini, A. D. (eds.) (1985) *Play Language and Stories: the Development of Children's Literate Behaviour*. Norwood, NJ: Ablex.

Gallacher, L-A. and Gallagher M. (2008) Methodological immaturity in childhood research? *Childhood*, 15 (4): 499–516.

Garajová, K. (2001) *Fremdsprachen in Primaschulbereich*. Marburg: Tectum.

Garcia, E. E., Frede, E. A. and Perkins, D. (eds.) (2010) *Young English Language Learner: Current Research and Emerging Directions for Practice and Policy*. New York: Teachers' College Press.

Garcia, O. (2008) *Bilingual Education in the 21st century: A Global Perspective*. Oxford: Wiley and Blackwell.

Garcia Mayo, M. P. (2003) Age, length of exposure and grammaticality judgements in the acquisition of English as a foreign language. In M. P. Garcia Mayo and M. I. Garcia Lecumberri (eds.), *Age and the Acquisition of English as a Foreign Language*. Clevedon: Multilingual Matters, pp. 77–93.

Garcia Mayo, M. P. and Garcia Lecumberri, M. L. (eds.) (2003) *Age and the Acquisition of English as a Foreign Language*. Clevedon: Multilingual Matters.

Gardner, H. (1983) *Frames of Mind: Theory of Multiple Intelligences*. New York: Basic Books.

Gardner, S. F. and Yaacob, A. (2007) Researcher-initiated role play and third space discourses. Unpublished paper, University of Warwick.

Garvie, E. (1990) *Story as a Vehicle*. Clevedon: Multilingual Matters.

Gauvain, M. and Rogoff, B. (1989) Collaborative problem solving and children's planning skills. *Developmental Psychology*, 25: 139–51.

Genelot, S. and Tupin, F. (2001) Evaluation des practiques pédagogiques: Les atouts d'une approche methodologique plurielle le cas du programme Evlang (Comunication au quatrième congres international d'actualité de la recherche en éducation et en formation), Lille.

Genesee, F. (1983) Bilingual education of majority language children: The immersion experiments in review. *Applied Psycholinguistics*, 4: 1–46.

Genesee, F. (1987) *Learning Through Two Languages*. Cambridge, MA: Newbury House.

Genesee, F. (ed.) (1994) *Educating Second Language Children*. New York: Cambridge University Press.

Genesee, F. (2003) Rethinking bilingual acquisition. In J.-M. Dewaele, A. Housen and Li Wei (eds.), *Bilingualism: Beyond Basic Principles*. Clevedon: Multilingual Matters, pp. 204–28.

Genesee F. and Hamayan, E. (1980) Individual differences in young second language learners. *Applied Psycholinguistics*, 1 (1): 95–110.

Genesee, F., Holobow, N., Lambert, W. E., Cleghorn, A. and Walling, R. (1985) The linguistic and academic development of English speaking children in French schools: Grade four outcomes. *Canadian Modern Language Review*, 41 (4): 669–85.

Genesee, F. and Nicoladis, E. (2007) Bilingual first language acquisition. In E. Hoff and M. Shatz (eds.), *Blackwell Handbook of Language Development*. Oxford: Blackwell, pp. 324–44.

Genesee, F., Nicoladis, E. and Paradis, J. (1995) Language differentiation in early bilingual development. *Journal of Child Language*, 22: 611–31.

Gerngross, G. and Puchta, H. (1996) *Do and Understand*. Harlow: Addison Wesley Longman.

Geva, E. and Wang, M. (2001) The development of basic reading skills in children: A cross-language perspective. *Annual Review of Applied Linguistics*, 21: 182–204.

Gibbons, P. (2002) *Scaffolding Language, Scaffolding Learning: Teaching Second Language Learners in the Mainstream Classroom*. Portsmouth, NH: Heinemann.

Gleitman, L. R. (1990) The structural sources of verb meanings. *Language Acquisition*, 1: 3–55.

Goh, C. and Taib, Y. (2006) Metacognitive instruction in listening for young learners. *ELT Journal*, 60 (3): 222–32.

Gopnik, A. and Choi, S. (1995) Names, relational words and cognitive development in English and Korean speakers: Nouns are not always learnt before verbs. In M. Tomasello and W. Merriman (eds.), *Beyond Names for Things: Young Children's Acquisition of Verbs*, Hillsdale, NJ: Lawrence Erlbaum, pp. 63–114.

Gordon, T. (2006) *Teaching Young Children a Second Language*. Santa Barbara, CA: Praeger.

Graham, C. (1978) *Jazz Chants for Children*. Oxford: Oxford University Press.

Green, J. M. and Oxford, R. (1995) A closer look at learning strategies, L2 proficiency, and gender. *TESOL Quarterly*, 29 (2): 261–97.

Gregory, E., Long, S. and Volk, D. (2004) *Many Pathways to Literacy*. New York, NY: Routledge Falmer, Taylor and Francis Group.

Grieve, R. and Hughes, M. (eds.) (1997) *Understanding Children*. Oxford: Blackwell.

Grimshaw, T. and Sears, C. (2008) 'Where am I from? Where do I belong?' The negotiation and maintenance of identity by international school students. *Journal of Research in International Education*, 7 (3): 259–78.

Grosjean, F. (1982) *Life with Two Languages: An Introduction to Bilingualism*. Cambridge, MA: Harvard University Press.

Grosjean, F. (1994) Individual bilingualism. *The Encyclopedia of Language and Linguistics*. Oxford: Pergamon, pp. 1656–60.

Gu, P. Y., Hu, G. and Zhang L. J. (2005) Investigating language learners' strategies among lower primary school pupils in Singapore. *Language and Education*, 19 (4): 281–303.

Guasti, M. T. (2002) *Language Acquisition: The Growth of Grammar.* Cambridge, MA: MIT Press.

Gunning, P. (1997) The learning strategies of beginning ESL learners at the primary level. Master's thesis, Concordia University, Montreal.

Hakuta, K. (1986) *Mirror of Language: The Debate on Bilingualism.* New York: Basic Books.

Hakuta, K., Bialystok, E. and Wiley, E. (2003) Critical evidence: A test of the critical-period hypothesis for second-language acquisition. *Psychological Science,* 14 (1): 31–8.

Halford, G. S. (1992) Analogical reasoning and conceptual complexity in cognitive development. *Human Development,* 35: 193–217.

Halliday, M. A. K. (1975) *Learning How to Mean: Explorations in the Development of Language.* London: Edward Arnold.

Halliwell, S. (1992) *Teaching English in the Primary Classroom.* London: Longman.

Harding-Esch, E. and Riley, P. (2003) *The Bilingual Family: A Handbook for Parents.* Cambridge: Cambridge University Press.

Harley, B. (1986) *Age in Second Language Acquisition.* Clevedon: Multilingual Matters.

Harley, B. (1998) The role of focus-on-form tasks in promoting child L2 acquisition. In K. Doughty and J. Williams (eds.), *Focus on Form in Classroom Second Language Acquisition.* Cambridge: Cambridge University Press, pp. 156–76.

Harley, B. and Hart, D. (1997) Language aptitude and second language proficiency in classroom learners of different starting ages. *Studies in Second Language Acquisition,* 19: 379–400.

Harley, B., Hart, D. and Lapkin, S. (1986) The effects of early bilingual schooling on first language skills. *Applied Psycholinguistics,* 7 (4): 295–322.

Harter, S. (1996) Developmental changes in self-understanding across the 5 to 7 shift. In A. J. Sameroff and M. M. Haith (eds.), *The Five to Seven Year Shift.* Chicago: University of Chicago Press, pp. 207–36.

Harter, S. (1998) The development of self-representations. In N. Eisenberg (ed.), *Handbook of Child Psychology 3: Social, Emotional and Personality Development.* New York: Wiley, pp. 553–618.

Hartup, W. W. (1978) Peer interaction and the process of socialisation. In M. J. Guralnick (ed.), *Early Intervention and the Integration of Handicapped and Non-handicapped Children.* Baltimore, MD: University Park Press, pp. 27–51.

Hartup, W. W. (1996) The company they keep: friendships and their developmental significance. *Child Development,* 67: 1–13.

Hasselgren, A. (2005) Assessing the language of young learners. *Language Testing,* 22/3: 337–54.

Hasselhorn, M. (1992) Task dependency and the role of category typicality and metamemory in the development of an organisational strategy. *Child Development,* 63: 202–14.

Hawkins, E. (1984) *Awareness of Language: An Introduction.* Cambridge: Cambridge University Press.

Hawkins, M. (2005) Becoming a student: identity work and academic literacies in early schooling. *TESOL Quarterly,* 39 (1): 59–82.

Haynes, J. (2007) *Getting Started with English Language Learners: How Educators Can Meet the Challenge.* Alexandria, VA: Association for Supervision and Curriculum Development.

Haznedar, B. (1997) *Child Second Language Acquisition of English: A Longitudinal Study of a Turkish Speaking Child.* Durham, UK: University of Durham.

Heining-Boynton, A. L. and Haitema, T. (2007) A ten-year old chronicle of student attitudes toward foreign language in the elementary school. *The Modern Language Journal*, 91 (2): 149–68.

Henny, L. and Rixon, S. (1990) *Look Alive!* London: Heinemann.

Hewings, M. (1991) The interpretation of illustrations in ELT materials. *ELT Journal*, 45: 237–44.

Hill, M. (1997) Participatory research with children: research review. *Child and Family Social Work*, 2: 117–28.

Hill, M. (2005) *Ethical Considerations in Researching Children's Experiences*. London: Sage.

Hill, J. D. and Flynn, K. M. (2006) *Classroom Instruction that Works with English Language Learners* Alexandria, VA: Association for Supervision and Curriculum Development.

Hoffman, C. (1998) Luxembourg and the European schools. In J. Cenoze and F. Genesee (eds.), *Beyond Bilingualism: Multilingualism and Multilingual Education*. Clevedon: Multilingual Matters, pp. 143–74.

Holmes, R. M. (1998) *Fieldwork with Children*. London: Sage Publications.

Hughes, M. and Grieve, P. (1980) On asking children bizarre questions. *First Language*, 1: 149–60.

Hyltenstam, K. and Abrahamsson, N. (2000) Who can become native-like in a second language? All, some or none? On the maturational constraints controversy in second language acquisition. *Studia Linguistica*, 54 (2): 150–66.

INTRAC (International NGO Training and Research Centre) (1997) *Involving Children in Research for Planning, Programming and Monitoring: A Pilot INTRAC Training Course*. Oxford: INTRAC.

Ionnou-Georgiou, S. and Pavlou, P. (2003) *Assessing Young Learners: Resource Books for Teachers*. Oxford: Oxford University Press.

Ireland, L. and Holloway, I. (1996) Qualitative health research with children. *Children and Society*, 10: 155–64.

Jacobson, R. (1960) Closing statement: Linguistics and poetics. In T. A. Sebeok (ed.), *Style in Language*. Cambridge, MA.: MIT Press.

Jaeggli, O. and Safir, K. (1989) The null subject parameter and parametric theory. In O. Jaeggli and K. Safir (eds.), *The Null Subject Parameter*. Dordrecht: Foris, pp. 1–44.

James, A. and Prout, A. (1997) *Constructing and Reconstructing Childhood*. London: Falmer Press.

Jantscher, E. and Landsiedler, I. (2000) Foreign language education at Austrian primary schools: An overview. In M. Nikolov and H. Curtain (eds.), *An Early Start: Young Learners and Modern Languages in Europe and Beyond*. Strasbourg: Council of Europe, pp. 13–28.

Jia, G. and Aaronson, D. (2003) A longitudinal study of Chinese children and adolescents learning English in the United States. *Applied Psycholinguistics*, 24: 131–61.

Jia, G. and Fuse, A. (2007) Acquisition of English grammatical morphology by native Mandarin-speaking children and adolescents: Age-related differences. *Journal of Speech, Language and Hearing Research*, 50: 1280–99.

Jimenez Raya, M., Faber, P., Gewehr, W. and Peck, A. J. (eds.) (2001) *Foreign Language Teaching in Europe: Effective Foreign Language Teaching at the Primary level*. Bern: Peter Lang.

Johnson, J. and Newport, E. (1989) Critical period effects in second language learning: The influence of maturational state on the acquisition of English as a second language. *Cognitive Psychology*, 39: 215–58.

Johnson, K. (2008) Teaching children to use visual research methods. In P. Thomson (ed.), *Doing Visual Research with Children and Young People*. London: Routledge, pp. 77–94.

Johnson, R. K. and Swain, M. (eds.) (1997) *Immersion Education: International Perspectives*. Cambridge: Cambridge University Press.

Johnston, J. R. and Slobin, D. I. (1979) The development of locative expressions in English, Italian, Serbo-Croatian, and Turkish. *Journal of Child Language*, 16: 531–47.

Johnstone, R. (1999) *Education Through Immersion in a Second or Additional Language at School: Evidence from International Research*. Stirling: Scottish CILT.

Johnstone, R. (2002) Addressing the age factor: Some implications for language policy. Strasbourg: Council of Europe.

Josel, C. A. (2002) *Ready-to-use ESL Activities for Every Month of the School Year*. Jerusalem: Centre for Applied Research in Education.

Justice, E. M., Baker-Ward, L., Gupta, S. and Jannings, L. R. (1997) Means to the goal of remembering: Developmental changes in awareness of strategy use-performance relations. *Journal of Experimental Child Psychology*, 65: 293–314.

Kachru, B. B. (1992) *The Other Tongue: English across Cultures*. Champaign, IL: University of Illinois Press.

Kail, R. (1993) The role of a global mechanism in developmental change in speed of processing. In M. L. Howe and R. Pasnak (eds.), *Emerging Themes in Cognitive Development 1: Foundations*. New York: Springer Verlag.

Kail, R. (1997) Processing time, imagery and spatial memory. *Jourrnal of Experimental Child Psychology*, 64: 67–78.

Karmiloff-Smith, A. (1986) Some fundamental aspects of language development after age 5. In P. Fletcher and M. Garman (eds.), *Language Acquisition*. Cambridge: Cambridge University Press, pp. 455–74.

Karmiloff Smith, A. (1992) Beyond modularity: A developmental perspective on cognitive science. Cambridge, MA: MIT Press/Bradford Books.

Keil, F. C. (1981). Constraints on knowledge and cognitive development. *Psychological Review*, 88 (3): 197–227.

Kellett, M. (2005) *How to Develop Children as Researchers: A Step-by-Step Guide to Teaching the Research Process*. London: Sage.

Kellett, M. (2010) *Rethinking Children and Research: Attitudes in Contemporary Society* London: Continuum.

Kellett, M. and Ding, S. (2004) Middle childhood. In S. Fraser, V. Lewis, S. Ding, M. Kellett and C. Robinson (eds.), *Doing Research with Children and Young People*. London: Sage. pp. 161–74.

Kennedy, C. and Jarvis, J. (eds.) (1991) *Ideas and Issues in Primary ELT*. London: Nelson.

Kennedy, T. J., Nelson, J. K., Odell, M. R. L and Austin, L. K. (2000) The FLES attitudinal inventory. *Foreign Language Annals*, 33 (3): 278–89.

Kim, K. H. S., Relkin, N. R., Lee, K.-L. and Hirsch, J. (1997) Distinct cortical areas associated with native and second language. *Nature*, 388: 171–4.

Kim, Y. (2008) The effects of integrated language-based instruction in elementary ESL learning. *The Modern Language Journal*, 92 (3): 431–51.

King, K. and Mackey, A. (2007) *The Bilingual Edge: Why, When and How to Teach Your Child a Second Language*. New York: Collins Publishing.

Kiss, C. and Nikolov, M. (2005) Developing, piloting and validating an instrument to measure young learners' aptitude. *Language Learning*, 55 (1): 99–150.

Kitchener, K. S., Lynch, C. L., Fischer, K. W. and Wood, P. K. (1993) Developmental range of reflective judgment: The effect of contextual support and practice of developmental stage. *Developmental Psychology*, 29: 893–906.

Klein, E. C. (1995) Second versus third language acquisition: Is there a difference? *Language Learning*, 45: 419–65.

Knell, E., Siegel, L. S., Haiyan, Q., Lin, Z., Miao, P., Wei, Z. and Yanping, C. (2007) Early immersion and literacy in Xi'an, China. *The Modern Language Journal*, 91 (3): 395–417.

Kormos, J. and Csiszér, K. (2007) An interview study of inter-cultural contact and its role in language learning in a foreign language environment. *System*, 35: 241–58.

Kovačević M. (1993) Foreign language acquisition in children: some evidence from testing English with first Graders. In M. Vilke and Y. Vrhovac (eds.), *Children and Foreign Languages*. Zagreb: University of Zagreb.

Krashen, D., Long, M. and Scarcella, R. C. (1979) Age, rate and eventual attainment in second language acquisition. *TESOL Quarterly*, 13/4: 573–82.

Kubanek-German, A. (1998) Primary foreign language teaching in Europe – trends and issues. State of the art survey article. *Language Teaching*, 31: 193–205.

Kunzinger, E. L. (1985) A short term longitudinal study of memorial development during early grade school. *Developmental Psychology*, 21: 642–6.

Lakoff, G. (1987) *Women, Fire, and Dangerous Things*. Chicago: University of Chicago Press.

Lamb, M. (2003) Integrative motivation in a globalizing world. *System*, 32: 3–19.

Lan, R. and Oxford, R. (2003) Language learning strategy profiles of elementary school students in Taiwan. *IRAL*, 41: 339–79.

Lantolf, J. (2006) Sociocultural theory and L2: State of the art. *Studies in Second Language Acquisition*, 28: 67–109.

Lanvers, U. (1999) Infant bilingualism: A longitudinal case study of two bilingual siblings. Exeter University, UK.

Lanza, E. (1997) *Language Mixing in Infant Bilingualism: A Sociolinguistic Perspective*. Oxford: Clarendon Press.

Larsen-Freeman, D. and Long, M. (1991) *An Introduction to Second Language Acquisition Research*. Harlow: Longman.

Lasagabaster, D. (1997) *Creatividad y conciencia metalingüística: Incidencia en el aprendizaje del inglés como L3*. Leioa: University of the Basque Country.

Lasagabaster, D. (2000) Three languages and three linguistic models in the Basque educational system. In J. Cenoz and U. Jessner (eds.), *English in Europe: The Acquisition of a Third Language*. Clevedon: Mutlilingual Matters, pp. 179–97.

Law, B. and Eckes, M. L. (2000) *The More-Than-Just-Surviving Handbook: ESL for Every Classroom Teacher*. Winnipeg, Manitoba: Portage & Main Press.

Ledesma, H. M. L. and Morris, R. D. (2005) Patterns of language preference among bilingual (Filipino-English) boys. *The International Journal of Bilingual Education and Bilingualism*, 8 (1): 62–80.

Legutke, M. K., Müller-Hartmann, A., Schocker-v. Ditfurth, M. (2009) *Teaching English in the Primary School*. Stuttgart: Klett Lerntraining.

Lenneberg, E. H. (1967) *Biological Foundations of Language*. New York: Wiley.

Leopold, W. (1949) Original invention in language. *Symposium*, 3: 66–75.

Leseman, P. P. M. (2000) Bilingual vocabulary development of Turkish preschoolers in the Netherlands. *Journal of Multilingual and Multicultural Development*, 21: 93–112.

Lewis, A. (1992) Group child interviews as a research tool. *British Educational Research Journal*, 18 (4): 413–21.

Lewis, G. (2004) *The Internet and Young Learners Resource Books for Teachers*. Oxford: Oxford University Press.

Light, P. and Perrett-Clermont, A. (1989) Social context effects in learning and testing. In A. R. H. Gellatly, D. Rogers and J. Sloboda (eds.), *Cognition and Social Worlds*. Oxford: Clarendon Press, pp. 99–112.

Lightbown, P. and Spada N. (1994) An innovative programme for primary ESL students in Quebec. *TESOL Quarterly*, 28 (3): 563–79.

Lightbown, P. and Spada, N. (1999) *How Languages are Learned*. Oxford: Oxford University Press.

Likata, T. (2003) Interkulturelle Bildung und Erziehung im Fremdsprachenunterricht der Grundschule. Begründung- Konzepte- Bewährung. Dissertation, Passau University.

Likert, R. (1932) A technique for the measurement of attitudes. *Archives of Psychology*, 140: 1–55.

Lindholm, K. J. (1997) Two way bilingual education programs in the United States. In J. Cummins and D. Corson (eds.), *Encyclopaedia of Language and Education 5: Bilingual Education*. Dordrecht: Kluwer Academic Publishers, pp. 271–80.

Lindholm-Leary, K. J. (2001) *Dual Language Education*. Clevedon: Multilingual Matters.

Lippi-Green, R. (1997) *English with an Accent: Language Ideology and Discrimination in the United States*. London: Routledge.

Llinares Garcia, A. (2007) Young learners' functional use of the L2 in a low-immersion EFL context. *ELT Journal*, 61 (1): 39–45.

Lloyd, P. (1991) Strategies used to communicate route directions by telephone: A comparison of the performance of 7-year-olds, 10-year-olds and adults. *Journal of Child Language*, 18: 171–89.

Lloyd, P., Baker, E. and Dunn, J. (1984) Children's awareness of communication. In L. Feagans, G. Golinkoff and C. Garvey (eds.), *The Origins and Growth of Communication*. Norwood, NJ: Ablex Publishing, pp. 281–96.

Low, L., Brown, S., Johnstone, R. and Pirrie, A. (1995) *Foreign Languages in Primary Schools: Evaluation of the Scottish Pilot Project 1993–1995: Final Report*. Stirling: Scottish CILT.

Lucchini, R. (1996) Theory, method and triangulation in the study of street children. *Childhood*, 3 (2): 167–70.

Lundberg, G. (2007) Developing teachers of young learners: In-service for educational change and improvement. In M. Nikolov, J. Mihaljević Djigunović, M. Mattheoudakis, G. Lundberg and T. Flanagan (eds.), *Teaching Modern Languages to Young Learners: Teachers, Curricula and Materials*. European Centre for Modern Languages, Brussels: Council of Europe, pp. 21–34.

Lundy, J. E. B. (1999) Theory of mind: Development in deaf children. *Perspectives in Education and Deafness*, 18 (1): 1–5.

Mackey, A, Kanganas, A. P. and Oliver, R. (2007) Task familiarity and interactional feedback in child ESL classrooms. *TESOL Quarterly*, 41 (2): 285–312.

Mackey, A., Oliver, R. and Leeman, J. (2003) Interactional input and the incorporation of feedback: An exploration of NS-NNS and NNS-NNS adult and child dyads. *Language Learning*, 53 (1): 35–66.

Mahon, A., Glendinning, C., Clarke, K. and Craig, G. (1996) Researching children: Methods and ethics. *Children and Society*, 10 (2): 145–54.

Mandler, J. M. (1984) *Stories, Scripts, and Scenes: Aspects of Schema Theory*. Hillsdale, NJ: Erlbaum.

Marinova-Todd, S. H. (2003) Know your grammar: What the knowledge of syntax and morphology in an L2 reveals about the critical period for second/foreign language acquisition. In M. P. Garcia Mayo and M. L. Garcia Lecumberri (eds.), *Age and the Acquisition of English as a Foreign Language*. Clevedon: Multilingual Matters, pp. 59–76.

Marinova-Todd, S., Bradford Marshall, H. D. and Snow, C. (2000) Three misconceptions about age and L2 learning. *TESOL Quarterly*, 34 (1): 9–34.

Mayall, B. (2008) Conversations with children: Working with generational issues. In P. Christensen and A. James (eds.), *Research with Children: Perspectives and Practices*. London: Routledge, pp. 109–22.

Mayberry, R. I., Lock, E. and Kazmi, L. (2002) Development: Linguistic ability and early language exposure. *Nature*, 417: 38.

McGarrigle, J. and Donaldson, M. (1974) Conservation accidents. *Cognition*, 3: 341–50.

McGilly, K. and Siegler, R. S. (1990) The influence of encoding and strategic knowledge on children's choices among serial recall strategies *Developmental Psychology*, 26: 931–41.

McKay, P. (2006) *Assessing Young Language Learners*. Cambridge: Cambridge University Press.

McKay, P. and Guse, J. (2007) *Five-minute Activities for Young Learners*. Cambridge: Cambridge University Press.

McLaughlin, B. (1994) *Second Language Acquisition in Childhood, Vol. 1 Preschool Children* Hillsdale, NJ: Lawrence Erlbaum Associates.

McLaughlin, B. and Nayak, N. (1989) Processing a new language: Does knowing other languages make a difference? In H. W. Dechert and M. Raupach (eds.), *Interlingual Processes*. Tübigen: Gunter Narr, pp. 5–16.

McNaughton, G. and Smith K. (2005) Transforming research ethics: The choices and challenges of researching with children. In A. Farrell (ed.), *Ethical Research with Children*, Maidenhead: Open University Press, pp. 112–23.

McNaughton, G., Rolfe, S. A. and Siraj-Blatchford. I. (eds.) (2001) *Doing Early Childhood Research: International Perspectives on Theory and Practice*. Maidenhead: Open University Press.

McNaughton, S. (1995) *Patterns of Emergent Literacy: Processes of Development and Transition*. Auckland: Oxford University Press.

McWhinney, B. (1991) *The CHILDES Project: Tools for Analysing Talk*. Hillsdale, NJ: Lawrence Erlbaum.

Meadows, S. (1993) *The Child as a Thinker*. London: Routledge.

Meara. P. (1996) The vocabulary knowledge framework Vocabulary Acquisition Research Group. University of Wales: Swansea. Available at www.lognostics.co.uk/vlibrary/meara1996

Medgyes, P. (1994) *The Non-native Teacher*. London: Macmillan Publishers.

Meisel, J. M. (1994) Code-switching on young bilingual children: The acquisition of grammatical constraints. *Studies in Second Language Acquisition*, 16: 413–41.

Mercer, N. (1995) *The Guided Construction of Knowledge: Talk amongst Teachers and Learners*. Clevedon: Multilingual Matters.

Mercer, N. (2000) *Words and Minds: How we Use Language to Think Together*. London: Routledge.

Mercer, N. and Littleton, K. (2007) *Dialogue and the Development of Children's Thinking*. London: Routledge.

Mercer, N., Wegerif, R. and Dawes, L. (1999) Children's talk and the development of reasoning in the classroom. *British Educational Research Journal*, 25 (1): 95–111.

Mihaljević Djigunović, J. (2009) Impact of learning conditions on young FL learners' motivation. In M. Nikolov (ed.), *Early Learning of Modern Foreign Languages: Processes and Outcomes*. Clevedon: Multlilingual Matters, pp. 75–89.

Mihaljević Djigunović, J. and Vilke, M. (2000) Eight years after: Wishful thinking versus facts of life. In J. Moon and M. Nikolov (eds.), *Research into Teaching English to Young Learners*. Hungary: University of Pécs Press, pp. 74–9.

Miller, G. A. (1956) The magical number seven, plus or minus two: some limits on our capacity for processing information. *The Psychological Review*, 63 (1): 81–97.

Miller, P. H. (1989) *Theories of Developmental Psychology*. New York: Freeman.

Miller, J. (2003) *Audible Differences: ESL and Social Identity in Schools*. Clevedon: Multilingual Matters.

Mitchell, R. and Lee, C. N. (2008) Learning a second language in the family. In J. Philp, R. Oliver and A. Mackey (eds.), *Second Language Acquisition and the Young Learner: Child's Play?* Amsterdam: John Benjamins, pp. 255–78.

Möhle, D. (1989) Multilingual interaction in foreign language production. In H. W. Dechert and M. Raupach (eds.), *Interlingual Processes*. Tübingen: Gunter Narr, pp. 179–94.

Moon, J. (2000) *Children Learning English*. Oxford: Macmillan.

Morrow, V. (1999) 'It's cool . . . . cos you can't give us detentions and things, can you?!' Reflections on researching children. In P. Milner and B. Carolin (eds.), *Time to Listen to Children*. London: Routledge, pp. 203–15.

Morrow, V. (2005) Ethical issues in collaborative research with children. In A. Farrell (ed.), *Ethical Research with Children*. Maidenhead: Open University Press, pp. 150–65.

Morrow, V. and Richards, M. (1996) The ethics of social research with children: An overview. *Children and Society*, 10: 90–105.

Moyer, A. (2004) *Age, Accent and Experience in Second language Acquisition*. Clevedon: Multilingual Matters.

Muñoz, C. (2000) Bilingualism and trilingualism in school students in Catalonia. In J. Cenoz and U. Jessner (eds.), *English in Europe: The Acquisition of a Third Language*. Clevedon: Mutlilingual Matters, pp. 157–78.

Muñoz, C. (2006) The effects of age on foreign language learning: The BAF project. In C. Muñoz (ed.), *Age and the Rate of Foreign Language Learning*. Clevedon: Multilingual Matters, pp. 1–40.

Muñoz, C. (2007) Age related differences and second language learning processes. In R. M. DeKeyser (ed.), *Practice in a Second language: Perspectives from Applied Linguistics and Cognitive Psychology*. Cambridge: Cambridge University Press, pp. 229–55.

Murphy, E. (2003) Monolingual international schools and the young non-English-speaking child. *Journal of Research in International Education*, 2 (1): 25–45.

Nagy, K. (2009) What primary school pupils think about learning English as a foreign language. In M. Nikolov (ed.), *Early Learning of Modern Foreign Languages: Processes and Outcomes*. Bristol: Multilingual Matters, pp. 229–42.

Nassaji, H. and Cumming A. (2000) What's in a ZPD? A case study of a young ESL student and teacher interacting through dialogue journals. *Language Teaching Research*, 4 (2): 95–121.

Nation, R. and McLaughlin, B. (1986) Novices and experts: An information processing approach to the 'good language learner' problem. *Applied Psycholinguistics*, 7: 41–56.

Nayak, N., Hansen, N., Krueger, N. and McLaughlin, B. (1990) Language-learning strategies in monolingual and multilingual adults. *Language Learning*, 40: 221–44.

Nelson, K. (1996) *Language in Cognitive Development*. Cambridge: Cambridge University Press.

Newcomb, A. F. and Bagwell, C. L. (1995) Children's friendship relations: A meta-analytic review. *Psychological Bulletin*, 117: 306–47.

Nicoladis, E. and Genesee, F. (1998) Parental discourse and code-mixing in bilingual children. *International Journal of Bilingualism*, 2: 85–100.

Nicoladis, E. and Secco, G. (2000) The role of a child's productive vocabulary in the language choice of a bilingual family. *First Language*, 58: 3–28.

Nicholas, H. and Lightbown, P. M. (2008) Defining child second language acquisition, defining roles for L2 instruction. In J. Philp, R. Oliver and A. Mackey (eds.), *Second Language Acquisition and the Young Learner: Child's Play?* Amsterdam: John Benjamins, pp. 27–52.

Nikolov, M. (1999a) Natural born speakers of English: Code switching in pair- and group-work in Hungarian primary classrooms. In S. Rixon (ed.), *Young Learners of English: Some Research Perspectives*. Harlow: Longman, pp. 72–88.

Nikolov, M. (1999b) Why do you learn English? Because the teacher is short. A study of Hungarian children's foreign language learning motivation. *Language Teaching Research*, 3 (1): 33–56.

Nikolov, M. (2000) The critical period hypothesis reconsidered: Successful adult learners of Hungarian and English. *International Review of Applied Linguistics in Language Teaching*, 38 (2): 109–24.

Nikolov, M. (2006) Test-taking strategies of 12- and 13-year old Hungarian learners of EFL: Why whales have migraines. *Language Learning*, 56 (1): 1–51.

Nikolov, M. (ed.) (2009a) *Early Learning of Modern Foreign Languages: Processes and Outcomes*. Clevedon: Multilingual Matters.

Nikolov, M. (ed.) (2009b) *The 'Age Factor' and Early Language Learning: Studies on Language Acquisition*. Berlin: Mouton de Gruyter.

Nikolov, M. and Curtain, H. (eds.) (2000) *An Early Start: Young Learners and Modern Languages in Europe and Beyond*. European Centre for Modern Languages, Strasbourg: Council of Europe Publishing.

Nikolov, M., Mihaljević Djigunović, M., Mattheoudakis, M., Lundberg G. and Flanagan, T. (2007) *Teaching Modern Language to Young Learners: Teachers, Curricula and Materials*. Brussels: Council of Europe.

O'Kane, C. (2008) The development of participatory techniques: Facilitating children's views about views about decisions which affect them. In P. Christensen and A. James (eds.), *Research with Children: Perspectives and Practices*. London: Routledge, pp. 125–55.

Ohta, A. S. (2001) *Second Language Acquisition Processes in the Classroom: Learning Japanese*. London: Lawrence Erlbaum Associates.

Oliver, R. (1998) Negotiation of meaning in child interactions. *The Modern Language Journal*, 82 (3): 372–86.

Oliver, R. (2002) Age differences in negotiation and feedback in classroom and pairwork. *Language Learning*, 50 (1): 119–51.

Olson, L. and Samuels, S. (1973) The relationship between age and accuracy of foreign language pronunciation. *Journal of Educational Research*, 66: 263–7. Reprinted (1982) in S. Krashen, R. Scarcella, and M. Long (eds.), *Child-Adult Differences in Second Language Acquisition*. Rowley, MA: Newbury House.

Ornstein, P. A., Naus, M. J. and Liberty, C. (1975) Rehearsal and organisational processes in children's memory. *Child Development*, 46: 818–30.

Ornstein, P. A., Stone, B. P., Madlin, R. G. and Nauss, M. J. (1985) Retrieving for rehearsal: An analysis of active rehearsal in children's memory. *Developmental Psychology*, 21: 633–41.

Oshima-Takane, Y., Goodz, E., Derevensky, J. L. (1996) Birth order effects on early language development: Do second born children learn from overheard speech? *Child Development*, 67 (2): 621–34.

Oxford, R. (1990) *Language Learning Strategies: What Every Teacher Should Know*. Boston: Heinle and Heinle.

Oyama, S. (1976) A sensitive period for the acquisition of a non-native phonological system. *Journal of Psycholinguistic Research*, 5: 261–84.

Oyama, S. (1978) The sensitive period and comprehension of speech. *Working Papers in Bilingualism*, 16: 1–17. Reprinted (1982) in M. Krashen, R. Scarcella and M. Long (eds.), *Child-Adult Differences in Second Language Acquisition*. Rowley, MA: Newbury House.

Painter, C. (1999) *Learning Through Language in Early Childhood*. London: Cassell.

Pan, B. A. (1995) Code-negotiation in bilingual families: 'My body starts speaking English'. *Journal of Multilingual and Multicultural Development*, 16: 315–27.

Papapavlou, A. N. (1999) Academic achievement, language proficiency and socialisation of bilingual children in a monolingual Greek Cypriot-speaking school environment. *International Journal of Bilingual Education and Bilingualism*, 2 (4): 252–67.

Paradis, J. (2001) Do bilingual two-year-olds have separate phonological systems? *International Journal of Bilingualism*, 5 (1): 19–38.

Paradis, J. (2005) Grammatical morphology in children learning English as a second language: Implications of similarities with specific language impairment. *Language, Speech, and Hearing Services in Schools*, 36: 172–87.

Paradis, J. (2007) Second language acquisition in childhood. In E. Hoff and M. Shatz (eds.), *Blackwell Handbook of Language Development*. Oxford: Blackwell Publishers, pp. 387–405.

Paradis, J. and Genesee, F. (1996) Syntactic acquisition in bilingual children: autonomous or independent? *Studies in Second Language Acquisition*, 18: 1–25.

Paradis, J., Nicoladis, E. and Genesee, F. (2000) Early emergence of structural constraints on code-mixing: Evidence from French-English bilingual children. In F. Genesee (ed.), *Bilingualism: Language and Cognition*. Cambridge: Cambridge University Press, pp. 245–61.

Patkowski, M. (1980) The sensitive period for the acquisition of syntax in a second language. *Language Learning*, 30: 449–72.

Patkowski, M. (1990) Accent in a second language: A reply to James Emil Flege. *Applied Linguistics*, 11: 73–89.

Patterson, C. and Kister, M. (1981) The development of listening skills for referential communication. In W. Dickson (ed.), *Children's Oral Communication Skills*. New York: Academic Press, pp. 143–66.

Patterson, J. L. and Pearson, B. Z. (2004) Bilingual lexical development: Influences, contexts and processes. In B. A. Goldstein (ed.), *Bilingual Language Development and Disorders in Spanish-English Speakers*. Baltimore, MD: Brookes Publishing, pp. 77–104.

Peal, E. and Lambert, W. (1962) The relation of bilingualism to intelligence. *Psychological Monographs*, 76: 1–23.

Pearson, B. Z., Fernandez, S. C. and Oller, D. K. (1993) Lexical development in bilingual infants and toddlers. *Language Learning*, 43: 93–120.

Peñate Cabrera, M. and Bazo Martínez, P. (2001).The effects of repetition, comprehension checks, and gestures on primary school children in an EFL situation. *ELT Journal*, 55 (3): 281–8.

Penfield, W. and Roberts, L. (1959) *Speech and Brain Mechanisms*. Princeton, NJ: Princeton University Press.

Peng, J. and Zhang, L. (2009) An eye on the target language use in elementary English classrooms in China. In M. Nikolov (ed.), *Early Learning of Modern Foreign Languages: Processes and Outcomes*. Bristol: Multilingual Matters, pp. 212–28.

Perera, K. (1986) *Children's Writing and Reading: Analysing Classroom Language*. London: Blackwell.

Peterson, C. and Siegal, M. (1995) Deafness, conversation, and theory of mind. *Journal of Child Psychology and Psychiatry*, 36: 459–74.

Phillips, S. (1999) *Drama with Children*. Oxford: Oxford University Press.

Philp, J., Oliver, R. and Mackey, A. (2006) The impact of planning time on children's task-based interactions. *System*, 34: 547–65.

Philp, J., Oliver, R. and Mackey, A. (eds.) (2008) *Second Language Acquisition and the Young Learner: Child's Play?* Amsterdam: John Benjamins.

Piaget, J. (1926/1955) *The Language and Thought of the Child*. London: Routledge and Kegan Paul.

Piaget, J. and Inhelder, B. (1956) *The Child's Conception of Space*. London: Routledge and Kegan Paul.

Pinter, A. (2006) *Teaching Young Language Learners*. Oxford Handbooks for Language Teachers. Oxford: Oxford University Press.

Pinter, A. (2007) Benefits of peer-peer interaction: 10-year-old children practising with a communication task. *Language Teaching Research*, 11 (2): 1–19.

Polio, C. G. and Duff, P. A. (1994) Teachers' language use in university foreign language classrooms: A qualitative analysis of English and TL alternation. *Modern Language Journal*, 78: 313–26.

Pollard, A. (1996) *The Social World of Children's Learning*. London: Cassell.

Potowski, K. (2007) *Language and Identity in a Dual Immersion School*. Clevedon: Multlingual Matters.

Punch, S. (2002) Research with children: the same or different from research with adults? *Childhood*, 9 (3): 321–41.

Raven J., Court, J. and Raven, J. C. (1995) *Manual for Raven's Progressive Matrices and Vocabulary Scales*. Oxford: Oxford Psychologists Press.

Reilley, J. and Reilley, V. (2005) *Writing with Children*. Oxford: Oxford University Press.

Richardson, K. and Sheldon, S. (eds.) (1988) *Cognitive Development to Adolescence*. Hove: Psychology Press.

Riderinkhof, K. R. and Molen, M. W. van der (1997) Mental resources, processing speed and inhibitory control: A developmental perspective. *Biological Psychology*, 45: 241–61.

Rixon, S. (1981) *How to Use Games in Language Teaching*. London: Macmillan.

Rixon, S. (ed.) (1999) *Young Learners of English: Some Research Perspectives*. London: Longman.

Rixon, S. (2000) Collecting eagle's eye and more intimate data on young learners of English. In M. Crook and A. Hughes (eds.), *Teaching English to Young Learners: First International TEYL Research Seminar Papers*. York, UK: EFL Unit, University of York.

Robinson, C. and Kellett, M. (2004) Power. In S. Fraser, V. Lewis, S. Ding, M. Kellett, and C. Robinson (eds.), *Doing Research with Children and Young People*. London: Sage, pp. 81–96.

Robinson, E. J. and Robinson, W. P. (1983) Children's uncertainly about the interpretation of ambiguous messages, meanings and reality. *British Journal of Developmental Psychology*, 36: 305–20.

Robinson, W. P. (1986) Children's understanding of the distinction between messages and meaning: Emergence and implications. In M. Richards and P. Light (eds.), *Children of Social Worlds*. Cambridge: Polity, pp. 213–32.

Rodino, A. M. and Snow, C. E. (1997) 'Y.. no puedo decir más nada': distanced communication skills of Puerto Rican children. In G. Kasper and E. Kellerman (eds.), *Communication Strategies*. London and New York: Longman, pp. 168–91.

Rogoff, B. (1990) *Apprenticeship in Thinking: Cognitive Development in Social Context*. Oxford: Oxford University Press.

Romaine, S. (1995) *Bilingualism*. Oxford: Blackwell.

Ronjat, J. (1913) *Le Développement du langage observé chez un enfant bilingue*. Paris: Champion.

Satchwell, P. and de Silva, J (2009) *Speak Up! Young Pathfinder 15*. London: CILT.

Saunders, G. (1982) *Bilingual Children: From Birth to Teens*. Clevedon: Multilingual Matters.

Scardamalia, M. (1977) Information processing capacity and the problem of horizontal decalage: A demonstration using a combinatorial reasoning task. *Child Development*, 48: 28–37.

Schneider, W. (2006) Memory development in childhood. In U. Goswami (ed.), *Blackwell Handbook of Childhood Cognitive Development*. Oxford: Blackwell Publishing, pp. 236–56.

Schneider, W. and Bjorklund, D. F. (1992) Expertise, aptitude and strategic remembering. *Child Development*, 63: 461–73.

Schneider, W. and Bjorklund, D. F. (2003) Memory and knowledge development. In J. Valsiner and K. J. Connolly (eds.), *Handbook of Developmental Psychology*. London: Sage. pp. 370–404.

Schneider, W. and Pressley, M. (1997) *Memory Development Between Two and Twenty*. Mahwah, NJ: Erlbaum.

Schwartz, B. D. (2003) Child L2 acquisition: Paving the way. In B. Beachley, A. Brow and F. Conlin (eds.), *Proceedings of the Boston University Conference on Language Development 27*. Somerville, MA: Cascadilla, pp. 26–50.

Scott, C. (2008) *Teaching Children English as an Additional Language: A Programme for 7–11 year olds*. London: Routledge.

Scott, J. (2008) Children as respondents: The challenge for quantitative methods. In P. Christensen and A. James (eds.), *Research with Children: Perspectives and Practices*. London: Routlegde, pp. 87–108.

Scott, W. A. and Ytreberg, L. H. (1990) *Teaching English to Children*. Harlow: Pearson Education.

Selinker, L. (1972) Interlanguage. *International Review of Applied Linguistics*, 10: 209–31.

Selman, R. L. and Jaquette, D. (1977) Stability and oscillation in interpersonal awareness: A clinical-developmental analysis. In C. B. Keasey (ed.), *The Nebraska Symposium on Motivation 25*. Lincoln: University of Nebraska Press.

Shaffer, D. (1973) Children's responses to a hypothetical proposition. Unpublished manuscript. Kent State University.

Shaffer, D. and Kipp, K. (2010) *Developmental Psychology: Childhood and Adolescence*. Belmont, CA: Wadsworth.

Shak, J. and Gardner, S. (2008) Young learners' perspectives on four focus on form tasks. *Language Teaching Research*, 12 (3): 387–408.

Shatz, M. and Wilkinson, L. C. (eds.) (2010) *The Education of English Language Learners: Research to Practice (Challenges in Language and Literacy)*. New York: Guilford Press.

Shin, S. J. (2005) *Developing in Two Languages*. Clevedon: Multilingual Matters.

Shrubshall, P. (1997) Narrative, argument and literacy: A comparative study of the narrative discourse development of monolingual and bilingual 5–10 year old learners. *Journal of Multilingual and Multicultural Development*, 18 (5): 402–21.

Siegler, R. S. (1981) *Developmental Sequences Within and Between Concepts*. Monographs of the Society for Research in Child Development, 46.2 Serial number 189.

Siegler, R. S. (1995) How does change occur: A microgenetic study of number conservation. *Cognitive Psychology*, 28: 225–73.

Siegler, R. S. (1996) *Emerging Minds: The Process of Change in Children's Thinking*. New York: Oxford University Press.

Simard, D. (2004) Using diaries to promote metalinguistic reflection among elementary school students. *Language Awareness*, 13 (1): 34–48.

Simon, H. A. (1974) How big is a chunk? *Science*, 183: 482–8.

Simpson, J. and Wigglesworth, G. (eds.) (2008) *Children's Language and Multilingualism*. London: Continuum.

Sinclair, J. M. H. and Coulthard M. (1975) *Towards an Analysis of Discourse: The English used by Teachers and Pupils*. Oxford: Oxford University Press.

Singleton, D. (1987) Mother- and other-tongue influence on learner French. *Studies in Second Language Acquisition*, 9: 327–46.

Singleton, D. (2003) Critical period or general age factors. In M. P. Garcia Mayo and M. L. Garcia Lecumberri (eds.), *Age and the Acquisition of English as a Foreign Language*. Clevedon: Multilingual Matters, pp. 3–22.

Singleton, D. and Ryan, L. (2004) *Language Acquisition: The Age Factor*. Clevedon: Multilingual Matters.

Skinner, B. F. (1957) *Verbal Behaviour*. New York: Appleton-Century-Crofts.

Skutgabb-Kangas, T. and Toukomaa, P. (1976) *Teaching Migrant Children's Mother Tongue and Learning the Language of the Host Country in the Context of the Sociocultural Situation of the Migrant Family*. Helsinki: The Finnish National Commission for UNESCO.

Slattery, M. and Willis, J. (2001) *English for Primary Teachers*. Oxford: Oxford University Press.

Smith, P. K., Cowie, H. and Blades M. (1998) *Understanding Children's Development*. Oxford: Blackwell.

Snow, C. (1986) Conversations with children. In P. Fletcher and M. Garman (eds.), *Language Acquisition: Studies in First Language Development*. Cambridge: Cambridge University Press, pp. 69–89.

Snow, C. and Höfnagel-Höhle, M. (1977) Age differences in the pronunciation of foreign sounds. *Language and Speech*, 20: 357–65.

Snow, C. and Höfnagel-Höhle, M. (1978a) Age differences in second language acquisition. In E. Hatch (ed.), *Second Language Acquisition: A Book of Readings*. Rowley. MA: Newbury House, pp. 333–46.

Snow, C. and Höfnagel-Höhle, M. (1978b) The critical period for language acquisition: Evidence from second language learning. *Child Development*, 49: 1114–28. Reprinted (1982) in S. Krashen, R. Scarcella and M. Long (eds.), *Child-Adult Differences in Second Language Acqusition*. Rowley, MA: Newbury House, pp. 84–92.

Sonnenschein, S. (1986) Development of referential communication: Deciding that a message is uninformative. *Developmental Psychology*, 22: 164–68.

Spencer, J. R. and Flin, R. (1990) *The Evidence of Children: The Law and Psychology*. London: Blackstone.

Strutt, G. F., Anderson, D. R. and Well, A. D. (1975) A developmental study of the effects of irrelevant information on speeded classification. *Journal of Experimental Child Psychology*, 20: 127–35.

Suárez-Orozco, M. M., Suárez Orozco, C. and Baolian Qin, D. (eds.) (2005) *The New Immigration*. London: Routledge.

Sundin, K. (2000) English as a first foreign language for young learners: Sweden. In M. Nikolov and H. Curtain (eds.), *An Early Start: Young Learners and Modern Languages in Europe and Beyond*. Strasbourg: Council of Europe, pp. 151–8.

Swain, M. (1981) Target language use in the wider environment as factor in its acquisition. In R. Andersen (ed.), *Second Languages: A Cross-linguistic Perspective*. Rowley, MA: Newbury House.

Swain, M. (1985) Communicative competence: Some roles of comprehensible input and comprehensible output in its development. In S. Gass and C. Madden (eds.), *Input in Second Language Acquisition*, Rowley, MA: Newbury House, pp. 235–53.

Swain, M. (2000) The output hypothesis and beyond: Mediating acquisition through collaborative dialogue. In J. P. Lantolf (ed.), *Sociocultural Theory and Second Language Learning*. Oxford: Oxford University Press, pp. 97–114.

Swain, M. and Lapkin, S. (1989) Interaction and second language learning; Two adolescent French immersion students working together. *The Modern Language Journal*, 82 (3): 320–37.

Swain, M. and Lapkin, S. (1995) Problems in output and the cognitive processes they generate: A step towards second language learning. *Applied Linguistics*, 16 (3): 371–91.

Swain, M. and Lapkin, S. (2003) Talking it through: Two French immersion learners' response to reformulation. *International Journal of Educational Research*, 37: 285–304.

Tabors, P. O. (1997) *One Child: Two Languages: A Guide for Preschool Educators of Children Learning English as a Second Language*. Baltimore, MD: Brookes Publishing.

Tagoilelagi-Leota, F., McNaughton, S., MacDonald, S. and Farry, S. (2005) Bilingual and biliteracy development over the transition to school. *The International Journal of Bilingual Education and Bilingualism*, 8 (5): 455–79.

Takeuchi, M. (2006) The Japanese language development of children through the one-parent-one language approach in Melbourne. *Journal of Multilingual and Multicultural Development*, 27 (4): 319–31.

Tammivaara, J. and Enright, D. S. (1986) On eliciting information: Dialogues with child informants. *Anthropology and Education Quarterly*, 17: 218–38.

Tang, E. and Nesi, H. (2003) Teaching vocabulary in two Chinese classrooms: Schoolchildren's exposure to English words in Hong Kong and Guangzhou. *Language Teaching Research*, 7 (1): 65–97.

Tannenbaum, M. and Howie, P. (2002) The association between language maintenance and family relations: Chinese immigrant children in Australia. *Journal of Multilingual and Multicultural Development*, 23 (5): 408–24.

Tardiff, T. (1996) Nouns are not always learnt before verbs: Evidence from Mandarin speakers' early vocabularies. *Developmental Psychology*, 32: 492–504.

Tharp, R. G. and Gallimore, R. (1988) *Rousing Minds to Life: Teaching, Learning and Schooling in Social Context*. Cambridge: Cambridge University Press.

Thatcher, R. W. (1994) Cyclic cortical reorganisation: Origins of human cognitive development. In G. Dawson and K. W. Fisher (eds.), *Human Behaviour and the Developing Brain*. New York: Guilford, pp. 232–66.

Thatcher, R. W., Lyon, G. R., Rumsey, J. and Krasnegor, J. (1996) *Developmental Neuroimaging*. San Diego, CA: Academic Press.

Thomas, W. and Collier, V. (2003) The multiple benefits of dual language. *Educational Leadership*, 61: 61–4.

Thompson, J. G. and Myers, N. A. (1985) Inferences and recall at ages four and seven. *Child Development*, 56: 1134–44.

Thomsen, H. (2003) Scaffolding target language use. In D. Little, J. Ridley and E. Ushioda (eds.), *Learner Autonomy in the Foreign Language Classroom: Teacher, Learner, Curriculum and Assessment*. Dublin: Authentik, pp. 29–46.

Thomson, P. (ed.) (2008) *Doing Visual Research with Children and Young People*. London: Routledge.

Thornton, S. (2008) *Understanding Human Development*. Basingstoke and New York: Palgrave Macmillan.

Tinson, J. (2009) *Conducting Research with Children and Adolescents: Design, Methods and Empirical Cases*. Oxford: Goodfellow Publishers Limited.

Tisdall, K., Davies, J. B. and Gallagher, M. (2009) *Researching with Children and Young People: Research Design, Methods and Analysis*. London: Sage Publications.

Toda, S., Fogel, A. and Kawai, M. (1990) Maternal speech to three-months-old infants in the United States and Japan. *Journal of Child Language*, 17: 279–94.

Tomasello, M. (1995) Language is not an instinct. *Cognitive Development*, 10: 131–56.

Tomasello, M. (1999) *The Cultural Origins of Human Cognition*. Cambridge, MA: Harvard University Press.

Tomasello, M. (2003) *Constructing a Language: A Usage-based Theory of Language Acquisition*. Cambridge, MA: Harvard University Press.

Toohey, K. (2000) *Learning English at School: Identity, Social Relations and Classroom Practice*. Clevedon: Multilingual Matters.

Trott, K., Dobbinson, S. and Griffiths, P. (2004) *The Child Language Reader*. London: Routledge.

Turnbull, M. (1999) Multidimensional project-based second language teaching: Observations of four grade 9 core French teachers. *Canadian Modern Language Review*, 56: 3–35.

Turnbull, M. (2001) There is a role for L1 in second and foreign language teaching but... *Canadian Modern Language Review*, 57 (4): 531–40.

Turnbull, M., Lapkin, S., Hart, D. and Swain, M. (1998) Time on task and immersion graduates' French proficiency. In S. Lapkin (ed.), *French Second Language Education in Canada: Empirical Studies*. Toronto: University of Toronto Press, pp. 31–55.

United Nations (1989) *United Nations Convention on the Rights of the Child*. New York: United Nations.

Urpunen, M. I. (2004) Ultimate Attainment in Post-puberty Second Language Acquisition. Unpublished doctoral thesis. Boston, MA: Boston University.

Vale, D. and Feunten, A. (1995) *Teaching Children English*. Cambridge: Cambridge University Press.

Van den Branden, K. (1997) Effects of negotiation on language learners' output. *Language Learning*, 47 (4): 589–636.

Verhallen, M. and Schoonen, R. (1993) Lexical knowledge of monolingual and bilingual children. *Applied Linguistics*, 14 (4): 344–63.

Verhelst, M. (2006) A box full of feelings: promoting infants' second language acquisition all day long. In K. Van den Branden (ed.), *Task-based Language Education: From Theory to Practice*. Cambridge: Cambridge University Press, pp. 197–216.

Verhelst, M. and Van den Branden, K. (1999) Observeren in Kleuterklassen. Indicatoren voor krachtige leeromgevingen voor taalvaardigheidsonderwijs. Unpublished internal document. Leuven: Steunpunkt NT2.

Victori, M. and Tragant E. (2003) Learner strategies: Cross-sectional and longitudinal study of primary and high school EFL learners. In M. P. Garcia Mayo and M. L. Garcia Lecumberri (eds.), *Age and the Acquisition of English as a Foreign Language.* Clevedon: Multilingual Matters, pp. 182–209.

Vihman, M. (1998) A developmental perspective on code-switching: Conversations between a pair of bilingual siblings. *International Journal of Bilingualism*, 2: 45–84.

Volterra, V. and Taeschner, T. (1978) The acquisition and development of language by bilingual children. *Journal of Child Language*, 5: 311–26.

Vurpillot, E. (1968) The development of scanning strategies and their relation to visual differentiation. *Journal of Experimental Child Psychology*, 6: 632–50.

Vygotsky, L. (1978) *Mind in Society.* Cambridge, MA: Harvard University Press.

Wajnryb, R. (2003) *Grammar Dictation.* Oxford: Oxford University Press.

Wang, X. (2008) *Growing Up with Three Languages: Birth to Eleven.* Bristol: Multilingual Matters.

Warriner, D. S. (2007) Transnational literacies: Immigration, language learning and identity. *Linguistics and Education*, 3–4: 201–14.

Watson, M. (1990) Aspects of self development as reflected in children's role playing. In D. Cicchetti and M. Beeghly (eds.), *The Self in Transition: Infancy to Childhood*, pp. 281–307. Chicago: University of Chicago Press.

Weber-Fox, C. M. and Neville, H. J. (1996) Maturational constraints on functional specializations for language processing: ERP and behavioural evidence in bilingual speakers. *Journal of Cognitive Neuroscience*, 8 (3): 231–56.

Weber-Fox, C. and Neville, H. (1999) Functional neural subsystems are differentially affected by delays in second language immersion: ERP and behavioural evidence in bilinguals. In D. Birdsong (ed.), *Second Language Acquisition and the Critical Period Hypothesis.* Mahwah, NJ: Lawrence Erlbaum, pp. 23–38.

Wells, G. (1986) *The Meaning Makers: Children Learning Language and Using Language to Learn.* Portsmouth, NH: Heinemann.

Wells, G. (1981) *Learning through Interaction: The Study of Language Development.* Cambridge: Cambridge University Press.

Wells, G. and Chang-Wells, G. L. (1992) *Constructing Knowledge Together: Classrooms as Centres of Inquiry and Literacy.* Portsmouth, NH: Heinemann.

White, L. and Genesee, F. (1996) How native is near-native? The issue of ultimate attainment in adult second language acquisition. *Second Language Research*, 12: 238–65.

Whitehurst, G. J. and Sonnerschein, S. (1981) The development of informative messages in referential communication: Knowing when versus knowing how. In W. Dickson (ed.), *Children's Oral Communication Skills.* New York: Academic Press.

Whong-Barr, M. and Schwartz, B. D. (2002) Morphological and syntactic transfer in child L2 acquisition of the English dative alternation. *Studies in Second Language Acquisition*, 24: 579–616.

Wightman, M. (1981) *The French Listening Comprehension Skills of Grade Six English Programme Students; Second Year of Testing.* Ottawa: Research Centre, Ottawa Board of Education.

Williams Fortune, T. and Tedich, D. J. (eds.) (2008) *Pathways to Multilingualism: Evolving Prespectives on Immersion Education.* Clevedon: Multilingual Matters.

Willet, J. (1995) Becoming first graders in an L2: An ethnographic study of L2 socialisation. *TESOL Quarterly*, 29 (3): 473–503.

Winer, G., Craig, R. K. and Weinbaum, E. (1992) Adults' failure on misleading weight-conservation tests: A developmental analysis. *Developmental Psychology*, 28: 109–20.

Winitz, H., Gillispie, B. and Starcev J. (1995).The development of English speech patterns of a 7-year old Polish-speaking child. *Journal of Psycholinguistic Research*, 24 (2): 117–43.

Wong-Fillmore, L. (1983) The language learner as an individual: Implications of research on individual differences for the ESL teacher. In M. A. Clarke and J. Handscombe (eds.), *On TESOL '82: Pacific Perspectives on Language Learning and Teaching*. Washington, DC: TESOL, pp. 157–71.

Wong-Fillmore, L. (1991) Second-language learning in children: Models of language learning in social context. In E. Bialystok (ed.), *Language Processing in Bilingual Children*. Cambridge: Cambridge University Press, pp. 49–69.

Wood, D. (1998) *How Children Think and Learn*. Oxford: Blackwell Publishers Limited.

Wood, D., Bruner, J. and Ross, G. (1976) The role of tutoring in problem solving. *Journal of Child Psychology and Psychiatry*, 17: 89–100.

Wright, A. (1997) *Creating Stories with Children*. Oxford: Oxford University Press.

Young, A. and Helot, C. (2003) Language awareness and/or language learning in French primary schools today. *Language Awareness*, 12 (3–4): 234–46.

Index